Social Policy and Welfare

Social Policy and Welfare
A Clear Guide

Tom Burden

Pluto  Press

LONDON · CHICAGO, ILLINOIS

First published 1998 by Pluto Press
345 Archway Road, London N6 5AA
and 1436 West Randolph, Chicago, Illinois 60607, USA

British Library Cataloguing in Publication Data
A catalogue record for this book is available from the British Library

ISBN 0 7453 0965 8 hbk

Library of Congress Cataloging in Publication Data
A catalog record for this book is available from the Library of Congress

Designed and produced for Pluto Press by
Chase Production Services, Chadlington, OX7 3LN
Typeset from disk by Stanford DTP Services, Northampton
Printed in the EC by TJ International, Padstow

Contents

List of Tables

Introduction

The study of social policy

The term 'social policy' refers to forms of state intervention which affect the social opportunities and conditions under which people live. The study of social policy has normally focused on areas of intervention such as education, social security, welfare and health services, and housing provision – the kinds of activities which we think of as making up the welfare state. Indeed, the study of social policy has closely followed the development of separate national welfare systems or welfare states. Accordingly, there is a substantial body of literature on social policy and the welfare state in the older industrial capitalist countries such as Britain, the US, Australia, Germany and France.

However, in the past three decades major shifts have taken place in the study of social policy. Since the 1960s there has been an increase in studies dealing with comparative social policy. These usually involve comparing the features of social provision in two and sometimes more states, normally from the developed world. It is now commonly accepted that social policies can be much better understood when they are viewed in the light of the kinds of provision made elsewhere. One reason for this is that states themselves do not make policies in isolation – they often closely monitor the policy initiatives of other states – sometimes employing the policies as a model for their own or maybe attempting to avoid mistakes made elsewhere.

Since the 1970s there has been a further expansion of the literature to deal with a wider range of states such as the socialist regimes of pre-1989 Eastern Europe, the countries of the third world and the newly developing states of the Pacific Rim. The focus has thus shifted to cover a much wider range of societies in which social policies are found.

In the 1980s the West witnessed something close to a triumphalism of the right in the area of economic and social policy with the resurgence of economic liberalism and major cuts in welfare programmes. The ideological move to the right went along with a growing timidity in the reformist programmes of major political parties of the centre and left. However, there are now indications of a renewed concern with the social consequences of poverty and unemployment. The scene is set for a conflict between those who would like to finish off the remnants of the welfare states and those who would like to reassert some of the principles on which they were based.

In the past decade or so a further important shift in the study of social policy has begun. Increasing attention is being paid to the fact that social policies are not only made by and within national states — they are also made by international organisations. In western Europe people are familiar with the social policy role of the European Union (EU). However, it is also clear that a major role in social policy is now played by a range of organisations operating on a wider stage than the regional arena in which the EU functions. The World Health Organization and bodies like the World Bank and the International Monetary Fund have a role in social policy-making which has influenced social provision made in many states. These changes invite the study of social policy to adopt a 'global' perspective. This new perspective in the study of social policy is in line with developments in the other social sciences in which the theme of globalisation is coming to the fore.

The approach taken here

This book attempts to take this shift to a more global perspective seriously though without abandoning more traditional approaches to studying social policy. The national perspective on the study of social policy is employed in parts of this book but it is located within the framework of a comparative approach so that variations in the nature of social provision between states can be explored. A global perspective is used to review some of the international influences on social provision which affect societies today, and which may become increasingly important as we move into the next century.

Perspectives on the politics of social policy

Social policy is often at the centre of ideological and political divisions and debates. This is certainly true when we look at the divisions between political parties. Social-policy issues such as state provision for health, or policies towards the unemployed normally play a central role in politics. The ideological dimension will be given considerable weight in this book because social policies, in common with most acts of government, cannot be very well understood if they are simply treated as 'neutral' attempts to deal with 'problems'. Indeed, what is to count as a problem is itself generally a matter of political debate. The concepts and perspectives of modern political theory are an important element in current debates about social policy. An understanding of the underlying ideological and political divisions is therefore vital for those wishing to understand the nature of social policy.

In addition, there are important debates and divisions amongst the academics who write about social policies. The study of social policy, in common with other areas of social science, is 'contested terrain'. Scholars and researchers come to it with different assumptions and presuppositions which colour their approach to the subject. For those seeking to understand the literature on social policy it is important to be able to identify and make sense of the ideological and political positions taken up, implicitly or explicitly, by those authors who deal with it.

In making sense of both political thought and social policy it is useful to distinguish three main approaches. These are most commonly understood under the headings 'right', 'centre' and 'left'. When we come to consider the social policies undertaken in different states, or in the same state at different times, we can learn a great deal by looking at the ideologies held by the governments which introduced particular policies. An understanding of these three approaches is also of importance when we consider the different interpretations which are found in the academic literature on social policy. Broadly speaking, in the study of social policy, there are three major perspectives which parallel the political differences described above. These perspectives on social policy are as follows.

THE RIGHT-WING APPROACH

In this view extensive state welfare provision is generally seen as undesirable though it may be required in order to maintain social order by ameliorating the conditions faced by the most hard-pressed members of society. Those holding this view generally prefer a relatively restricted range of state social provision.

THE REFORMIST APPROACH

In this view state welfare provision is seen as a form of collective intervention which is designed to meet a range of social needs and solve important social problems in the general interest. Proponents of this view normally support social policies which are designed to establish minimum standards of provision though without radically transforming the existing social order.

THE RADICAL APPROACH

In this view state welfare provision is usually seen as a means by which ruling groups stifle dissent, and reinforce their own dominance, whilst failing to make any substantial reductions in the inequalities which are the source of the inadequate living conditions the policies are presented as being designed to improve. Supporters of this view would generally like to see welfare provision being used as a means of substantially reducing social inequalities.

The three perspectives sketched above are painted with a very broad brush. In reality, within each viewpoint there can be found a variety of schools of thought. Each of these schools puts together a coherent representation of policy using a particular selection and combination of the ingredients found within the broader viewpoint. Throughout the book these schools of thought are outlined where they have played a significant part in the development of understanding of particular policies.

We are aware that major contributions have been made to the study of social policy by authors writing from a feminist perspective. These contributions have covered a range of issues such as the significance of women in the making of social policy, the role of women in the delivery of social policies and the impact of social policy on women. More recently, more general questions of gender have been raised, particularly in relation to the issue of 'masculinity'. These issues are also treated in this book although feminism is not treated throughout as a single distinct political perspective with something to say on every issue, since, arguably, it does not have the inclusive and politically unified focus of the perspectives treated broadly here as 'left', 'centre' and 'right'.

The changing context of social policy

The book is designed to give an overall understanding of the nature of social policy using a comparative approach and with more emphasis than has been customary being put on a global perspective. However, the readership of the book is likely to be found predominantly in the developed English-speaking states, and where national social policies and welfare states have been examined particular attention has been paid to the social policies that these readers are likely to have experience of, though the general features of the analysis given can be applied elsewhere.

The broader global context has seen the collapse of Soviet communism and the economic and political restructuring of Eastern Europe. At the same time, there has been growing evidence of the economic strength of the countries of the Pacific Rim. The nature of global political conflict has also fundamentally altered with the end of the cold war. We are now witnessing the emergence of new lines of conflict around revivals of fundamentalist belief and the resurgence of nationalism. All these changes have important implications for social policies at a national and global level. The economic dominance of the established Western capitalist democracies is under threat and welfare polices are often blamed for their increasing competitive weakness. Debate over the role of welfare policies as instruments of economic recovery and of social integration is therefore sharpening.

The study of social policy is a major area of debate and dispute in which some of the outlines of the shape of society in the future are being determined. The role of social policy and its relationship with the economic organisation of society are crucial questions. It is to be hoped that an appreciation of the issues examined in this book will help in understanding the options available in the future as the present flux of events begins to crystallise in the social forms which are emerging as we approach the twenty-first century.

The aims of this book

This book covers a very broad range of issues and the emphasis throughout is on the overall framework of ideas rather than on the exposition of the details of particular policies, though the reader will be guided to appropriate sources where these can be explored. The book is designed to allow the examination of a wide range of national and international social policy issues in a consistent and coherent way. The book as a whole does not present a sequential argument. However, each chapter does give a coherent though not necessarily a comprehensive treatment of the area which it covers. The presentation of individual topics is not designed to be comprehensive but to offer an overall view in a simplified but not simple-minded form. This is done in the belief that a more complex understanding is only possible if the basic structure of an argument is understood. The book is designed to be used primarily as a resource for teaching and learning.

The substantive aims of the book are to:

- analyse the political ideologies underlying social policy
- examine varying interpretations of key concepts in the study of social policy
- examine different strategies used in the social-policy formation
- explore alternative theoretical approaches to explaining the development of social policy
- examine central issues in social policy and perspectives on them
- examine the ideological and political basis of the diversity of provision in a range of welfare states
- explore the emerging global character of social policy.

Using this book

Each topic is treated by giving a brief summary of the issue and significant debates around it. Given the limitations of space, the arguments are always presented in condensed form with only the bare outline given. However, an attempt has been made to treat the issues in a sophisticated way in that the complexities of debate have not, one hopes, been avoided even though they can only be recounted in summary form.

Extensive use has also been made of quotations where passages have been found which summarise arguments cogently. These may also help to give readers a flavour of the arguments in some of the key sources and maybe encourage them to explore the literature further.

Readers are encouraged to use this book as a *hypertext*, in which the reader can move from place to place following material on a particular issue, rather than a linear account. Various features of the book make this possible.

1. *Detailed table of contents* lists all the topics dealt with in the book chapter by chapter. This can usefully be scanned by anyone wishing to see the overall framework of the book.
2. *Cross-references* are given in those places in the text where a concept is employed which is more fully explained elsewhere in the book. In addition, where mention is made of a *topic* which is treated elsewhere in the book, this is shown in italics.
3. *Related topics* are given for each of the topics treated. The topic title and its section number are given. Using these allows the reader to follow up linked ideas or to explore key concepts in more detail where they are covered elsewhere in the book.
4. *Further reading* is given for the topics covered allowing readers to widen their understanding through consulting other more detailed sources. An effort has been made to avoid sources which are too inaccessible in terms of both comprehensibility and likely availability.
5. The *Index* at the end of the book can be used in searching for material on particular issues and concepts.

Student use

Where students have not been given specific advice by their tutors, they may wish to use this book for the following purposes:

1. To identify relevant topics using the *Detailed table of contents*.
2. To examine a whole series of related issues by looking at a complete chapter that covers a topic area they are currently concerned with.
3. To follow up linked topics using the *Related topics* for those topics they are interested in.
4. To examine different perspectives on a major social policy issue or concept.
5. To search for information on given topics using the *Index*.

For teachers

The book is designed for ease of use by teachers and their students. It could be used alone or as a resource in conjunction with a conventional textbook. It can be used to support a range of different courses in the area of social policy. These courses could focus on any selection from, or combination of, the material dealt with in the different chapters including: explanatory perspectives, central concepts, social policy development, social policy strategies, social policy issues, vulnerable groups, different welfare states and global social policy. In order to assist teachers who wish to use this book additional resources are available on the Pluto Books Website. Readers can access the Pluto Books Website on:

http://www.leevalley.co.uk./plutopress

The Website contains material relating to this book which teachers are free to download and use for their teaching. The downloaded text can be copied and pasted into a word-processing program and then edited. The material available includes:

1. The *References* listed at the end of the book. These can be downloaded and items selected for use in student reading lists.
2. The complete list of topics covered as printed in the *Detailed table of contents* along with the *Related topics* and *Further reading* for each item. This can be downloaded and then edited to select particular topics or sections relevant to the course being taught. A study guide for students could then be produced which contains topics, *Related topics* and *Further reading*, with the teacher's own additions included.
3. Suggested course outlines using materials from this book are provided for the following topics. Each outline is based on a course covering twelve topics. These can be downloaded, edited and used as required. At the time of writing the following course outlines are available. We would be interested to hear further suggestions for new outlines and to add outlines to the list which have been provided by readers:

   - theoretical approaches to social policy
   - social policy in Britain
   - right-wing thought and social policy
   - reformist thought and social policy
   - radical thought and social policy
   - central concepts in social policy (various options)
   - the development of social policy
   - interpreting the history of welfare states
   - alternative strategies for social policy
   - major issues in social policy (various options)

- social policy and the vulnerable
- the range of welfare states
- Anglo-American welfare states
- the Anglophone welfare states
- understanding global social policy.

The Website also contains suggestions as to how the book might be used by teachers on courses covering various professional and external courses in social policy, including the following.

Courses

Social Work
Probation
Youth and Community Work
Institute of Health Services Management
HND Social Care
A-level Social Policy (various boards)

Tom Burden
August 1997

CHAPTER 1

General explanatory perspectives

Part 1 Ideological Perspectives

1.1 PUBLIC POLICY AND SOCIAL POLICY

We need to start by clarifying what we mean by public policy. The term 'public policy' is problematic though at first sight its meaning seems obvious. It is usually used to refer to state intervention which takes place in the pursuit of clearly defined objectives using specially chosen modes of implementation. Public policy is made up of the whole array of government interventions. Social policy is part of public policy as a whole.

This approach to the study of policy often begins with the examination of explicit policy statements and discussions. This can cause problems, since it defines policy in the terms used by the authorities. This prevents any consideration of the notion that policy might not be what it is avowed to be and that it may have hidden objectives. Governments often produce 'policy statements' which purport to describe what they are doing and why they are doing it. However, in these statements policy may be portrayed in terms which are socially acceptable so as to provoke less opposition than revealing the objectives actually being pursued where these are different.

Various ministries or government departments carry policies out under the control of the minister responsible. In Britain there are departments dealing with economic policy such as the Treasury and the Department of Trade and Industry and others dealing with social policy such as the Department of Health and Social Security and the Department for Education and Employment.

In the standard approach, health policy would be seen as what the Department of Health does. But we can be seriously misled by identifying policy with the work of the particular department which is officially given responsibility for it. The policies of other departments have such important implications for health that they too might be seen as involved with health policy. For example, in Britain the Treasury influences smoking through taxation and this has a big impact on health, while the Department of the Environment deals with policy towards motor vehicles, which is

1

also a major factor in health. In fact, it is very difficult to draw up the limits of many areas of social policy, since they go beyond the work of the ministries explicitly designated as the source of policy. Social policy may in reality be an aspect of the work of a wide range of departments, many of which are not labelled in ways which indicate their social-policy functions.

RELATED TOPICS

9.1 Globalisation

FURTHER READING

Ham and Hill (1984) Chap 1
Hogwood and Gunn (1984) Chap 2

1.2 SOCIAL POLICY AND THE SOCIAL SERVICES

In Britain until the mid-1960s courses on what is now usually called social policy were usually referred to as 'social administration'. Social administration involved a study of the social services with an emphasis on the moral progress from the harshness of the Victorian Poor Law to the beneficence of the welfare state. The term 'social services' was used to mean the five major areas of government policy which made up the 'welfare state':

1. health services
2. public housing
3. social security
4. state education
5. welfare or 'personal' social services.

In the social-administration approach, social policy was seen to benefit society by:

• creating greater social cohesion
• improving economic efficiency
• improving living standards
• increasing opportunities for the recipients of services.

The motivation for the establishment of the welfare state was seen as humanitarian. The main focus in the study of public administration was on how the services were organised and delivered. There was little discussion of ideological issues, and the social services and the welfare state were generally assumed to be desirable institutions which benefited society. This view of the social services as benevolent and beneficial institutions implies a particular kind of definition of social policy:

... the mainspring of social policy may be said to be the desire to ensure every member of a community certain minimum standards and certain opportunities. (Hagenbuch, quoted in Titmuss, 1974: 29)

Ideological issues did not receive much attention because it was assumed that the social services were both widely supported and desirable. Insofar as this approach to the welfare state was based on a theory, it was that of *Fabianism*. Definitions of social policy which stressed its benevolence only really came under challenge when alternative theoretical viewpoints from *Marxism* and from the ideas of the *new right* became more widely debated from the late 1960s.

RELATED TOPICS

1.20 Fabianism
3.5 Social betterment

FURTHER READING

Brown (1983)
Marshall (1975) Introduction
Titmuss (1968) Chap 1

1.3 TITMUSS: THE SOCIAL DIVISION OF WELFARE

Titmuss challenged the idea that the social services alone were the proper object of study. Titmuss suggested we also needed to look at the way social policies could promote 'illfare' as well as welfare. Titmuss divided welfare provision into three sectors:

... all collective interventions to meet certain needs of the individual and/or to serve the wider interests of society may now be broadly grouped into three major categories of welfare: social welfare, fiscal welfare, and occupational welfare. (Titmuss, 1964: 42)

For Titmuss:

* *social welfare* meant the social services
* *fiscal welfare* meant allowances and reliefs from tax, which he viewed as a transfer payment
* *occupational welfare* meant benefits such as children's school fees, which are received as a result of holding a particular job and paid for by tax reliefs given to employers.

Titmuss's influence transformed social administration into an analytic study of social policy, a search for explanations of how and why state power affects the social allocation of every type of financial, welfare and environmental resource. (Kincaid, 1983: 294)

Titmuss was a social reformist who abhorred the continued existence of privilege and poverty but was also reticent about using political power to attack privilege because of the threat this posed to individual freedom.

FURTHER READING

Kincaid (1983)
Mann (1992) Chaps 1 and 2
Titmuss (1964)

1.4 THREE PERSPECTIVES ON SOCIAL POLICY

Up until the mid-1960s studies of social policy were usually based on a *reformist* or *Fabian* approach. This assumed that the social problems of capitalist societies were soluble through carefully planned state action. For a long time this view was largely unchallenged.

1. In the 1960s radical viewpoints, including *Marxism*, challenged the reformist orthodoxy. The radical approach tended to ask how social policy worked to reinforce the capitalist system and the capitalist class. It was seen as a means of blunting working-class political opposition and of increasing capitalist profits through the provision of a 'social infrastructure', such as free education, which increased labour efficiency.
2. Reformist thought includes *Fabianism* in social policy, *Keynesian* ideas in economics and *pluralism* in political science. The reformist approach tends to assume that the welfare state is a beneficent institution which works to the benefit of everyone. It is the means by which the undesirable by-products of the (otherwise beneficial) operations of an industrial society can be ameliorated.
3. In the 1970s there was a resurgence of *liberalism*, which challenged both reformism and radicalism. This *new-right* approach saw the welfare state as damaging the operation of the market system. It did this by destroying personal and business incentives through high taxation and by interfering in the operation of free markets.

A number of authors have developed typologies of social policy which employ these three basic perspectives or variants of them. Some of these authors also include other perspectives which do not fit within these categories, particularly *feminist* and *green* approaches, and where relevant these are also considered.

RELATED TOPICS
1.12 Supporting the market
1.17 Neo-liberalism (the new right)
1.20 Fabianism
1.22 Keynesian welfare state
1.23 Welfare pluralism
1.26 Marxism: 1 Capital logic
3.6 Pluralism

FURTHER READING
George and Wilding (1985)

1.5 TITMUSS: THREE MODELS OF WELFARE

Titmuss identified three models of welfare: the *institutional redistributive*, the *industrial achievement performance* and the *residual*. The residual and institutional models are based on the work of Wilensky and Lebeaux (1965).

Table 1.1 Three models of welfare

	The institutional redistributive	The industrial achievement performance	The residual
Role of the state	Universalist state-run services should redistribute income and reduce social inequality	The state should meet needs on the basis of productivity and work performance	State should only intervene if the market and the family cannot meet needs
Priorities	Meeting social needs is given priority over concerns for economic productivity	Social needs are met but the success of the economy is viewed as the primary concern	The liberal values of the market predominate and private provision is favoured
Status of recipients	All members of society are recipients with the status of full citizens	Recipients are viewed as potential productive resources to be supported for economic reasons	Recipients of state welfare are stigmatised as failures
Political position	Left	Centre	Right

RELATED TOPICS

1.17 Neo-liberalism
1.20 Fabianism
1.21 Logic of industrialism

FURTHER READING

Titmuss (1964) Chap 2
Wilensky and Lebaux (1965)

1.6 ESPING-ANDERSEN: WELFARE REGIMES

Esping-Andersen (1990) criticises theories which suggest a tendency towards uniformity amongst capitalist welfare states based on a presumed *logic of industrialism*. He finds links between the extent of *decommodification* (non-reliance on the market) in the provision of pensions, sickness and unemployment benefits and labour market policies, and the type of 'political regime' in the 18 Organization for Economic Co-operation and Development (OECD) states.

Political regimes are distinguished in terms of the extent of three factors:

1. Left influence and working-class mobilisation in government
2. Electoral support for Catholic conservatism
3. A history of authoritarian rule or a restricted franchise.

This produces three types of political regime which are described as *liberal, conservative* and *socialist*.

1. *Liberal* welfare states lack working-class mobilisation and a history of absolutism. They make extensive use of means-tests, with limited social-insurance benefits and with state encouragement of private benefits. Examples are the US, Canada and Australia.
2. *Conservative corporatist* welfare states have a Catholic conservative tradition and absolutist tendencies in their political history. They employ social insurance more than means-tested or private benefits though income redistribution is kept to a minimum. Examples are Austria, Italy, France and Germany.
3. Socialist (i.e. social democratic *reformist*) welfare states have strong working-class mobilisation in government and influential social democratic parties. They have wide-ranging and redistributive benefits systems with labour market measures to support the unemployed. Examples are Sweden, the Netherlands, Denmark and Norway.

RELATED TOPICS

1.12 Supporting the market

1.21 Logic of industrialism
1.22 Keynesian welfare state
4.4 Means-testing and selectivity
4.6 National Insurance
4.7 Universalism
4.10 Decommodification

FURTHER READING

Esping-Andersen (1990)

1.7 GEORGE AND WILDING: IDEOLOGY AND SOCIAL WELFARE

Most discussion of the nature of social policy has tended to take place in a theoretical vacuum. Social policy is analysed as if it were an autonomous set of social institutions unconnected with the social and political system in which it is set and which it serves. (George and Wilding, 1976: 1)

George and Wilding distinguished four ideologies in their analysis of social policy: Marxism, Fabian socialism, Reluctant collectivism and Anti-collectivism. See Table 1.2.

RELATED TOPICS

1.17 Neo-liberalism (the new right)
1.20 Fabianism
1.22 Keynesian welfare state
1.27 Marxism: 2 Balance of social forces

FURTHER READING

George and Wilding (1976)

1.8 GEORGE AND WILDING: WELFARE AND IDEOLOGY

George and Wilding have added feminist and green perspectives to their latest survey of ideologies in social policy. See Table 1.3.

RELATED TOPICS

1.17 Neo-liberalism (the new right)
1.20 Fabianism
1.29 Illich and anti-industrialism
3.11 Feminism

FURTHER READING

George and Wilding (1994) Chap 1

Table 1.2 Ideology and social welfare

	Marxism	**Fabian socialism**	**Reluctant collectivism**	**Anti-collectivism**
Values	Freedom, economic and social equality, public ownership, democracy, cooperation	Humanitarianism, equality of opportunity, planning	Equality of opportunity to benefit individuals and increase economic efficiency	Property, freedom, competition and individualism
Authors	Marx, Engels, Lenin	Titmuss, Crosland, Tawney	Keynes, Beveridge, Galbraith	Hayek, Friedman
Equality	Society should be classless with a high degree of economic equality	Society should have a degree of equality with unnecessary privilege and extremes of poverty and wealth eliminated	Society should only have whatever inequalities are necessary for efficient economic functioning	Society should be based on competitive individualism and personal responsibility
Economy	There should be public ownership of all productive facilities and economic planning to regulate production	There should be a mixed economy containing both nationalised industries and privately owned firms	The state can intervene to create the conditions where everyone is able to fend for themselves, e.g. free education	State social intervention should reinforce the disciplines of the market and avoid creating dependency
Social provision	Extensive free social services should be provided	There should be a balance between free services for all and means-tested provision for the needy	Keynesian methods to secure full employment can be used but intervention should be kept to a minimum	The scope of social intervention should be strictly limited

Table 1.3 Welfare and ideology

Ideology	Reasons for development of the welfare state	Attitudes towards the welfare state	Welfare and the ideal society
The New Right	War, Keynesianism; bureaucratic and professional self-interest	Damages the spontaneous order of the market; misunderstands human nature; undermines individual responsibility, creates inefficiency	Minimal role for state; free markets, individual freedom
The Middle Way	Pressure from below and initiatives from above; morality and social betterment	Belief in state-organised social improvement; support for mixture of public and private provision	Social harmony; mixed economy; balance of individual and social responsibility
Democratic Socialism	Outcome of long period of campaigning; linked to growth of industrialism	Unreserved support; belief that social services increase economic efficiency	Advancing and developing social democracy; ethically based socialist society
Marxism	The needs of capital; class conflict	Viewed as designed to reproduce capitalism; welfare expenditure can damage process of accumulation	Society that meets all needs; fully democratic; a high degree of equality
Feminism	Emphasises contribution of women; welfare state seen as reinforcing the subordination of women	Critical of failure to meet women's needs; desire more emphasis on gender equality	Full citizenship for women; socialisation of domestic labour; services designed to meet needs of women
Greenism	Logic of industrialism; the capitalist character of economic growth	Needs to adjust to environmental limits to economic growth; high technology in medicine is damaging; individualism receives too much encouragement	An eco-centric society; greater respect for the environment; emphasis on sustainable development; smaller-scale communities

1.9 CLARKE, COCHRANE AND SMART: IDEOLOGIES OF WELFARE

'Ideologies of welfare' are relatively systematic theories of the relationship between needs, welfare, the state and policy. They link abstract analyses of welfare concepts such as need, justice, equality and freedom with concrete political programmes of welfare reform. Clarke, Cochrane and Smart see a continuing conflict between four main ideologies of welfare throughout the twentieth century – *laissez-faire, Fabianism, socialism* and *feminism*.

Table 1.4 Ideologies of welfare

Laissez-faire	Socialism	Fabianism	Feminism
Laissez-faire welfare ideology is derived from classical political economy with support for private provision and the market and hostility to state intervention	Socialism is dubious about the ability of 'reforms' to achieve fundamental and lasting improvements within a capitalist society	Fabianism has a view of the state as a vehicle for social advancement guided by the careful study of social problems	Feminist welfare ideology has raised the question of how the welfare state reinforces gender divisions
Since the late 1970s the new right has dominated policy making and attempted to re-model the welfare state in line with a stress on incentives, efficiency and cuts in spending	It views the welfare state as employed to blunt reduce working-class radicalism and to exercise control through welfare officials and professionals	The broad Fabian approach to welfare maintains an influence because it is the basis of the caring professions and because of its stress on practical plans for reform	It has challenged divisions between the public and the private, and the political and the personal, and argues for measures to remove the disadvantages faced by women

RELATED TOPICS

1.17 Neo-liberalism (the new right)
1.20 Fabianism
1.27 Marxism: 2 Balance of social forces
3.11 Feminism

FURTHER READING

Clarke, Cochrane and Smart (1987) Introduction

1.10 WILLIAMS: PERSPECTIVES REVISITED

Race and gender are issues that have been neglected ... in terms of a failure to, first, acknowledge the experiences and struggles of women and of Black people over welfare provision; secondly, to account for racism and sexism in the provision of state welfare; thirdly, to give recognition to work which does attempt to analyse the relationship between the welfare state and the oppression of

Table 1.5 Race, gender and social policy

	Gender	Race
Anti-collectivism *Neo-liberalism* This focuses on economic freedom and the operation of the market *Neo-conservatism* This stresses the role of authority in the creation of social order	The family is seen as a 'natural' social institution and women's main role is in the 'private sphere' not the public worlds of work and politics	The free market is impersonal and should work against racism and discrimination. 'Race' involves deep-seated cultural differences which may undermine national unity — a cohesive multi-cultural society is not possible
Social reformism *Beveridge* *Fabianism*	Women do work, 'which is vital, though unpaid, without which their husbands could not do their paid work and without which the nation could not continue...' (Beveridge, 1942: 49) The inter-war Family Endowment Movement sought to enhance childrearing — but Fabianism has neglected inequality within the family	Both Beveridge (see 4.6) and the early Fabian tradition are linked to the belief that social policy can be used to reinforce national military and economic strength and to the view that biological inferiority is a factor in social problems
Political economy of welfare (*Marxism*)	Women's role is explained in terms of state reinforcement of their contribution to the capitalist economy but state support for patriarchy is not examined	Race issues are neglected in the Marxist social-policy analyses of Ginsburg and Gough — and race struggles tend to be viewed in 'class' terms

women and of Black progressive welfare strategy which incorporates the needs and demands which emerge from such strategies and analyses. (Williams, 1989: xi)

Williams revisits the perspectives and puts a particular emphasis on their treatment of the issues of gender and race.

RELATED TOPICS

1.16 Eugenics
1.20 Fabianism
3.9 Marxism
3.11 Feminism
8.6 Great Britain: race
9.15 Race

FURTHER READING

Williams (1989) Chap 5
Williams (1987)

Part 2 Right-wing approaches

1.11 RIGHT-WING APPROACHES: GENERAL FEATURES

Political and social thought on the right takes a variety of forms, although there are essentially two main strands, *conservatism* and *liberalism*.

1. *Conservatism* emphasises that a prerequisite of society is the maintenance of 'order'. Conservatism stresses the importance of the nation and of tradition and religion as sources of order and identity. In some versions of conservatism the exercise of power needs to be based on *paternalism*. Rulers therefore have a fatherly duty to look after those who cannot care for themselves. Conservatism employs an 'organic' view of society in which all the parts contribute to the maintenance of society as a whole. Social stability requires a stable hierarchy with an established and respected ruling group exercising power.
2. *Liberalism* emphasises individualism and personal freedom. Personal freedom means freedom from interference, especially by the state, which should have a minimal role. The state should ensure internal and external order and establish orderly conditions for freely undertaken economic activity – markets must operate freely.

For the new right, then, a major explanation for the spiralling cost of the welfare state could be found in the power of certain groups who saw that it was in their interests perpetually to expand spending on public services. The task, therefore, was to reduce the power of these groups by cutting state spending, thereby reducing taxation and enabling consumers to make their own choices based on the money in their own pockets. The liberty of the individual was thus to be extended through a reduction of state compulsion. (Dearlove and Saunders, 1984: 323)

All versions of political and social thought on the right support private property. State intervention designed to reduce economic inequalities is strongly opposed.

The right was originally opposed to democracy. Many liberal thinkers thought that only property owners should be entrusted with political rights and supported a restricted franchise, often with the propertyless (and women) excluded. Conservatism distrusted democracy, which it originally viewed as undermining the authority of traditional ruling groups. The key differences between these political theories can be summarised as follows:

- for liberals, social policies should support the market
- for conservatives, social policies should help to maintain order.

RELATED TOPICS

2.2 The individual in society: right-wing view
9.2 Liberalism

FURTHER READING

Dearlove and Saunders (1984) pp 321–30

1.12 SUPPORTING THE MARKET

Modern social policy largely developed through the use of the power of the state to create the conditions for a capitalist market economy to operate successfully. Social policies for dealing with the unemployed, the poor and the old were associated with the development of industrial capitalism and a free market for labour. Industrial capitalism produced factory labour and the widespread employment of women and children. Economic instability and cyclical fluctuations increased.

Many reformers felt that these new conditions required a more disciplined and orderly society – people needed to be made to adjust to the new demands of a competitive market economy. It was generally assumed everyone should take complete responsibility for maintaining themselves without relying on the state. If there were people unable to fend for themselves, however, it was the job of the state to help or force them to do this.

Various social problems and conditions that had previously been treated with a degree of tolerance were now to be dealt with by the state. New residential institutions were set up specifically designed to re-form or re-moralise their inmates. A range of 'total institutions' including prisons, lunatic asylums and reformatories were set up to do this in the early period of capitalist industrialisation.

> ... the conditions in the new institutions mimicked the discipline necessary for the factory system. The quasi-military authority structure of the total institution seemed ideally suited to be the means of establishing 'proper' work habits among these marginal elements of the workforce who were apparently most resistant to the monotony, routine, and regularity of industrialised labour ... one of the attractions of places like asylums and prisons was the promise they held out of instilling the virtues of bourgeois rationality into those segments of the population least amenable to them. (Scull, 1984: 26)

Those who were destitute could apply for admission to a 'workhouse'. Workhouse inmates were subjected to a regime carefully planned to alter their behaviour and their values:

- Conditions were designed to be 'less eligible' (i.e. worse than) the standards of the poorest paid worker to discourage all but the most desperate
- The inmates would be turned into self-reliant members of a competitive society
- Then they could then take their place in a competitive market economy
- State expenditure would be kept to a minimum.

RELATED TOPICS

1.17 Neo-liberalism (the new right)
1.21 Logic of industrialism
2.11 Community: right-wing view

FURTHER READING

Goffman (1961)
Scull (1984) Part 2

1.13 BISMARCKIANISM

Bismarckianism is named after Bismarck, the first Chancellor of Germany when it was unified in 1871. Bismarck was an authoritarian conservative nationalist who sought to use social policy to reduce support for socialism and to create internal unity and economic strength in order to increase Germany's international influence.

Bismarck faced an internal threat from the Social Democratic Party, which adopted a Marxist programme and had substantial support. Bismarck introduced a scheme of *National Insurance* for workers. This required government, workers and their employers to contribute to a fund which was used to provide unemployment and sickness benefits. It showed that the state was concerned to improve working-class living conditions and it decreased economic insecurity. This form of state intervention was *conservative* in that it sought to maintain order. But it was also in line with *liberal* principles, since it reinforced the idea of 'self-help' through insurance contributions.

His policies created interest throughout Europe where there were growing pressures for democracy and increasing support for socialist parties. In many European countries traditional ruling groups were looking for ways to stay in power and neutralise the threats posed by socialism and democracy. The British government sent a delegation to study the scheme and partly used it as model for the National Insurance legislation of 1911.

RELATED TOPICS

1.12 Supporting the market
1.15 Conservative paternalism
1.19 The new liberalism
4.6 National Insurance

FURTHER READING

Hennock (1981)

1.14 SOCIAL IMPERIALISM

In Britain at the end of the nineteenth century, *liberal* doctrines of free trade and minimal state intervention were coming under attack from other forces on the right. This occurred as a response to:

- growing international competition
- consciousness of the adverse economic effects of working-class poverty
- fear of class conflict
- concern about the growth of support for socialism.

Social imperialism was a political and social doctrine based on the principles of 'national political economy'.

> What marks national political economy ... is its tendency to treat the nation as a single strategic commercial and industrial enterprise, competing with other similar enterprises in the world economy. Liberal political economy treats the nation as an

association of individuals pursuing their own separate purposes within a framework of law. The nation has no purpose other than the purposes of the individuals who compose it ... For national political economy there is a national interest beyond the purposes of individuals, which it is the task of the permanent agencies of the state to identify, formulate and secure. (Gamble, 1981: 170)

In Britain, Joseph Chamberlain launched a campaign for 'tariff reform' in the early years of the twentieth century. Tariff reform meant using import controls to encourage domestic employment and to stimulate imperial trade and economic development. Increased tax revenues from the tariff and from economic growth would be used to:

- finance social welfare policies designed to benefit the working class
- increase the efficiency of the labour force
- reduce class conflict
- create social harmony.

Many on the right supported it because it meant high tax revenues for social and military spending without taxing property owners. However, the policy of tariff reform was rejected in the general election of 1906, when its opponents argued that it would mean higher food prices. As a result Britain remained committed to a policy of free trade, which lasted until the protectionist measures of the 1930s. There are some parallels between the European Union and the strategy of social imperialism in that a free trade area with an external tariff is used in the EU to provide funds for social expenditure.

RELATED TOPICS

1.13 Bismarckianism
1.15 Conservative paternalism
9.6 The European Union

FURTHER READING

Gamble (1981) pp 166–74
Semmel (1960) pp 23–8 and 90–7

1.15 CONSERVATIVE PATERNALISM

Paternalism refers to the exercise of a fatherly form of authority which is both stern and caring. Paternalist concern for the poor has been an element in the development of social policy. Paternalism is an aspect of conservative thought which has its origins in the obligation of feudal superiors to their vassals.

The paternal tradition in social policy has deep roots in Britain. In 1794, during a period of wartime inflation, popular radicalism, unemployment and economic dislocation, a meeting of magistrates agreed to pay poor relief in cash or kind whenever the price of bread reached a certain threshold. This early form of index-linked benefit was known as the 'Speenhamland system' after the place where the magistrates had met. The relief was paid whether or not the applicants were in paid work, thus violating *liberal* principles on maintaining work incentives.

This paternalist tradition was strengthened by the Conservative leader Disraeli following the Reform Act of 1867 which broadened the franchise allowing many working-class men to vote for the first time. Disraeli wrote that 'the palace is not safe when the cottage is not happy'. He also criticised mid-Victorian England as 'two nations' (rich and poor) which became the origin of the term 'one nation conservatism'. This referred to a paternalistic conservatism, often known as Toryism, which attempted to shield the poor from the worst economic effects of capitalist industry.

> Social legislation ... is not merely to be distinguished from Socialist legislation but it is its most direct opposite and its most effective antidote. Socialism will never get possession of the great body of public opinion ... among the working class or any other class if those who wield the collective forces of the community show themselves desirous to ameliorate every legitimate grievance and to put Society upon a proper and more solid basis. (A. J. Balfour, future Tory leader, 1895, quoted in Fraser, 1973: 129)

Tory paternalism also played a part when the Conservative Party in Britain, after being re-elected in 1951, did not set out to reverse the welfare reforms establishing the welfare state which had been brought in by the Labour Party.

RELATED TOPICS

1.13 Bismarckianism
1.14 Social imperialism
2.8 The family: right-wing view

FURTHER READING

Weale (1978)

1.16 EUGENICS

Eugenics is based on 'scientific' laws of heredity showing that human characteristics are inherited and that social problems are caused by people who are biologically inferior. A belief in the biological inferiority of the lower classes was widely held in the second half of the nineteenth century and the first half of the twentieth century. This viewpoint has been called 'Social Darwinism', since it rested on the application of Darwin's ideas on the role of 'natural selection' and competition between species in ensuring the 'survival of the fittest'.

In Britain a Eugenics Society was founded in 1907, supported by many leading supporters of *Fabianism* such as George Bernard Shaw, Beatrice and Sidney Webb, and representatives of the *new liberalism* such as John Maynard Keynes and William Beveridge (see 4.6). It had an important influence on legislation.

The 1913 Mental Deficiency Act classified mental defectives into four types: idiots, imbeciles, the feeble-minded and moral imbeciles. Feeble-mindedness was seen as hereditary, and as the main cause of poverty, unemployment, crime, prostitution, promiscuity, alcoholism and vagrancy. Under the act, members of these categories could be, and were, compulsorily detained.

These policies were pursued until well into the second half of the twentieth century in Britain and in other advanced capitalist states including the United States, France and the Nordic countries. Ideas about the biological basis of social problems have continued to exercise an influence on social policy. 'Hereditarian' theories have been developed in several areas such as the debate about 'racial differences'. Some criminologists have viewed crime as having some hereditary determinants. Poverty continues to be viewed by many on the right as a hereditary condition.

> The balance of our population, our human stock is threatened ... a high and rising proportion of children are being born to mothers least fitted to bring children into the world and bring them up ... they are producing problem children, the future unmarried mothers, delinquents, denizens of our borstals, sub-normal educational establishments, prisons, hostels for drifters ... (Joseph, 1974)

Herrnstein and Murray (1994) have argued that intelligence is transmitted by genes and that racial groups have different scores. Black Americans have lower scores than whites and they see this as the reason for their high rates of poverty and the lower positions they tend to occupy in the class structure.

Developments in molecular biology have led to attempts to associate particular genes with crime and other forms of deviant behaviour. It has been suggested that 'genetic screening' would allow foetuses with these genes to be aborted. The views have been described as part of a 'new eugenics'.

Eugenics is also closely linked to the ideas developed in Sociobiology. Sociobiology emphasises the role of instincts in determining human behaviour. There is also a modern centre-left version of sociobiology known as 'evolutionary psychology'. This rests on the application of Darwinian ideas to the interpretation of social behaviour. It views various aspects of behaviour as a result of genetic characteristics which developed as an adaptation to the conditions of early human history. These dispositions are seen as setting limits to possible programmes of reform.

> Dispositions such as self-interest, material aggrandisement, sympathy, notions of fairness, equity, etc., are genetically hardwired, not social constructs. (Mulgan, quoted in Malik, 1996)

RELATED TOPICS

1.19 The new liberalism
1.20 Fabianism
2.17 Poverty: right-wing view
5.3 The causes of crime: right-wing view
6.8 Mental disability
8.6 Great Britain: race
9.20 Disability

FURTHER READING

Cronin and Curry (1996)
Herrnstein and Murray (1994) Chap 1
Jones (1980) pp 108–20
Mazumdar (1991)
Searle (1976)
Wilson (1975)

1.17 NEO-LIBERALISM (THE NEW RIGHT)

Neo-liberalism, sometimes termed the *new right*, is a new (neo) formulation of liberalism with distinctive economic, political and social doctrines. Its chief political theorist is Hayek (1980) who argued that the sovereignty of parliament should be limited, perhaps by a 'bill of rights', in order to prevent it from violating the rights of individuals. Hayek saw state social services as 'the road to serfdom' because extensive state intervention took away people's liberty.

> In Britain, neo-liberal ideas have been advanced by such bodies as the Institute of Economic Affairs and the Adam Smith Institute, and were particularly influential within the Thatcher government. (Leach, 1991: 82)

The economic and social-policy implications of neo-liberalism are most clearly worked out by Friedman. In principle, all services should be provided by the market, since then people can express their preferences freely in terms of what they are willing to pay for. Competition between providers in a free market will ensure that services will be produced efficiently. However, if for practical or historical reasons state social provision exists, it must be run on lines which are consistent with market principles. Consumers must be able to choose between providers. Providers must compete with one another. The recipients are seen as consumers (buying a product) rather than clients (receiving a professional service).

> The new right has a double strategy here: to cut back as far as possible on state expenditure ... a difficult task with high levels of unemployment and an ageing population; the second strand is to encourage the development of market-based forms of provision, private hospitals and insurance in the health field, encourage private education via the assisted places scheme, and occupational pensions by ensuring their portability. The strategy seems to be to create an environment more favourable to market allocation in this sphere, in the hope that, over time, people will look to the state less and less for welfare, taking more responsibility for their own lives. (Drucker et al., 1986: 12)

This policy involves the creation of *provider markets*, sometimes called 'quasi-markets', in which state services are provided by competing state-financed units with some degree of choice exercised by, or on behalf of, the recipients. State schooling in Britain was reformed using these principles in the 1980s and 1990s. The British National Health Service was reorganised in this fashion after 1989.

RELATED TOPICS

4.2 Privatisation
4.3 Provider markets
5.7 Schooling: right-wing view
8.4 Great Britain: health care

FURTHER READING

Friedman (1962)
Friedman and Friedman (1980)
Gamble (1988) Chap 2
Hayek (1980)
Loney (1987) Chap 1
Minford (1987)
Pierson (1991) pp 40–8
Room (1979) pp 48–56

Part 3 Reformist approaches

1.18 REFORMIST APPROACHES: GENERAL FEATURES

Modern social reformism combines ideas from a number of sources.

1. *Revisionism*: at the end of the nineteenth century some German Marxists became disillusioned with the prospects for revolution and began to support more limited, but immediate, social reforms – supporters of this approach were called 'revisionists' as they had revised classical Marxism.
2. *The new liberalism*: some liberals came to believe that support for free markets created such severe conditions that many people could never develop their capabilities to the full and therefore that the state should intervene to create the conditions where liberal aspirations for the full development of every individual could be met.
3. *Conservatism*: some varieties of conservative thought, especially those within a paternalist or Catholic tradition, argued for social reforms to increase social unity and, sometimes, to head off support for the left.

   Social reformism is characterised by a generalised commitment to progress, a faith in the capacity of human-beings to improve, an egalitarian impulse predisposing them to democracy, a faith in the role of the state as an instrument of social reform, a belief in the possibility and desirability of incremental social change and an antipathy to revolutionary movements and revolutionary change. (Coates, 1990: 267)

Reformist ideologies lie in the centre between the free-market ideas of *liberalism* and the organised egalitarianism of the radical left. Reformism involves the pursuit of gradual improvement and reform. All varieties of social reformism aim to solve social and economic problems through rationally designed state action. This is undertaken through democratic, parliamentary means.

The epitome of reformism is the *Keynesian welfare state*. Keynesianism uses state economic management to solve the social and economic problem of unemployment. The welfare state uses social provision to meet the needs of those who cannot secure an adequate standard of life through the market.

RELATED TOPICS

1.15 Conservative paternalism
1.22 Keynesian welfare state
8.7 Ireland: background
9.3 Reformism

FURTHER READING

Coates (1990)
Crosland (1964)
Room (1979) pp 56–66
Sullivan (1987) pp 29–39

1.19 THE NEW LIBERALISM

The *new liberalism* was a reforming tendency within the British Liberal Party, which developed in the early part of the twentieth century and exercised an influence over policy in the Liberal governments of 1906–14. Some leading Liberals felt the party could no longer continue to support laissez-faire principles. There was growing evidence of deep-seated poverty and other social problems which seemed to result from an uncontrolled market. There was also increasing concern about foreign economic competition and political rivalry. The new liberalism attempted to chart a new, reformist path for the Liberal Party. The new liberalism was closely linked to the 'national efficiency movement' which campaigned for policies to improve the health and strength of British workers to enhance industrial productivity and military strength.

> British Liberalism ... has not abandoned the traditional ambition of the Liberal Party to establish freedom and equality; but side by side with this effort it promotes measures for ameliorating the conditions of life for the multitude. (Lloyd George, speech, 1908, quoted in Hay, 1978: 13)

The new liberalism was not a coherent political theory but it did have some intellectual underpinnings. A central theoretical idea of the new liberalism was *citizenship* – making the working class full members of society. It also made extensive use of the concept of *poverty*. Seebohm Rowntree, a progressive industrialist from the Quaker chocolate manufacturers, demonstrated that wage levels were so low that they were insufficient to maintain a normal level of health and working efficiency for many workers. Rowntree's researchers (reported in *Poverty: A Study of Town Life*, 1901) established the modern study of *poverty* using a 'scientifically' calculated poverty line.

The social policies introduced by the new liberals included medical inspections for children (1907), old age pensions (1908), labour exchanges (1909) and *National Insurance* for sickness and unemployment (1911).

RELATED TOPICS

2.15 Citizenship: reformist view
2.18 Poverty: reformist view

FURTHER READING

Clarke, Cochrane and Smart (1987) pp 35–47
Freeden (1978)
Hay (1975) Chap 3
Pearson and Williams (1984) Chap 5
Searle (1971)
Weiler (1982)

1.20 FABIANISM

Fabianism has been the principal source of reformist plans and ideas within the British Labour Party. The Fabian Society was formed by a number of socialist intellectuals in 1883, and was named after Fabius Cunctator, a Roman general who defeated Hannibal by avoiding a head-on conflict.

The early Fabians viewed the main defects of capitalism as waste and inefficiency rather than inequality and exploitation. Two key figures in the Fabian movement were Sidney and Beatrice Webb, who played a major role in mobilising reforming opinion through personal contact with members of the elite. Many prominent intellectuals of the time were also members including George Bernard Shaw, the playwright and H. G. Wells, the novelist. Many of these were also supporters of the Eugenics Society. The Webbs also produced a massively detailed programme of reform in their Minority Report of the Royal Commission on the Poor Laws, which reported in 1909. The minority report proposed a comprehensive system of state welfare and its ideas remained influential in that it described a broad programme of reform of the kind that was implemented in the 1940s.

The strategy of the Fabians was rationalist, elitist and gradualist.

1. They were *rationalist* in that they believed that research and discussion could produce solutions to all social and economic problems.
2. They were *elitist* in that they believed that a small number of dedicated intellectuals could alone create effective pressures for reform and in that they sought to implement their ideas through 'permeation', i.e. by personal influence with decision makers.
3. They were *gradualist* in that they sought a steady progress towards socialism rather than a sudden revolutionary shift.

Fabian principles of gradual reform from above have remained a major influence on British Labour Party thinking. In recent years, however, Fabianism has come under strong attack from a range of alternative ideologies.

> After a balmy youth as the common sense of government in the Wilson era, this tradition has suffered sudden attack on three fronts. The success of reformism is challenged in the evidence that state welfare has not advanced equality; its popular appeal is overthrown by the 1979 and 1983 election victories; and the advent of feminist, Marxist and liberal critiques of Fabian theory demand a response. (Taylor-Gooby, 1985: 119)

RELATED TOPICS

1.16 Eugenics
1.19 The new liberalism
3.5 Social betterment
4.8 Administrative reorganisation

FURTHER READING

Shaw (1949)
Weeks (1984)

1.21 LOGIC OF INDUSTRIALISM

The logic of industrialism is a 'functionalist' approach (see 2.24), which rests on a form of technological determinism. Functionalist explanations claim that new policies have been instituted in order to meet the 'needs' of an 'industrial' or 'urban' or 'changing' society. Technological determinism sees technology as the major force shaping modern society, having more influence over our lives than any other social or political factor.

Theories based on technological determinism suggest that as modern industrial methods of production come to predominate in any society certain requirements are created which have to be met to ensure sustained economic expansion. These requirements consist of a system of competitive recruitment to occupational roles based on competence and a high level of consent to the existing order among the population.

> The state will be powerful. It will, at the minimum, have the responsibility for the economic growth rate; the over-all distribution of income among uses and among individuals; the basic security of individuals (the family formerly was the basic security unit); the stability of the system; providing the essential public services of education, transportation, recreational areas, cultural facilities, and the like; and the responsibility of providing

a favourable physical environment for urban man. (Kerr et al., 1973: 271)

In order to meet these requirements every industrial society will be under pressure to develop a similar income and occupational structure underpinned by social policies. This necessitates:

1. A mass educational system in order to ensure that the required skills and knowledge are available and that employers have the widest possible pool to draw from.
2. Health services to ensure a healthy and contented workforce.
3. Social services to reduce dependence on the extended family so allowing the social and geographical mobility which is needed for the efficient use of labour.

One strand in the story of the social services is the continuing endeavour to provide the environment required for industrial progress. The industrial revolution imposed a clear-cut distinction between those who were in work and those who were not. It called for a mobile, disciplined and increasingly educated labour force. It greatly intensified the poverty cycle afflicting children, their parents and old people. It created the big city, with its new problems of public health and public order. (Donnison, 1962: 28)

The logic of industrialism is the basis for the 'convergence thesis' which predicts a growing similarity in the social structure of all industrial societies.

RELATED TOPICS

1.20 Fabianism
2.24 Social needs and problems: reformist view
3.5 Social betterment

FURTHER READING

Kerr et al. (1973)
Mishra (1977) Chap 3
Pierson (1991) pp 12–21

1.22 KEYNESIAN WELFARE STATE

The term *Keynesian welfare state* refers to the kind of policies established in many Western capitalist countries after the Second World War. The Second World War created conditions favourable to social reform. The adoption of these policies has been seen as part of a 'post-war settlement' which was able to resolve social antagonisms and form the basis for a period of social harmony.

... everywhere these 'post-war settlements' included at their core a central premise: 'full' employment through governmental demand management and increased social welfare expenditure in return for relative social harmony and labour peace. There would be a better-managed capitalism, with considerable limits placed on private prerogative: a capitalism tilting toward a non-ideological social democracy. (Krieger, 1986: 23)

The two key thinkers whose ideas underpinned this development were Keynes and Beveridge (see 4.6). Both were associated with the *new liberalism* and both worked within the Liberal Party. Keynes's theories involved a system of government intervention to increase spending in order to create jobs while preserving the market and individual economic and political freedom. Beveridge's proposals for the welfare state were contained in his wartime report of 1942, which proposed a comprehensive social-security system along with full employment, a national health service and family allowances.

Much of the legislation for the British welfare state was brought in by the Labour government of 1945–50, though, ironically, the detailed plans were largely based on ideas found in the work of Keynes and Beveridge. When the Conservatives were re-elected in 1951 they maintained the commitment to Keynesian full employment policies and the welfare state.

RELATED TOPICS

1.19 The new liberalism
1.20 Fabianism
4.6 National Insurance
4.7 Universalism

FURTHER READING

Beveridge (1942 and 1944)
Cutler et al. (1986) Chap 1

1.23 WELFARE PLURALISM

The preference of the British Conservative government of 1979–97 for a 'mixed' system of welfare was based on a desire to reduce the role of the state, cut public spending and increase the role of the private sector. *Welfare pluralism* is concerned to reduce the role of the state in the provision of welfare – it is also sometimes known as the 'mixed economy of welfare'.

... social and health care may be obtained from four different sectors – the statutory, the voluntary, the commercial and the informal ... welfare pluralism implies a less dominant role for the state. (Hatch and Mocroft, 1983: 2)

These four sectors operate in different ways:

1. The *statutory* sector is based on legislation and operates through state-welfare organisations.
2. The *voluntary* sector uses voluntary effort but may be coordinated and partly financed by, and operate under contract to, the state sector.
3. The *private* sector operates for profit under contract and sometimes in partnership with other sectors.
4. The *informal* sector consists mainly of families who provide care to dependent members and members of the *community* who assist others.

An important theme in welfare pluralism is decentralisation. In local authorities a means of achieving this is the 'patch' system, in which small teams of social workers operate in a particular neighbourhood and get to know it well.

Critics on the left see welfare pluralism as a shift to the right by those Fabians who have promoted it and as a response to the economic crisis of the late 1970s and 1980s. Feminist critics argue that voluntarism will often involve relying on women's unpaid domestic labour.

RELATED TOPICS

1.20 Fabianism
2.12 Community: reformist view
3.6 Pluralism
4.2 Privatisation

FURTHER READING

Beresford and Croft (1984)
Hadley and Hatch (1981)
Moore (1993) Chap 9

1.24 COMMUNITARIANISM

The main idea of *communitarianism* is to balance individual rights and community responsibilities. Unrestrained individualism is seen as having undermined family and community relationships. The goal of communitarians is to promote *community* rather than equality. They believe that the modern state must have a broad sense of purpose greater than the sum of individual and group interests.

Communities need not be, and often are not, local or just residential. Union solidarity can provide community. So can a profession, a religious persuasion, a shared sub-culture. The main features are a web of interpersonal attachments and a shared set of values. Communities need to be evaluated, judged and often reformed, but not replaced with nothing. Communities that develop hierarchies, where those in power oppress others, are in particular need of restructuring. One must acknowledge, though, that full equality is a Utopian goal and one which we should not expect to achieve. Similarly one should not assume that equality is a cure-all; we still need to nourish and sustain bonds. (Etzioni, 1995: 25)

Communitarianism has become a key idea in those versions of reformism which down play economic egalitarianism and emphasise moral improvement. Communitarianism supports the concept of a 'peer marriage' with parents with equal rights and responsibilities committed to their children. Communitarianism supports an approach to dealing with crime which emphasises strong social bonds and creating a partnership between the community and the enforcement agencies.

Feminists have criticised the communitarian idea of community for ignoring gender and power inequalities. The left has criticised communitarianism for ignoring class exploitation, economic decay, job insecurity and poverty as causes of community decline.

RELATED TOPICS

2.3 The individual in society: reformist view
2.9 The family: reformist view
2.12 Community: reformist view

FURTHER READING

Etzioni (1993)
Frazer and Lacey (1993)
Galston (1991)

Part 4 Radical approaches

1.25 RADICAL APPROACHES: GENERAL FEATURES

Radical approaches to social policy have three main sources.

1. Disillusion with the social impact of *liberalism*. Radicals argue that modern industrial societies are characterised by alienation in the sense that they fail to create the social conditions needed for the full development of the human capabilities of the people who live in them. So instead of realising the liberal vision of a society

of free, equal and prosperous individuals, economic freedom produces a capitalist society based on exploitation, inequality and class conflict.

Miliband writes of 'a fundamental distinction' which Marx made between 'political emancipation' and 'human emancipation'. The former included civic rights such as the extension of the suffrage, representative institutions and the curbing of arbitrary power, and was attainable within the capitalist system. In contrast, 'human emancipation' cannot be achieved simply through political changes but depends upon the revolutionary transformation of the economic and social order. Capitalism cannot create a truly human environment. It cannot provide the economic and social conditions for men and women to realise their true potentialities. (George and Wilding, 1985: 96–7)

2. Disillusion with the failure of *reformism* to achieve lasting and thoroughgoing social improvement. In capitalist societies social policy is always influenced by the need to sustain capitalism, wage labour and inequality. Only through the abolition of capitalism and the establishment of a society based on common ownership and equality can the conditions be created for the real achievement of the freedom originally aspired to in reformist thought.

3. Revulsion at the character of developed capitalist industrialism. These societies have been seen as failing to offer a genuinely human experience, owing to their scale, technology, complexity and specialisation. An alternative non-Marxist radical response has been to seek to move to a society based on simpler technology and smaller organisations. This would create conditions in which people could live in closer harmony with nature and with each other.

Radical approaches to social policy have sometimes been adopted at local level. This occurred in some of the 'little Moscows' in the 1920s which pursued generous policies towards the unemployed. It also occurred in what was termed the 'new municipal socialism' of the early 1980s in Britain.

RELATED TOPICS

1.29 Illich and anti-industrialism
9.4 Radicalism

FURTHER READING

Dearlove and Saunders (1984) pp 313–21
Green (1987)
Mishra (1977) Chap 5
Westergaard and Resler (1975) pp 346–50

1.26 MARXISM: 1 CAPITAL LOGIC

One explanation of the nature and role of social policies in capitalist societies given by Marxism assumes that all public policies will be dominated by the need to ensure the survival of capitalism. Explanations of this kind are functionalist (see 2.24). The explanation starts by asking what functions social policy performs for 'capital', i.e. the survival of the capitalist system.

> the capitalistic state must try to fulfil two ... functions accumulation and legitimisation ... to maintain or create the conditions in which profitable capital accumulation is possible ... the state also must try to maintain or create the conditions for social harmony ... [social] services ... [can] lower the reproduction costs of labour ... An example of this is social insurance ... [S]ervices which are required to maintain social harmony ... fulfil the state's legitimization function ... The best example is the welfare system, which is designed chiefly to keep social peace among unemployed workers. (O'Connor, 1973: 5–6)

These approaches are sometimes called capital logic or state-derivation theories. This is because the nature of the (welfare) state is 'derived', i.e. deduced, from the needs of the capitalist system. 'Accumulation' refers to state policies designed to improve the profitability of capitalist production. 'Legitimation' refers to social policies designed to promote acceptance of capitalism and the society based on it.

The main weakness of this approach is that it seems to imply that all capitalist societies will have similar social policies and therefore it cannot account for the substantial variations between their social policies that exist in reality. In order to do this an alternative Marxist approach is needed which puts much greater emphasis on the distinctive character of the historical development and the *balance of social forces* found in different capitalist societies.

RELATED TOPICS

1.13 Bismarckianism
1.14 Social imperialism
3.9 Marxism

FURTHER READING

Burden and Campbell (1985) Chap 1
Gough (1979) pp 49–54
O'Connor (1973) Chap 1
Room (1979) pp 42–8

1.27 MARXISM: 2 BALANCE OF SOCIAL FORCES

Marxists who stress the balance of social forces see social policies as resulting from the political process within a capitalist society. The types of political parties and other significant social movements, their programmes and their levels of support all affect the policies which are brought in. All these factors can vary substantially between capitalist societies. While there may be a general pressure for social policies which sustain capitalism, these will vary markedly from one society to another. Important differences may arise from:

1. Social movements such as feminism or temperance campaigns, which may exercise a strong influence on policy.
2. Historical legacies, such as a strong (or a weak) labour movement or a dominant class which includes the residue of a pre-capitalist landowning class, as is the case in Britain.
3. International factors such as imperial possessions or ambitions which can affect social policies initiated by ruling groups.

The extent to which social policies are initiated by ruling groups will depend on their sense of security and the existence of a tradition of *paternalism*. As a result, welfare states may often incorporate social services which represent a range of different values and concerns.

> ... the welfare state ... simultaneously embodies tendencies to enhance social welfare, to develop the powers of individuals, to exert social control over the blind play of market forces; and tendencies to repress and control people, to adapt them to the requirements of the capitalist economy. (Gough, 1979: 12)

This kind of Marxism shares some features of *pluralism* except that it rests on the assumption that ultimately the most important influences on social policies are capitalism and class.

RELATED TOPICS

1.6 Esping-Andersen: welfare regimes
1.14 Social imperialism
1.15 Conservative paternalism
3.6 Pluralism
3.9 Marxism
3.10 New social movements

FURTHER READING

Burden and Campbell (1985) Chap 1
Ginsburg (1979) Chap 1
Gough (1979) Chaps 1 and 2
Pierson (1991) pp 45–58

1.28 LEGITIMATION CRISIS

The concept of *legitimation crisis* comes from the work of Habermas. He depicts society as made up of three sub-systems: the economic, the political and the socio-cultural. Each sub-system has to operate effectively for the society as a whole to continue to function. This is a functionalist argument (see 2.24). When unmanageable problems arise in the inputs or outputs of any of the sub-systems there is a crisis.

'Crisis' is a term taken from medicine, which refers to the stage in the course of an illness at which the patient may either begin to recover or enter a fatal decline. These crises can take several forms, which are often related to social policies.

1. A *rationality crisis* can occur when the state is incapable of implementing effective solutions to serious policy problems.
2. A *fiscal crisis* can occur when the levels of taxation needed to finance social policies damage the general profitability of capitalist enterprise.
3. A *motivation crisis* can occur if institutions involved with social policy such as schools and families do not succeed in socialising the young into the values necessary for the continuation of the society.

In combination, these specific crises can lead to a generalised legitimation crisis which threatens the survival of the society in its existing form.

> ... a legitimation crisis then, must be based on a motivation crisis – that is, a discrepancy between the need for motives declared by the state, the educational system and the occupational system on the one hand, and the motivation supplied by the socio-cultural system on the other ... (Habermas, 1976: 74–5)

Social policies can thus be viewed in terms of the role they play in contributing to, or resolving crises. Habermas puts forward an argument which has much in common with the Marxist approach based on the balance of social forces except that he does not view the economic system as necessarily exercising a predominant influence.

RELATED TOPICS

1.27 Marxism: 2 Balance of social forces
3.2 Overloaded government
3.6 Pluralism

FURTHER READING

Habermas (1976) Part 2

1.29 ILLICH AND ANTI-INDUSTRIALISM

This approach to social policy starts with a rejection of industrialism and industrial society rather than with a rejection of capitalism. The most important advocate of social policies based on these principles is Illich. Three aspects of modern industrial societies are criticised: advanced technology, large-scale organisation and occupational specialisation:

1. *advanced technology* because it is out of the control of those it affects and because it destroys many formerly meaningful human activities such as work;
2. *large-scale organisation* because its bureaucratic form is impersonal;
3. *occupational specialisation* because it sets strict limits to the exercise of human capabilities particularly when it takes the form of *professionalism*.

    ... it is possible to identify a natural scale. When an enterprise grows beyond a certain scale, it first frustrates the end for which it was originally designed, and then rapidly becomes a threat to society itself ... Society can be destroyed when further growth of mass production renders the milieu hostile, when it extinguishes the free use of the natural abilities of society's members, when it isolates people from each other and locks them into a man-made shell, when it undermines the texture of community by promoting extreme social polarisation and splintering specialisation ... (Illich, 1977a: 11)

Rejection of advanced technology may involve a preference for 'intermediate technology' with important implications for areas of social policy such as health care. Illich argues that professionalism is a threat to those subject to it. Professionalism in areas of social policy such as health care and education is seen as preventing these activities from being controlled or even influenced by those who are subject to them. Illich argues that modern medicine dehumanises patients and is itself a major threat to health. He supports a recasting of education and has advocated 'deschooling' society. In common with some ecologists, Illich seeks a smaller-scale society based on a simpler pattern of life but with a wider range of human activity for each of its members.

RELATED TOPICS

1.24 Communitarianism

2.13 Community: radical view
4.9 Participation
5.9 Schooling: radical view
5.21 Death and disease: radical view
5.25 Professionalism: radical view

FURTHER READING

Dickson (1974)
Illich (1977a) Chap 3
Schumacher (1993)

CHAPTER 2

General concepts in social policy

2.1 CENTRAL CONCEPTS

Concepts are the basic building blocks of theories. Each of the social sciences has its own family of concepts. A large part of learning a subject lies in becoming fluent in its concepts by being able to talk and think with them. The concepts included in this chapter are all central to debates about social policy. These concepts are 'contested' in the sense of being the subject of, or figuring in, contemporary and historical debates about social policy. Each concept is given a distinctive meaning by each of the three main perspectives employed in this book. In this chapter the *right-wing, reformist* and *radical* perspectives on each of the concepts are considered. The following concepts are examined:

1. *The individual in society* – this concerns individuality and human nature and their links with social order.
2. *Gender* – this concerns social definitions of the differences between men and women.
3. *Family* – this concerns family relationships and the social role of the family.
4. *Community* – this concerns the nature of the bonds uniting those with a common sense of identity.
5. *Citizenship* – this concerns the rights and obligations arising from membership of a national society.
6. *Poverty* – this concerns the recognition of, and response to, what is seen as an unacceptably low standard of living.
7. *Race* – this concerns social perceptions of the existence of biologically different groups.
8. *Social needs and social problems* – this concerns how issues become the subject of policy intervention.

RELATED TOPICS

5.1 Issues in social policy

FURTHER READING

A good way to study concepts is to use specialised dictionaries and encyclopaedias such as those listed below (full details are given in the References at the end of this book)
Abercrombie, N. et al. (1988)

Bottomore T. B. (ed.) (1991)
Bottomore, T. and Outhwaite, W. (eds) (1993)
Bullock, A. and Stallybrass, O. (eds) (1988)
Humm, M. (1995)
Mann, M. (1983)
Miller, D. et al. (eds) (1987)
Timms, N. and Timms, R. (eds) (1982)
Williams, R. (1976)

2.2 THE INDIVIDUAL IN SOCIETY: RIGHT-WING VIEW

Two rather different views of the individual in society are found in right-wing political and social theories. These views are associated with *liberalism* and *conservatism*.

1. The view associated with *liberalism* stresses rational motives and behaviour and the role of reason in social life. This doctrine takes an optimistic view of human nature and sees people as reasoning beings who will flourish and develop under conditions of minimal restrictions on their liberty.

In political theory this view is known as individualism. Liberal views are founded on the idea of a social contract. Individuals agree to abide by laws which protect everybody's freedom. Society is seen as no more than a collection of individuals. It is held together by the dealings they each undertake with each other in pursuit of their self-interest.

2. The view associated with *conservatism* sees people as driven by feelings as much as by reason. This doctrine takes a pessimistic view of human nature based on the Christian idea of original sin and the notion of human imperfectibility. Since people by nature are partly driven by impulse and emotion then social order requires that they be effectively controlled. The state needs to be a powerful centre of authority in society. *Paternalism* may play a part in sustaining social order.

With a strong state keeping order, people can live together in a civilised fashion. The conservative view may also rest on the idea of a social contract which people make in order to save themselves from their destructive impulses. A sovereign state with effective law-enforcing powers is the only guarantee of a secure existence. The authority of the state needs to be reinforced by respect for tradition and the social authority of established ruling groups. The maintenance of social order is more important than individual freedom.

Both versions of right-wing thought come to the conclusion that the state is needed so that individuals can live together in freedom and security.

RELATED TOPICS

1.15 Conservative paternalism
1.16 Eugenics
1.17 Neo-liberalism (the new right)

FURTHER READING

Forbes and Smith (1983) Chap 4
Lukes (1973) Chaps 9, 12 and 13
Morris (1969) Chap 1
Novak (1982) Chap 6

2.3 THE INDIVIDUAL IN SOCIETY: REFORMIST VIEW

The reformist conception of the individual shares with *liberalism* the view that, given individual freedom, people will generally flourish and prosper. In addition however, it recognises that for some people social conditions or individual disadvantage may make this impossible. Reformism rejects the extreme individualism of liberalism.

> ... for Mill humankind are not merely biological machines... they are for the most part conditioned by education, circumstance and the related causal laws of the mind... if we understand the role of each in forming human nature, we can mould education and circumstance into forms which serve the general purpose of encouraging the development of both emancipated individuals and an enlightened society. (Forbes and Smith, 1983: 44)

There is, therefore, a role for the state in providing the conditions under which everyone is able to make full use of the freedom they possess. This can include support for policies to relieve *poverty* and to ensure that everyone receives a good education. The provision of opportunities for all is seen as a means of holding society together. It also ensures that society is able to benefit from the availability of the widest possible pool of talent.

Reformism suggests that while individuals will pursue their self-interest they may also define this to include a concern for others. Reformism supports the idea of a social conscience. This can be expressed in various ways relevant to social policy:

1. in support for state welfare policies
2. in participation in campaigns for social reform
3. in active involvement in voluntary work designed to benefit others.

RELATED TOPICS

1.19 The new liberalism
3.5 Social betterment

FURTHER READING

Titmuss (1970) Chap 14

2.4 THE INDIVIDUAL IN SOCIETY: RADICAL VIEW

The radical conception of human nature views it as strongly influenced by the general character of a society. Human nature is a social product. Different types of society produce different types of human being. Marxism views the liberal conception of human nature as a reflection of the dominant values of capitalism rather than as a universal attribute of people everywhere. People are not 'naturally' individualistic or competitive but if they live in a society where these attributes are necessary for material survival then they will become so.

> ... personal liberty can be reconciled with the ideal of full and spontaneous participation in public affairs, once the evils of the present order are abolished. The self is not necessarily at odds with its social role; this fragmentation of the individual is a product of particular social conditions. Only true freedom, however, can permit reintegration and allow the development of a meaningful awareness of others' needs. (Jordan, 1976: 25)

Marxism also has a conception of human nature as a set of potential capabilities. In a capitalist society these remain under-developed. The abolition of capitalism and the end of the division of labour, would permit a full flowering of these capabilities.

> communist society ... makes it possible for me to do one thing today and another tomorrow, to hunt in the morning, fish in the afternoon, rear cattle in the evening, criticise after dinner, just as I have a mind, without ever becoming hunter, fisherman, shepherd or critic ... (Marx, 1965: 44–5, originally written in 1844)

In a capitalist society, people are 'alienated' (i.e. separated) from themselves. They may also be alienated from their own sexuality. Some Marxists have argued that social policies may be used to restrict the capabilities that people develop and mould their human characteristics into a form which benefits capital. Education for working-class children may be designed to habituate them to routine and discipline. This acts as a preparation for factory labour rather than as a means of fully developing their capabilities.

RELATED TOPICS

1.27 Marxism: 2 Balance of social forces
4.13 Empowerment

5.9 Schooling: radical view

FURTHER READING

Forbes and Smith (1983) Chap 2
Geras (1983)
Marcuse (1972) pp 11–19
Oakley (1972) Chap 2
Venable (1966) Chap 5

2.5 GENDER: RIGHT-WING VIEW

The conservative anti-feminist approach represents a traditionalist assertion of women's social role as homemaker and wife. Traditional ideologies of 'familism' (women's role as mothers) and domesticity (women's role in the household), looking after men, children and dependent relatives, are often emphasised. Conventional sociology in the form of the functionalist theory (see 2.24) of the family is an academic version of this viewpoint. The anti-feminist approach has a number of components:

- it employs traditional ideas of the biological superiority of men and the separate spheres of life of men and women
- it employs the results of 'scientific' research to try to demonstrate that gender inequalities have a basis in biological differences
- it claims that if women do not perform their 'natural' role within the family home their children will suffer
- it views *reformist* and *radical* policies towards gender as attempts to stir up political conflict.

Some *liberals* deny that there are any insurmountable barriers to the full equality of men and women. They argue that women need only to pursue their aspirations with vigour to achieve full equality. These 'libertarian feminists' see society from the viewpoint of individualism.

> ... some libertarian feminists retain the individualism of neo-liberalism but reject the biological determinism implicit in the writings of neo-liberal philosophers like Friedman, Hayek or Mount who see women's ability to bear children and 'natural instincts' determining their role as mothers and homemakers ... What they share is a belief in individualism and neo-liberalism. As such they have little to say about the organization of welfare since for them state intervention one way or another is not conducive to the improvement of women's lives ... (Williams, 1989: 43–4)

RELATED TOPICS

2.2 The individual in society: right-wing view

FURTHER READING

Burrows (1988) Chap 9
David (1986)
Goldberg (1994) Chap 1
Parsons and Bales (1956) pp 3–21
Williams (1989) pp 43–9

2.6 GENDER: REFORMIST VIEW

The reformist approach has its origins in nineteenth-century campaigns to achieve equal rights for women and the twentieth-century movement to secure *citizenship* and social rights for women.

> During the last three decades of the nineteenth century a series of campaigns emerged to improve women's legal and economic position. In particular, women campaigned to remove the legal disabilities of married women which denied them the right to own property, or to take custody of their children after separation or divorce, and which sanctioned a double standard of morality in divorce. They also opened up secondary and higher education to women by establishing women's schools and colleges and gaining women the right to sit for degrees, and to enter certain of the professions which previously barred women ... (Dale and Foster, 1986: 5–6)

Reformist perspectives on gender emphasise the concepts of discrimination and prejudice. Sexism is seen as largely a matter of personal motivation. Education and legislation against discrimination are viewed as effective means to combat sexism.

In many capitalist countries in the 1960s and 1970s a reformist policy was pursued based on legislation against discrimination. This approach dominated policy and much academic writing until recently. The emphasis is on equal opportunities and action to make them a reality. An important focus of this work is on educational change, which encourages girls and young women to enter subject areas in which their numbers are low. Another important area of policy in this perspective is employment, where efforts are made to prevent discrimination against women, and to provide the conditions which enable women to work. This can involve recognition by employers of women's child-care responsibilities through provision of nurseries for children of employees along with working hours and periods of leave which take account of women's domestic responsibilities.

2.7 GENDER: RADICAL VIEW

The two main radical views on gender are Marxist feminism and radical feminism.

Marxist thought revolves around capitalism and class. Other social divisions such as gender and ethnicity are explained within the context of class. The position of women is explained in terms of the contribution they make to the operation of the capitalist system. *Marxist feminism* views women as making up part of the 'reserve army of labour'. They are employed during periods of labour shortage to keep wage costs down, as are other groups making up this reserve army, such as migrant labourers and the old. The development of crisis conditions leads to the degradation of women's status because labour surpluses develop and they are no longer required.

Women also make a major contribution to the 'reproduction' of the present and the future labour force through their domestic labour. This largely involves looking after men and bringing up the new generation of workers.

Marxist feminists argue that class divisions mean that some women are in a more privileged position than others in terms of life experiences and life chances. Only a minority of women have the opportunity of gaining higher education along with access to higher-status and better-paid jobs, and the ability to buy child care and domestic services which free them from their dual roles.

Marxists argue that the need for capitalism to be reproduced through the domestic labour undertaken by women within the family has had a major influence on social policy. Social policies have played an active role in defining gender relations as major reports such as Beveridge (see 4.6) show. These policies may:

- reinforce women's role as mothers
- encourage domestic labour to be seen as more important than wage labour for women
- differentiate between the education to be provided for boys and girls.

... the Beveridge Report on Social Insurance and Allied Services (1942), the Wolfenden Report on Homosexual Offences and Female Prostitution (1957), and Newsom's book *The Education of Girls* (1948) ... touch upon the same matrix of practices: marriage, the family, sexuality and procreation, understood through a particular set of ideologies. Beveridge explicitly forges a link between the question of procreation and the reproduction of labour power by the use of particular ideologies for women, Newsom is concerned with the reproduction of a sex specific form of labour power through the state education system ... while Wolfenden attempts to classify and regulate (legally and ideologically) 'perverse' sexualities, by awarding primacy to reproductive sexuality. (Bland et al., 1979: 78)

Marxism has been criticised because it does not account for:

- gender inequalities and divisions which pre-date capitalism
- those inequalities which exist in non-capitalist societies
- the exclusion of women from areas which are not linked to production such as religion or the arts
- violence against women.

Radical feminism views 'gender' as the primary dimension of social inequality and as a problem of central theoretical importance in social policy studies. Gender divisions are explained in terms of patriarchy. Women are seen to serve the interests and needs of men rather than those of capitalism. Radical feminists argue that women's opportunities are limited, owing to the power of men who exclude women and close off opportunities to them. Major social institutions such as the law, the armed forces, schools and parliament are all controlled by men.

Sexism is seen as built into the operation of major social institutions and organisations. It has deep roots in the dominant patriarchal culture. Radical feminists see violence against women as another expression of men's dominance and power over women. In policy terms, radical feminism puts great stress on an active policy of anti-sexism. Some radical feminists have also raised the issue of 'masculinity' as a key concept in understanding how men treat women and a range of social problems such as youth crime.

The radical feminist approach has been criticised for assuming that all women's situations are the same. It tends to ignore the fact that issues such as class are a major determinant of life chances.

RELATED TOPICS

1.26 Marxism: 1 Capital logic
1.27 Marxism: 2 Balance of social forces
3.11 Feminism

6.5 The old: social status

FURTHER READING

Barrett (1980) Chap 5
Campbell (1993) Chap 1
Doyal (1979) Chap 6
Ginsburg (1979) pp 79–94
McIntosh (1978)

2.8 THE FAMILY: RIGHT-WING VIEW

The right views the family as playing a major role in holding society together. For the right, the family means two married parents and their children living together as a single household. It holds a traditional view of family relationships with a clear division of labour and authority between husband and wife.

This view was reinforced by the functionalist theory (see 2.24) of the family. The traditional family had evolved as a successful social institution because of what it offered to each of its members and the benefits it yielded for society. In it, the father offered the 'instrumental role model' introducing children to the public world of work. The mother offered the 'affective role model' introducing children to the private world of feelings and emotions.

The family is viewed as a microcosm of society.

- It is seen as the model for *paternalism* in which authority takes the form of the firm but benevolent rule of the father
- It is the means by which the values of society are passed on from one generation to another
- It offers the new generation a model of how life should be lived.

The 'breakdown of the family' is viewed as a serious threat to social order. The widespread adoption of alternative household arrangements is seen as a cause of numerous social problems such as delinquency, crime and drug abuse. Single-parent families have been seen as part of an 'underclass' (see 2.17) and the cause of major social problems. The underclass has been described as the 'new rabble'.

Characteristics of the New Rabble
Low-skilled working class, poorly educated.
Single-parent families are the norm.
Largely dependent on welfare and the black economy.
High levels of criminality, child neglect and abuse and drug use.
Impervious to social welfare policies that seek to change their behaviour. (Murray, 1994).

The right also emphasises the 'responsibilities' of the family for looking after its members. The Poor Law was partly based on the idea of 'liable relatives' who had a legal obligation to look after members of their family. Policies designed to encourage 'community care' often, in effect, require families to take back part or all of the responsibility for caring for dependent members.

> ... the strategy to dismantle the welfare function of the state is predicated in the neo-liberal thesis that those goods and services would be better provided by private enterprise and more efficiently utilised by a 'family' which could, through market relations, determine its own welfare needs. Thus the 'family' is no longer to have the status, as neo-liberals argue it has under social democracy of being a passive client; it is now to enjoy the 'freedoms' of the market and become the consumer of welfare. (Fitzgerald, 1983: 47)

RELATED TOPICS

1.15 Conservative paternalism
5.3 The causes of crime: right-wing view

FURTHER READING

Berger and Berger (1983) Chap 9
Bremner (1968)
Fitzgerald (1983)
Morgan (1975) pp 25–38
Murray (1994)

2.9 THE FAMILY: REFORMIST VIEW

Reformists generally see support for the family as one of the central purposes of social policy. State support for the family is seen to date from the early period of industrialisation. The establishment of factory production separated work from home and families no longer operated as a unit of production. Subsequently, the state began to play a role in child care and socialisation through state schooling and medical care.

In the twentieth century the state took on further responsibility for child care through family allowances. These were instituted in Britain in 1944 after a long campaign. Other areas of social policy such as social work have been largely organised around the principle of supporting the family.

> The family does not function in a social vacuum. How it functions today is ... profoundly affected by the forces of indus-trialisation. It is simultaneously benefited and damaged by those forces. The rapidity of change in highly industrialised societies

during the last one hundred years has put the family on the defensive. Its responsibilities have grown; it has been placed in more situations of divided loyalties and conflicting values; it has been forced to choose between kinship and economic progress; and it has been constantly subjected to the gales of creative instability ... we need to see the social services in a variety of stabilising, preventive, and protective roles. Interpreted in this way, and not as the modern equivalent of Bismarckian benevolence, the social services become an ally – not an enemy – of industrial and technological progress. (Titmuss, 1964: 117–18)

In the past reformist support for the family has often assumed a traditional family structure. The post-war social security system in Britain was set up along the lines proposed in the Beveridge report (see 4.6). Most women paid lower contributions and received lower benefits than men. The assumption was that married women should be largely supported by their husbands. Reformists nowadays often accept the fact of the current diversity of household types and have campaigned for help for single-parent families. However, *communitarianism* supports the idea of encouraging two-parent families.

RELATED TOPICS

1.24 Communitarianism
5.16 Social work: reformist view

FURTHER READING

Bowlby (1952) Part II Chap 7
Craven et al. (1982) Part 4
Fletcher (1967) pp 177–99
Williams (1989)

2.10 THE FAMILY: RADICAL VIEW

Classical Marxism saw the 'bourgeois family' as having its origins in the need to provide a secure basis for the hereditary transmission of property. Family law and sexual exclusivity ensured that the legitimate heirs would receive their inheritance. The bourgeois family and the rules of behaviour associated with it were seen as products of the unequal system of property ownership. Marxists thus believed that the end of capitalism would lead to the relaxation of rules governing sexual behaviour.

Modern Marxists have been more interested in how the nuclear family has contributed to the functioning of the capitalist economy. The family is the main institution through which the function of 'reproduction' takes place. Daily reproduction involves the labour force being fed, clothed and sheltered and made ready for the next day's work. Generational reproduction involves rearing the new generation of workers.

These reproductive activities are mainly undertaken within the *family* as the result of domestic labour. The inequalities within the family have meant that women have performed most of this reproductive work. These inequalities existed before the development of capitalism but social policies have often been used to reinforce them by increasing women's dependence on men.

This line of analysis also argues that women are disadvantaged as members of the labour force. They face discrimination, exclusion and segregation and they form part of a reserve army of labour (see 2.7). They may find work during periods of labour shortage but are likely to lose their jobs during periods of recession.

Marxism and *radical feminism* differ in their interpretation of the allocation of the bulk of domestic labour to women.

> ... there is controversy on the general question ... as to whose interests are served by women's labour in the household. On the one side Marxists argue that it serves capital, by reproducing labour power at very low cost; on the other side feminists argue that it serves men's interests by providing personal services and relieving them of family obligations. (Barrett, 1980: 210)

RELATED TOPICS

1.27 Marxism: 2 Balance of social forces
2.7 Gender: radical view

FURTHER READING

Barrett (1980) Chap 6
Burden and Campbell (1985) Section 4.4
Creighton (1985)
Engels (1962)
Oakley (1982) Chap 7
Rowbotham (1973b)
Williams (1989) Chap 6

2.11 COMMUNITY: RIGHT-WING VIEW

Right-wing views of community can be either *conservative* or *liberal*.

Conservatism gives a central place to the imagery of community. The idea of community has played an important part in the development of conservative social thought.

1. It is harmonious – there is no social conflict
2. It is deferential – everyone 'knows their place'

3. It is hierarchical – there is no pursuit of social equality
4. It is consensual – common values based on religion, tradition and respect for established authority form a basis for social unity.

The traditional *family* is seen as playing a key part in the maintenance of this version of community. Conservatism looks back to an imagined and idealised picture of feudal society and generally sees contemporary communities as based on a model of village life.

The classical *liberal* view of community sees it as based on tolerance and on support for a social contract in which everyone agrees to purse their own interests while respecting the rights of others.

> The liberal ideal is of a society composed of enlightened individuals, capable of rational decision-making and self-determination. Their enlightenment is derived from their all-round education and first hand knowledge of a number of social issues. This ideal is most nearly realised in societies with a large middle class which ... is active in numerous political, communal and voluntary civic organizations. Membership of a multiplicity of different groups and organizations exposes individuals to numerous points of view ... Liberals thus see democracy as flourishing where informed individuals participate equally in national political issues ... (Jordan, 1976: 38)

Neo-liberalism, by contrast, has no clear view of community. Its social ideal is a society made up of independent individualists. Conservative views of community may be seen as a sentimental irrelevance. Friendship and voluntary social obligations are seen as purely private matters beyond the scope of social policy. Any attempts to create or reinforce community are decried as social engineering.

RELATED TOPICS

1.14 Social imperialism
2.8 The family: right-wing view
5.11 Urban problems: right-wing view

FURTHER READING

Nisbet (1973) Chap 3

2.12 COMMUNITY: REFORMIST VIEW

The idea of community has played a central role in reformist approaches to social policy. In the early twentieth century the garden-city movement proposed the use of town planning to create 'mixed' communities in which members of different classes did not live in separate areas, in order to foster social unity.

In the 1960s social research identified the decline of older working-class communities as a problem for social policy. Community 'breakdown' or 'decay' became a key target of social intervention. The breakdown of community was seen as evidenced in giant and soulless public-housing schemes which contrasted with the vibrant community life of the slums that they had replaced.

Community breakdown also began to be seen as a factor in a range of other social problems. In Britain the lower educational achievement of working-class children was viewed as a problem of community in the Plowden report of 1968. The Seebohm report on the reorganisation of social work proposed that 'community development' should be given a new importance. Community work became a new specialism within social work.

> Community identity can be encouraged indirectly by the creation and development of the appropriate social and physical environment and here the social service department should be involved in social planning, acting in concert with, for example, housing, planning and other departments of local and central government concerned with new towns, schemes for urban renewal and other developments which affect the community environment. Community identity may also be developed through organizations such as community centres, clubs, play centres and tenants' associations, where the social service department could provide technical and professional help, information, stimulation and grant-aid. (Seebohm, 1968: para. 482)

Community also figures in the rhetoric of 'community care' though in reality this often means care by women in the family. The notion of community care itself looks back to the mythical conservative ideal of the integrated rural or small-town community and to the tight-knit community which developed in older working-class areas during the first half of the twentieth century.

The idea of the community in the 1970s and 1980s has shifted to became a 'resource' to be utilised in schemes based on notions of 'partnership' between the authorities and 'the community'. The meaning of the term 'community' has also expanded to take in a range of different groups and interests which began to be called communities, for example the 'gay community'. In the 1990s *communitarianism* constructed an entire programme of reform around the idea of reviving the spirit of community.

RELATED TOPICS

1.24 Communitarianism
5.12 Urban problems: reformist view
5.16 Social work: reformist view

FURTHER READING

Pahl (1970) pp 100–7
Seebohm (1968) Chap 16

2.13 COMMUNITY: RADICAL VIEW

Marxism views capitalism as the antithesis of community. It sees it as creating a form of society based on extreme individualism which sets people against one another.

> ... the bourgeoisie has pitilessly torn asunder the motley feudal ties that bound man to his natural superiors and has left remaining no other nexus between man and man than naked self-interest, than callous 'cash payment'. (Marx and Engels, 1962: 36, written in 1848)

In the radical approach, community is normally based on 'struggle'. A sense of community will develop on the basis of the shared experience of oppression and exploitation. The common experience of wage labour can create a bond between the workers in a firm. In industrial cities members of the same class are likely to live close together in similar housing and this can create a community based on common social experience. The bonds created at work may also be carried over into the community when the workers live together in the same area. This pattern is found in many traditional working-class communities based on a single industry, such as mining villages.

In Britain the community development projects of the late 1960s and 1970s formulated a radical view of community and the role of (radical) community workers in helping to encourage effective community action. Non-Marxist radicals also refer to other groups as communities, e.g. the 'black community'. Some modern radicals have developed the concept of *new social movements* to describe the 'struggles' of these communities.

RELATED TOPICS

3.10 New social movements
5.13 Urban problems: radical view
5.17 Social work: radical view

FURTHER READING

Jordan (1976) Chap 3

2.14 CITIZENSHIP: RIGHT-WING VIEW

In *conservative* thought citizenship has not usually been conceived of in terms of social and economic rights but in terms of a duty of loyalty owed by 'subjects' (not citizens) to the state.

Liberal political thought originally viewed citizenship in terms of the right to take part in the exercise of political power. This was confined to those males who owned property as in the restricted franchise of early Victorian England. This allowed only males who also owned property to vote. Under the Victorian Poor Laws recipients of poor relief were denied the right to vote. Citizenship was viewed as incompatible with the receipt of state benefits. Welfare recipients are still stigmatised, partly as a consequence.

> As we grow up, the most authentic rights we acquire and exercise are those we use in the roles of buyers and sellers in the market-place. We do not have to be persuaded that we have rights to what we buy. The idea of paying through taxes or holding authentic claims by virtue of citizenship remains largely an intellectual conceit of the social scientist and the socialist. For the majority the idea of participant citizenship in distributive processes outside the market-place has very little meaning. (Pinker, 1971: 141–2)

Citizenship has also been viewed in terms of nationality. This sets boundaries to the rights given by the state and non-members are excluded. Laws on immigration and the treatment of aliens are an important element of this.

Neo-liberalism has further developed the idea of citizenship. In Britain, the Citizens' Charter of 1991 is a *new right* initiative on citizenship. It depicts the citizen as a consumer empowered by the state. State provided services such as law and order, health, education and benefits are covered by the charter. Standards of service, the right of redress, and choice, are guaranteed. Another element of citizenship promoted by the *new right* is the 'active citizen'. The active citizen is public spirited and engages in forms of voluntary work which benefit the community.

RELATED TOPICS

FURTHER READING
Pinker (1971) Chap 4
Plant and Barre (1990)

2.15 CITIZENSHIP: REFORMIST VIEW

Citizenship was a key idea for the *new liberalism* and has remained a central element in reformist ideas about social policy. It has been linked to the idea of *universalism* involving socially guaranteed minimum standards of provision in various areas of social policy.

Marshall saw citizenship as the culmination of a long historical process of *social betterment*. He also saw the development of the status of citizenship as a means by which class inequalities could be legitimated. He viewed citizenship as a legal status made up of the possession of three kinds of rights; civil, political and social.

1. *Civil rights* such as the right to own property and freedom of speech developed in the eighteenth century
2. *Political rights* such as the right to vote or form a party developed in the nineteenth century
3. *Social rights* involving guaranteed minimum standards of income, health and education developed in the twentieth century.

Critics have pointed out that while these rights may have developed in this way for adult males, this has not occurred for other groups such as women, ethnic minorities and the disabled.

> In very different ways both racial minorities and women have been denied full participation in the activities and market earning power of our society because of social custom, values and prejudices. To give them full access and rights of citizenship will involve changing our laws which, by changing behaviour, may begin to modify built-in, barely appreciated prejudices. (Glennerster, 1983: 223)

There is a European Convention on Human Rights established in 1951 under the Council of Europe. The Labour government elected in Britain in 1997 intends to allow British citizens to enforce their rights under this convention in the British courts. Membership of the *European Union* involves a further development of rights of citizenship. The European Social Chapter includes a range of employment rights, social security entitlements and rights to legal services. European social policy legislation provides for social rights to have a legal basis in that national governments can be required to legislate in conformity with it.

FURTHER READING

Andrews (1991) pp 50–64
Marshall (1963) Chap 4 pp 86–7 and 120–7
Mishra (1977) Chap 2
Parker (1975) Chap 9

2.16 CITIZENSHIP: RADICAL VIEW

Radical approaches emphasise the limitations of the achievement of citizenship rights in a capitalist society. In Marxism 'abstract' legal equality is seen as a cloak for actual inequality. Real equality of status as citizens cannot be achieved without the removal of the structural basis of inequality. The private ownership of productive property and class divisions have to be eliminated. In a capitalist society only those who own property have real freedom. Only in a democratic socialist society would equal rights guarantee substantive equality.

Other radicals have seen the pursuit of democratic rights at the workplace as a way forward. These would pose a threat to the (absolute) rights of property owners to control their possessions.

Some activists have sought radical change through seeking clearly defined *welfare* rights. This involves support for social groups and *new social movements* seeking recognition of these rights.

The kind of citizenship offered by the *Keynesian welfare state* has been criticised as passive and disempowering by Keane. He calls for a revival of 'civil society', invoking a form of active citizenship of the left.

> Civil society ... has the potential to become a non-state sphere comprising a plurality of public spheres – productive units, households, voluntary organizations and community-based services – which are legally guaranteed and self-organizing. (Keane, 1988: 14)

FURTHER READING

Alcock (1989)
Hall and Held (1989)
Pierson (1991) pp 196–207

2.17 POVERTY: RIGHT-WING VIEW

The right employs a conception of *absolute poverty* which is set at subsistence level. This idea was first given a definitive form in the workhouse principle of less eligibility (see 1.12), in which the inmates were to be provided with a standard of living just sufficient for subsistence, which was also below that of the worst-paid 'independent labourer'.

> The first and most essential of all conditions, is that the situation of the individual relieved shall not be made really or apparently so eligible as the situation of the independent labourer of the lowest class ... we do not believe that a country in which that distinction has been completely effaced, and every man, whatever be his conduct or his character, ensured a comfortable subsistence, can retain its prosperity, or even its civilisation. (from the Commission of Enquiry into the Poor Laws of 1834, quoted in George, 1973: 12)

On the right, inequality is valued as the basis of social incentives and rewards. Social policy should not redistribute income from rich to poor. The right views poverty as normally being caused by the failings of those who experience it. The 'cycle of deprivation' theory sees the poor as trapped by their own inadequacies in a 'culture of poverty' which perpetuates itself over the generations. Individuals should be held responsible for their own failure to secure an adequate income.

The right has recently revived the old idea of poverty as being associated with an 'underclass'. Members of this underclass are concentrated in run down inner-city and peripheral public housing estates. They are often seen as threatening social order. The underclass has a dependency culture characterised by laziness, rejection of work and reliance on social benefits. Poverty can only be eliminated through the adoption of values of self-help and individual responsibility. Cutting social benefits can help produce this.

RELATED TOPICS

1.12 Supporting the market
1.16 Eugenics
2.8 The family: right-wing view
5.3 The causes of crime: right-wing view

FURTHER READING

Boyson (1971) pp 1–9
Eysenck (1973) Chap 4
Holman (1978) Chap 3
Murray (1994)
Pearson (1975) pp 148–76
Rose (1972) Chap 5
Saunders (1990) Chap 4

2.18 POVERTY: REFORMIST VIEW

Reformists employ a concept of relative *poverty* with a 'poverty line' which may rise with a general increase in incomes. Poverty refers to a socially unacceptable level of income which prevents a person from leading a normal life.

> ... poverty [exists when people] lack the resources to obtain the types of diet, participate in the activities and have the living conditions which are customary, or at least widely encouraged or approved in the societies in which they belong. (Townsend, 1979: 15)

Poverty is seen as an unfortunate aspect of society from which people should be protected by state action. The views of Beveridge (see 4.6) and Rowntree dominated policy on poverty in the post-war welfare state. Using the idea of a poverty line, the problem of poverty can be solved by making provision for particular groups, such as the old, unemployed, sick and disabled, amongst whom the poor are found.

Until the mid-1960s this conception of poverty dominated both political debate and academic research. The British Labour government of 1964–70 began a partial shift towards redefining poverty as multi-deprivation. This covers a range of factors as health, housing and education as well as income. Multi-deprivation was to be tackled by a range of urban-regeneration policies.

The *European Union* supports a relative conception of poverty, which it defined in 1984 as 'persons, families and groups of persons where resources (material, cultural and social) are so limited as to exclude them from the minimum acceptable way of life in the member states in which they live'.

RELATED TOPICS

1.20 Fabianism
2.3 The individual in society: reformist view
3.5 Social betterment
5.12 Urban problems: Reformist view
9.6 The European Union

FURTHER READING

Field (1981) Chap 2
Holman (1978) Chap 4
Kincaid (1973) Chap 3
MacGregor (1981) Chap 4
Marshall (1975) Chap 12
Townsend (1979) Chap 1

2.19 POVERTY: RADICAL VIEW

Radicals see poverty as a normal and ineradicable feature of capitalism. Policies intended to relieve poverty can never fully succeed because of powerful capitalist interests and the inherently exploitative nature of the system. Periodically poverty is 'rediscovered' by reformist or *Fabian* researchers demonstrating that the benefit system has again failed to secure adequate incomes for all. Radicals have argued that this rediscovery then leads to calls for further adjustments in the benefit system to cater for newly identified groups in need: later, poverty is 'rediscovered' again.

Marxism views the conventional *reformist* definition of poverty as helping to reinforce the ideology of capitalism. It does this by suggesting that poverty is a manageable problem that can be eliminated by properly designed income-support policies. It also diverts attention away from issues concerned with inequality by completely ignoring the question of wealth.

> ... poverty is to be regarded not as an unfortunate mishap but as functional in helping to preserve the existing divisions of society ... The existence ... of a group identifiable as the poor serves to set them apart from the rest of the population ... the working class is divided and thereby weakened ... Further, the poor act as a warning. They demonstrate the fate of those who do not conform to prevailing work and social standards ... those in poverty act as scapegoats, a vulnerable group on whom the blame for social problems can be placed. (Holman, 1973: 438)

The working class as a whole is affected by the instability of the capitalist economy. Members of the reserve army of labour (see 2.7), such as women and migrant workers, are especially subject to economic insecurity because their employment prospects constantly fluctuate. Classical Marxism also identified a 'lumpen-proletariat' as a permanently submerged group. This is similar to the right-wing idea of an underclass (see 2.17).

Radicals believe that poverty can only be abolished by a process of *decommodification*, which removes the link between personal incomes and the value of people's labour in the market. Incomes should be primarily based on need. One means of moving towards this would be to provide everyone with a standard regular payment in form of a 'citizen's income' or 'basic income'.

Many feminists believe that poverty has become 'feminised'. Poverty is seen as a particular issue for women, since:

- the proportion of women dependent on state benefits is higher than the proportion of men
- women are more likely to depend on low wages
- women have often been treated unfavourably by the social-security system
- they have greater caring responsibilities.

RELATED TOPICS

1.26 Marxism: 1 Capital logic
1.27 Marxism: 2 Balance of social forces
4.10 Decommodification
4.13 Empowerment

FURTHER READING

Breitenbach et al. (1990) pp 30–2
George (1973) Chap 2
Kincaid (1973) Chap 3
Lukes (1974) pp 74–95
Novak (1984) Chaps 1 and 4

2.20 RACE: RIGHT-WING VIEW

The right-wing view normally emphasises white racial superiority. This variety of racism may combine some of the following beliefs:

- the biological superiority of white people
- the cultural superiority of the way of life of the native-born white population
- that racist ideas can be verified by scientific research demonstrating that inequalities have a basis in biological differences
- that people of different cultures do not like to mix
- that 'racial' problems can only be solved by repatriation, either forced or assisted
- that reformist institutions constitute a 'race-relations industry' which only benefits those who work in it
- that anti-racism is an attempt to stir up political conflict and is 'anti-white'.

Racism is an ideology which identifies individuals as belonging to a group on the basis of some real or imaginary biological or inherent characteristic. It is common for the group to be identified by reference to some immediately evident physical characteristic(s) – skin colour, size of nose, shape of forehead ... The group ... is then also defined as having some other social or psychological characteristic(s) which is regarded unfavourably. This combination of characteristics and evaluations is interpreted to indicate a difference, a 'race' ... all those who share these characteristics are necessarily deficient or inferior and so should be treated less favourably than other groups not so identified. (Miles and Phizacklea, 1984: 10)

Critics see these ideas as having a long history. They argue that they have had a considerable influence on social policies since the origins of the welfare state. Legislation on aliens and restrictions on immigration are seen as examples of racist policies. Many state institutions such as the police also operate racist policies, though these may often be expressed in a 'coded' form such as through the selective presentation of crime statistics with an ethnic breakdown.

RELATED TOPICS

1.16 Eugenics
2.2 The individual in society: right-wing view
2.17 Poverty: right-wing view

FURTHER READING

Barker (1990) Chap 2
Jacobs (1988) Chap 5
Solomos (1989) Chap 10
Williams (1987)

2.21 RACE: REFORMIST VIEW

The reformist approach often uses the concepts of discrimination or prejudice. It sees racism as largely a matter of personal motivation. Racism involves an intolerant attitude on the part of a minority of whites and loss of confidence in institutions by blacks.

Education and legislation against discrimination are viewed as effective means to combat racism. In Britain from the 1960s policies were developed which incorporated the reformist approach. The Race Relations Act of 1965 established the Race Relations Board. Another act in 1968 widened its scope to include employment and housing and also set up the Community Relations Council. However, this approach had little impact on the racial division of labour. The Race Relations Act 1976 covered 'indirect discrimination' and formed the Commission for Racial Equality.

This deals with discrimination in employment though the annual number of applications upheld is very small, often under 40 in a year.

> ... the existence of a 'problem' of 'race relations' ... was to be resolved through the immigrants' assimilation into a richer cultural and political pluralism after an understandable but hopefully brief period of tension between the 'hosts' and the 'strangers' newly arrived within their midst. (Coates, 1984: 177)

According to critics, the academic work associated with this approach fails to deal properly with the legacy of racism which began with *Fabianism*. Racism is incorporated explicitly or implicitly into a great deal of welfare legislation. This tradition also treats race as a marginal issue in the study of social policy.

A new variant of the reformist view has developed in recent years in the *European Union* employing the concept of social exclusion. This views racism as involving what Max Weber (Gerth and Mills, 1970: 186–70) called 'negatively privileged status groups'. According to Weber, these groups have:

- a common lifestyle and culture
- a negative evaluation of status
- exclusion from intimate social contact with groups of a higher status
- a restriction of material opportunities due to group membership.

In this approach racism is seen as one case of a range of situations involving social exclusion rather than as something unique and on its own. Racism is thus placed alongside ideologies of caste, aristocratic ideologies of 'blue blood' and 'breeding', and degraded depictions of the disabled or the unemployed. The ideology of the Eugenics Movement shows that racism is not necessarily a matter of colour or culture or nationality, but of social and political exclusion. The Victorian and Edwardian belief that criminals, the Irish and the lowest stratum of casual workers were a separate race are also examples. There was no question of race in the sense of skin colour or appearance, but the notion of ascribed biological difference was present.

RELATED TOPICS

FURTHER READING

Banton (1985) Chap 7
Jenkins and Solomos (1987) Chap 3
Saggar (1991) Chap 3
Shaw et al. (1987) Chap 13

2.22 RACE: RADICAL VIEW

The two main radical perspectives on race are *radical anti-racism* and *Marxism*.

Radical anti-racism employs the concept of institutional racism. It sees racism as built into the operation of major social institutions and organisations. Racism is not a matter of personal motivation. It has deep roots in the dominant culture. It views racism as the central theoretical problem in social-policy studies. Race is also taken to be the primary dimension of social oppression, opposing the Marxist view that class issues are primary. This viewpoint puts great stress on an active policy of anti-racism.

Radical anti-racism often has difficulties in dealing with the vocabulary of race. One problem concerns the use of the undifferentiated term 'blacks', which implies uniformity. This also encourages the uncritical use of the term 'white' as a sweeping identification, as in 'white racism'. The class and ethnic divisions within the black and white populations are neglected.

Marxist accounts may start with the nature of the international capitalist system.

The roots of racism lie in the Empire, in the way in which colonial domination was justified in the nineteenth century. A culture was consolidated then in which the notion of distinct 'races' with distinct characteristics gained widespread currency: and an economic system was put in place which systematically under-developed colonies by extracting their surpluses to the 'mother country'. Colonial under-development spawned migration; and in conditions of labour scarcity in the UK in the 1950s and 1960s kept certain public services alive (in transport and health) and sustained under-capitalised industries (in textiles in particular) as cheap, unskilled, poorly organized and easily exploited colonial labour was locked into the bottom of the UK class structure. Once placed there, the routes up and out (through social mobility) for ethnic labour were then blocked. White workers co-operated to exclude black promotion and white house owners co-operated to head off ethnic expansion into suburbia so that the general diffusion of ethnic minority populations into the society was aborted. (Coates, 1991: 122)

The Marxist approach emphasises the notion of migrant labour. Race is seen as an additional factor on top of this, but not as the principal issue. Marxists argue that migrant labour is employed during periods of labour shortage to keep wage costs down. The degradation of the status of these groups is then encouraged when labour surpluses develop and they are no longer required. A comparison is made with the use of 'guest-workers' across the *European Union*. Migrant workers are part of the reserve army of labour (see 2.7). There is a similarity between the position of migrant labourers and other groups making up this reserve army, such as women and the old.

Marxism also relates racism to the development of crisis conditions. With the growing economic crisis of the 1970s in Britain the ideological depiction of 'immigrants' gradually became associated with criminality, illegal immigration, drugs, 'mugging' and finally with collective disorders in the inner cities. These changes in ideology are seen as related to the displacement of discontent caused by unemployment and deprivation on to a minority group.

RELATED TOPICS

1.25 Radical approaches: general features
6.5 The old: social status

FURTHER READING

Castles and Kosack (1973) Chap 11
Centre for Contemporary Cultural Studies (1984) Chap 1
George and Wilding (1985) Chap 1
Macey (1995)
Phizacklea and Miles (1980) Chap 1
Seidel (1986)
Williams (1989) Chap 4

2.23 SOCIAL NEEDS AND PROBLEMS: RIGHT-WING VIEW

Liberal social thought argues that if individual liberty and a fully functioning free market exist then interventionist social policies will not be necessary. Social intervention will only be required if the market is not operating properly because some people are unwilling to fend for themselves. The state may then need to create institutions to compel people to take responsibility for their own lives.

The concept of *needs* used by reformists and Marxists is not recognised. People have *wants* which are manifested by a willingness to pay to have them met.

... once it is accepted that some have a right to legislate for others about what they need the slippery slope to authoritarianism does seem more likely ... the New Right argue that the market ... is a morally superior as well as a more efficient method of allocating resources and defining goals. (Doyal and Gough, 1991: 10–11)

The *new right* does not subscribe to the notion of social injustice. According to Hayek, since the outcomes of the market are unintended and unforeseeable, those who do least well are not the victims of injustice and should have no claim on the state to compensate them. Conditions such as unemployment or *poverty* are not seen as social problems requiring state intervention. On the contrary, they are often the result of existing and past state intervention. State intervention both distorts the operation of the market and encourages dependence on the state.

The responsibilities of the state are limited to maintaining a stable currency, the rule of law and external security. But the precise form of the social order must be left to emerge as the unintended result of the individual choices made by all the members of the society acting in pursuit of their own interests.

RELATED TOPICS

1.12 Supporting the market
1.17 Neo-liberalism (the new right)

FURTHER READING

Soper (1981) Chap 1

2.24 SOCIAL NEEDS AND PROBLEMS: REFORMIST VIEW

Reformism involves the use of state intervention to solve social problems and meet social needs. In order to be solved the problems have to be widely recognised as such. Reformist authors often assume that there is a consensus on what needs are. There are three approaches to explaining how social needs come to be met by social policies.

1. An *individual* approach sees people as having certain needs. These are normally viewed as involving minimum levels of income, health, welfare, education and housing. These needs may be precisely specified, perhaps in the form of welfare rights, and more or less successfully met by the social services.
2. The *functionalist* approach sees societies as having certain needs. If these needs are not being met then social problems exist and society is subject to strain or social disorganisation. This leads

to a search for solutions. When these are found, new policies are introduced – the needs are now met and the social problems have been solved. The *logic of industrialism* is a version of this view.

3. The *interactionist* approach assumes that a state of affairs only becomes a social problem if it is successfully forced on to the political agenda. 'Moral entrepreneurs' may play a part by organising campaigns to highlight a particular social problem. They will aim to 'legitimate' the problem in order to develop a consensus that something should be done. If the problem is held to be legitimate then a policy decision may be taken. The policy will then be implemented. Each of these stages is problematic and the final outcome is not guaranteed to 'solve' the problem.

Rules are not made automatically. Even though a practice may be harmful in an objective sense to the group in which it occurs, the harm needs to be discovered and pointed out. People must be made to feel that something ought to be done about it. Someone must call the public's attention to these matters, supply the push necessary to get things done, and direct such energies as are aroused in the proper direction to get a rule created. Deviance is the product of enterprise in the largest sense; without the enterprise required to get rules made, the deviance which consists of breaking the rule could not exist. (Becker, 1963: 162)

RELATED TOPICS

1.20 Fabianism
1.21 Logic of industrialism
3.5 Social betterment

FURTHER READING

Becker (1963) Chap 8
Doyal and Gough (1984)
Doyal and Gough (1991)
Forder (1974) Chap 3

2.25 SOCIAL NEEDS AND PROBLEMS: RADICAL VIEW

According to the radical approach, what counts as a social problem is a state of affairs which threatens the interests of the dominant group. There are two major variants of this approach.

1. Some Marxists adopt a 'capital logic' or 'state derivation' perspective. This sees capitalism as developing through a series of identifiable stages. At each stage distinctive social problems emerge which threaten the process of accumulation. In the early stage of competitive capitalism where firms are small and technology is

relatively simple, there is little need for direct state support for capital beyond the maintenance of law and order, unless policies are required for *supporting the market*. At the later monopoly stage, technological advance requires state support for scientific progress and for the education of technically qualified workers. Policies are established to deal with these and allow capitalism to continue to develop.

2. Many Marxists and other radical theorists see the balance of class forces as a major factor in the identification of social problems and as a determinant of how they are dealt with. Subordinate classes such as the working class may seek to identify their poverty and economic insecurity as social problems and demand reforms to reduce them. Class conflict may involve trade-union and political action in pursuit of social reform.

> Marxists will see so-called social problems as the result not of industrialisation, urbanisation or conflicts between groups but as the result of the capitalist form of production and its accompanying forms of social relationships ... Marxists naturally maintain that since social problems are in the last resort caused by the capitalist system, social policies in a capitalist society cannot hope to achieve very much. (George and Wilding, 1985: 12–13)

A dominant class may seek to suppress behaviour and attitudes which threaten its position by defining them as social problems. For example, lifestyles which reject the work ethic are sometimes portrayed in this way. The dominant class may also seek to initiate some reforms which benefit poorer people in order to reduce opposition to its continued dominance. Some Marxists therefore see social reform as a means by which a dominant class can attempt to maintain 'hegemony', i.e. ideological dominance. This approach may be linked to *conservative paternalism*.

RELATED TOPICS

1.12 Supporting the market
1.14 Social imperialism
1.15 Conservative paternalism
1.26 Marxism: 1 Capital logic
1.27 Marxism: 2 Balance of social forces
3.10 New social movements
4.10 Decommodification

FURTHER READING

George and Wilding (1985) Chap 1
Wetherly (1996)

CHAPTER 3

Perspectives on social-policy development

3.1 THEORIES OF SOCIAL-POLICY DEVELOPMENT

Different general explanations from the left, centre and right which account for the development of social policies are shown in Table 3.1. In addition, the feminist perspective is considered at the end of the chapter.

RELATED TOPICS

1.11 Right-wing approaches: general features
1.18 Reformist approaches: general features
1.25 Radical approaches: general features

FURTHER READING

Carrier and Kendall (1977)

Part 1 Right-wing perspectives

3.2 OVERLOADED GOVERNMENT

The right wing concept of *overloaded government* criticises the expansion of the state. It argues that there are inherent tendencies for state social provision to expand. Sometimes this is augmented by government responses to an emergency such as war. Subsequently it proves difficult to cut expenditure back down to its previous levels because numerous vested interests have been created.

A number of processes are at work:

- Political parties seek votes by promising more public spending especially on social services. Each party will try to outbid the others thus raising the proposed extent and level of benefits.
- The expectations of the electorate will tend to increase over time, leading to more demands for increased expenditure.
- Civil servants running public-sector organisations will seek to expand their departments.
- Pressure for increased expenditure also comes from professionals who provide services, such as teachers and social workers.

Table 3.1 Left, centre and right theories of social-policy development

	Left	Centre	Right
Overall pattern	Social policies expand in an attempt to solve the contradictions, social tensions and pressures created by capitalism	Social policy develops as institutions are established to solve existing social problems and as new problems are identified	Social policy expenditure continues to grow as a result of failure to resist the pressure causing this to occur
Impetus for reform	This comes from the demands for social improvement and attempts by the dominant class to secure social harmony	This comes from pressure groups and reforming parties, progressive public opinion and advances in knowledge of social conditions	This comes from vested interests such as welfare professions and bureaucrats and from political parties seeking votes
The role of the state	A welfare state is established which reduces working-class economic insecurity and helps maintain the legitimacy of capitalism	The process of social reform culminates in the development of the welfare state in which the needs of all are met	This is excessive and is characterised by incompetence and inefficiency
Impact on society	New demands from exploited and oppressed groups are continually being made as society develops but reforms never fundamentally alter the system	Full citizenship is extended to all members of society based on a combination of universalist and selective social services	Incentives to work are undermined and over-taxation damages business
Examples covered	Marxism New social movements	Social betterment Pluralism Incrementalism Corporatism	Government overload Bureaucratic self-interest Democratic elitism and technocracy

• Businesses dependent on the state for benefits and subsidies also support increased state spending. Consumption is not restrained by goods and services having to be purchased by the recipients.

Britain, then has become harder to govern. The reason it has become harder to govern is that, at one and the same time, the range of problems that government is expected to deal with has vastly increased, and its capacity to deal with the problems, even many of the ones it had before, has decreased. (King, 1976: 25)

The government will tend to produce more goods than the majority of the electorate would choose under market conditions. The decisions made by providers will not necessarily be in accord with what people want. This occurs because in the absence of profit-seeking there is no clear criterion for deciding what to produce. Services will be inefficient because of the lack of market disciplines on producers. The government is 'overloaded' and its activities should be cut back.

RELATED TOPICS

1.17 Neo-liberalism (the new right)
1.28 Legitimation crisis
3.3 Bureaucratic self-interest

FURTHER READING

Dunleavy and O'Leary (1987) Section 3.3
King (1975)
King (1976) pp 3–29

3.3 BUREAUCRATIC SELF-INTEREST

The *liberal* theory of motivation which focuses on the rational pursuit of self-interest has been applied to political and administrative behaviour. These ideas have been used to create predictions about the behaviour of:

1. politicians 'rationally' seeking votes
2. voters 'rationally' seeking to obtain benefits through choosing which party to support
3. bureaucrats seeking to maximise their incomes and status.

Politicians seeking support are seen as having an incentive to promise increases in public expenditure, especially on social policies designed to increase the real incomes of voters. According to *neo-liberalism*, this builds in a tendency for rising social expenditure in democracies.

A 'rational-choice' model of bureaucracy has been developed by Niskanen. This model of bureaucratic behaviour is based on neo-classical economic theory. The model comes to orthodox neo-classical conclusions about the desirability and efficiency of free markets and private ownership. Every individual is seen as seeking the greatest possible rewards for themselves.

> Given the demand for service represented by the collective organization, all bureaux are too large, that is, both the budget and the output of all bureaux will be larger than that which maximises the net value of the sponsor. (Niskanen, 1971: 50)

State social intervention creates vested interests within the machinery of state. The welfare professionals such as teachers, social workers and nurses, whose jobs depend on state social spending, also have an interest in further expenditure. Just as firms seek to maximise their profits, so bureaucrats will attempt to maximise their budgets. A higher budget will provide more jobs and improve career prospects for bureaucrats. Bureaucrats involved in administering the social services thus have a vested interest in their perpetuation. Politicians often become advocates of the service provided by the bureaucracies they are supposed to control. Bureaucrats are able to increase their budgets because they have a near monopoly of information. In the rational-choice model, everyone would benefit if interventionist social policies and the bureaucracies that support them were abolished.

RELATED TOPICS

1.17 Neo-liberalism (the new right)
4.5 Managerialisation
4.8 Administrative reorganisation

FURTHER READING

Barry (1970) Chap 2
Downs (1957) Chap 1
Niskanen (1971)

3.4 DEMOCRATIC ELITISM AND TECHNOCRACY

Elite theories are based on the idea that power is always exercised by a minority. The mass of ordinary people are seen as having no real share in the exercise of power even in apparently democratic societies. This contrasts with *pluralism* which sees voters, and pressure groups supported by ordinary people, as key participants in the exercise of power.

Democratic elitism is the name given to the view that democracy is itself an elitist form of government. Political power is exercised by a system of competing party elites, not by 'the people'. It is not voters who control governments, but party elites who have themselves elected.

> ... democracy does not mean and cannot mean that the people actually rule in any obvious sense of the terms 'people' and 'rule'. Democracy means only that the people have the opportunity of accepting or refusing the men who are to rule them. (Schumpeter, 1965: 284–5)

Because modern government is so complex, scientific and technical experts play a key role. *Technocracy* is the term now used to describe the exercise of power by these experts. Technocrats often claim to be pursuing social welfare, efficiency, economic growth and stability in a non-ideological fashion. Decisions are made on 'rational', 'scientific' grounds, not on the basis of political ideology.

Cost-benefit analysis is an example of a technocratic approach to political decision-making. The belief that all decisions could and should be made 'rationally' according to the principles of cost-benefit analysis has been termed 'econocracy'. *Fabianism,* or at least the approach of the early Fabians, is often characterised as technocratic.

Modern social policies and their management show some signs of a technocratic approach. The claim that 'management' is a specific area of expertise which should control the delivery of social policies is a variant of technocracy. Proponents of this view often see social policy as a way of 'managing' difficult sections of the population.

Some radicals envisage a future in which the majority are lulled into passive acceptance of their inferior position through consumerism and welfarism. They see advances in communications technology as giving the elite greater power to manipulate opinion and prevent opposition from arising.

RELATED TOPICS

1.13 Bismarckianism
1.20 Fabianism
1.21 Logic of industrialism
3.6 Pluralism
4.5 Managerialisation

FURTHER READING

Schumpeter (1965) Chap 2
Touraine (1971) Chap 1

Part 2 Reformist perspectives

3.5 SOCIAL BETTERMENT

The history of social policy is often portrayed as a process of progressive *social betterment*. This is often linked to the idea of a gradually developing social conscience. This is a modern version of the 'Whig' interpretation of history, which viewed the history (of Britain) as 'progress'. This idea is often also associated with a 'great man' view of history, which emphasises the central role played by key reformers and statesmen. In the development of social policy in Britain this would include the work of prominent reformers or researchers such as Edwin Chadwick, Charles Booth or Seebohm Rowntree.

Many histories of social policy take a 'social-conscience' approach. Social reform is seen as an intrinsic and normal feature of society. There is often also an implicit functionalist perspective (see 2.24) which views social reform as a more or less automatic response to the appearance of new social needs or social problems.

> Social administrators in the social conscience tradition see the state as benevolent. The social services have as their aim the welfare of their users; the state provides the social services – the state has welfare as its aim. (Baker, 1979: 199)

Reforms are implemented when unacceptable social conditions are revealed by research and publicised by campaigners. Indeed a key role is often played by social enquiry of various kinds, official or unofficial. 'Progressive public opinion' may be seen as developing a consensus that some *social problem* should be dealt with. These accounts are validated by documentary evidence which shows that politicians are aware of these research results and justify reforms with reference to them.

RELATED TOPICS

1.20 Fabianism
1.21 Logic of industrialism
2.24 Social needs and problems: Reformist view
3.6 Pluralism

FURTHER READING

Baker (1979)
Self (1975)

3.6 PLURALISM

Pluralism is a theory about the links between pressure groups and the exercise of political power in a democracy. Pluralists view pressure-group activity as the essence of democracy. It is useful to distinguish between 'interest' groups, which seek advantages, and 'cause' groups, which advocate certain values. It is through pressure groups that the views of members of society are brought into the political process and influence policy. Pluralism assumes that there are a large number (a plurality) of pressure groups which may try to influence policy.

> ... most Western 'students of politics' tend to start ... with the assumption that power, in Western societies, is competitive, fragmented and diffused; everybody, directly or through organized groups, has some power and nobody has or can have too much of it. In these societies, citizens enjoy universal suffrage, free and regular elections, representative institutions, effective citizen rights, including the right of free speech, association and opposition ... no government, acting on behalf of the state, can fail, in the not very long run, to respond to the wishes and demands of competing interests. In the end, everybody, including those at the end of the queue, gets served. (Miliband, 1973: 4)

Pluralism has a number of key propositions:

1. policy is based on free and open debate amongst a politically informed public
2. numerous groups have their say and no one interest can dominate
3. the state is the guardian of the national interest
4. the state acts as a neutral umpire between conflicting groups and interests in society
5. public policy generally, including social policy, reflects the preferences of the public as expressed through pressure-group activity.

This approach denies that some kinds of group are intrinsically more influential than others. However, some critics suggests that there are 'insider' and 'outsider' groups. Outsider groups have little influence and have to try to mobilise public opinion. Insider groups may have a close relationship with government and may even capture control of policy, preventing other groups from having an influence – this is termed 'clientelism'. However, the 'neo-pluralism' developed by Lindblom (1968) suggests that business interests may be pre-eminent. This admission shifts neo-pluralism in the direction of *Marxism*.

RELATED TOPICS

4.9 Participation
4.13 Empowerment

FURTHER READING

Dunleavy and O'Leary (1987) Sections 2.3 and 6.3
Hall et al. (1975) pp 131–5

3.7 INCREMENTALISM

The term *incrementalism* is used to denote a pattern of policy-making in which decisions are made on the basis of small adjustments to existing policies. Policy-making is seen as a process in which decision makers within powerful organisations decide policy. The social pressures and movements described by other theories such as *Marxism* or *pluralism* are not given a central place in the analysis.

This approach developed as a critique of 'rational' models of decision-making which claim that policies are decided after a full and rational appraisal of alternatives. The incremental model suggests that normally only a limited range of alternatives are considered. These usually represent a marginal shift from the current situation.

> Lindblom ... puts up a strong argument for 'muddling through' an approach which is explicitly non-comprehensive and which he has described as 'disjointed incrementalism' ... Essentially this process is: incremental, usually involving only small changes; means oriented, in that ends are chosen that are appropriate to available means; serial, in that problems are not solved at one stroke but are successively attacked; remedial, in that decisions are made to move away from ills rather than towards objectives. The decision process is seen as disjointed for a large number of individuals and groups have access to it at different points. (Hambleton, 1979: 6)

Evidence from empirical studies of policy suggests that in practice policy makers tend to operate with something like the incremental model. They do not exhaustively consider the whole range of possible alternatives. Instead they review a limited range of realistic possibilities. Bargaining and compromise are important. Where a 'consensus' is sought the policy decision may well represent the best fit with the various interests involved rather than a 'rational' solution.

One important implication of this is that restructuring the management of services to create the basis for more 'rational' decision-making is likely to fail. Decision makers will soon fall back on rules of thumb, following precedents, backing hunches and other non-rational methods.

What the approach of incrementalism cannot explain is what happens when major shifts of policy do take place, as sometimes happens.

RELATED TOPICS

1.1 Public policy and social policy
3.4 Democratic elitism and technocracy
3.5 Social betterment
3.6 Pluralism

FURTHER READING

Ham and Hill (1984) pp 79–84
Hogwood and Gunn (1984) Chap 4

3.8 WELFARE CORPORATISM

Liberal democracy, pluralist democracy and corporatist democracy can be seen as three variants of democratic rule.

1. in a *liberal* democracy governments make decisions without giving organised interests a role in policy making
2. in a *pluralist* democracy government is strongly influenced by pressure-group activity
3. in a *corporatist* democracy policy is controlled by key organisations acting in partnership with government.

Corporatism has generally been used to refer to the process in which trade unions and employer associations were brought into partnership with government in making and implementing economic and industrial policies, particularly during the First and Second World Wars. The corporatist approach reduces public debate and open political conflict and settles issues through top-level negotiation.

Welfare corporatism can be seen as a feature of some areas of social policy making where policy tends to be dominated by a small number of influential bodies. One example is the British Medical Association (BMA) which represents doctors. This is a highly organised and influential producer group, which has often been able to exert pressure in the decision-making process. In other areas of policy which may lack powerful groups which can dominate the process, arrangements more characteristic of *pluralism* may prevail.

Policy making is sometimes 'captured' by those to whom policy is directed. This kind of relationship has been termed 'clientelism'. The result is that other interests, such as those of consumers, do not have an effective voice in the policy process.

In some social-democratic welfare states, such as Australia and Austria, governments have used a corporatist 'social partnership' to create a consensus on social policy. The partnership is based on policies to secure full employment with a market economy operating alongside a system of social welfare. The British Labour government of 1974–9 attempted to employ this strategy by making a 'social contract' with the trade-union movement in which the government would pursue welfare policies and the trade unions would agree to wage restraint.

There is also Catholic *corporatism*, which is based on Catholic social teaching. This has strongly influenced German and Irish social policy.

RELATED TOPICS

1.22 Keynesian welfare state
3.6 Pluralism
7.4 Germany
7.7 Austria
8.7 Ireland: background

FURTHER READING

Cawson (1982)
Wilensky (1976)

Part 3 Radical perspectives

3.9 MARXISM

One approach of *Marxism* to the growth of social policy is based on the idea that capitalism passes through different stages as it develops. At each stage:

- capitalism encounters different barriers to its further development
- the nature of class conflict changes
- the political demands facing the dominant class change
- the social policies developed will be distinctive.

In the early phase of 'competitive capitalism' the main barrier is an attachment to a traditional way of life and resistance to the strict demands of wage labour. At this stage the state is likely to be dominated by the capitalist class with restrictions on the right to vote. Firms are small and the technology employed relatively simple. Educational provision is often restricted. Appropriate policies would be those designed to enforce labour discipline *supporting the market* through the use of the workhouse (see 1.12) or similar polices. Traditional culture and attitudes unfavourable to regular work might also come under attack by the authorities.

Disorderly economic and social protest can be a feature of early capitalist industrialism. An organised system of policing would be likely to be established.

In the later phase of large-scale capitalism, sometimes called 'monopoly capitalism', new barriers to the further development of capitalism emerge. Firms become much larger and use more advanced technology. Scientific and technical training and the general level of education become more important. Health and working efficiency may also be considered important with services initiated to improve them. Trade unionism and organised political action increase along with pressure for more democracy. As working-class political influence grows, moves may be made to integrate the class into society through social policies designed to reduce poverty and economic insecurity.

However, owing to the uneven character of capitalist development on a world scale, states that develop later are able to miss out part or all of the earlier stage. For this reason an analysis making a sharp division between competitive and monopoly capitalism is not always relevant.

> The era of both monopoly capitalism and the welfare state is often contrasted with an earlier period of laissez-faire capitalism, characterised by small-scale capital and a minimal role for the state. This was true for only a very restricted range of countries, and possibly only for the United Kingdom, the leading capitalist country of the nineteenth century. In Italy, Russia and Japan, for example, the role of the state in creating the conditions for capitalist production and in abetting the development of monopoly capital were fused in time around the late nineteenth century: an intervening period of laissez-faire was unknown. This greatly affected the pattern of welfare legislation in these countries and served to differentiate it somewhat from the British. (Gough, 1979: 50)

RELATED TOPICS

1.26 Marxism: 1 Capital logic
1.27 Marxism: 2 Balance of social forces
2.25 Social needs and problems: radical view
4.10 Decommodification

FURTHER READING

Burden and Campbell (1985) Chap 1
Dunleavy and O'Leary (1987) Sections 5.3 and 5.4
Ginsburg (1979) Chap 3
Gough (1979) Chap 3
Hall et al. (1975) pp 135–40

O'Connor (1973) Chap 1
Saville (1983)

3.10 NEW SOCIAL MOVEMENTS

The term *new social movements* has been used to describe a range of social movements which became influential in the 1980s. Many of these movements dealt with issues central to social policy. These included groups campaigning for the rights of women, ethnic minorities, the disabled, the old and those with a minority sexual orientation. The student, anti-war and civil-rights movements of the 1960s were similar. In contrast to Marxist theories of politics, these movements are not based on class membership and do not pursue class interests.

... the 1970s witnessed the flowering of environmental, women's, anti-nuclear and peace movements, along with the eventual emergence of New Left-libertarian and 'Green' political parties in many European countries. At the same time divergent sub-cultural lifestyles emerged which celebrated 'alternative' cultural values. These developments were highly critical of the worship of economic growth in advanced capitalist societies and questioned the benefit of continued modernisation for both the metropolitan and Third World countries. (Fagan and Lee, 1997: 143)

Many new social movements are distinctive in rejecting orthodox lifestyles. They have been seen as expanding the boundaries of political debate to include new issues. These issues involved questions of 'identity' and what is sometimes called 'personal politics'.

Attempts were made to establish alliances of these movements as the basis for political and social change. Some supporters of the Labour Party in large local authorities such as the former Greater London Council employed these ideas in the 1980s. For this approach, social policy largely develops through social conflict initiated by emerging social movements.

Whether these movements are really a new development can be questioned. To go further back, the temperance movement was very influential in western Europe and the US in the early decades of the twentieth century. This was not class based and involved lifestyle and personal identity. The subsequent history of social policy contains numerous examples of non-class movements influencing policy.

RELATED TOPICS

4.12 Positive discrimination
4.13 Empowerment

FURTHER READING

Fagan and Lee (1997) pp 140–8
Green (1987)
Scott (1990)

3.11 FEMINISM

The approach of *feminism* to the development of social policy argues that conventional histories neglect the role of women in the process through which policy eventually comes to be made. Women are seen as 'hidden from history'.

The establishment of the welfare state in Britain in part involved the recognition of the needs of mothers, children and carers. Feminist historians have documented the role played by women in the political movements seeking welfare reform in the nineteenth and twentieth centuries. Women have also played a major role in the establishment of various areas of welfare provision, laying down the foundations for such services as *social work*, housing management and health visiting. Feminists in the early twentieth century campaigned to improve women's position in the 'public' sphere in terms of access to education, work and political rights. Later in the twentieth century women's role in the 'private sphere' of the *family* became the subject of debate.

Following on from this, some feminists have developed a broader critique which suggests that the main disciplines through which social policy is studied systematically neglect women and have often failed to place women on the research agenda or to develop the concepts through which women's role could be understood. Since the 1960s the feminist perspective in the study of social policy has grown and developed. It is argued that social policy and the welfare state cannot be properly understood without understanding how it deals with women.

> Much of this work offered new dimensions to key questions in social policy analysis: issues of caring, dependency, needs, of the relationship between work and income, of the relationships between the providers and users of welfare provision, as well as theoretical questions about the relationship between patriarchy, capitalism and the state. (Williams, 1989: xii)

This argument has been taken up by Marxist feminists, who have developed concepts for understanding the role played by women in the operation of the capitalist economy. Women perform vital 'reproductive' roles in the household caring for the current and the future generation of workers and also form part of the reserve army of labour (see 2.7). According to the Marxist feminist viewpoint, a great deal of social policy is designed to reinforce these roles.

RELATED TOPICS

2.5 Gender: right-wing view
2.6 Gender: reformist view
2.7 Gender: radical view
3.10 New social movements

FURTHER READING

Dale and Foster (1986) Chaps 1 and 2
David (1985)
Pascall (1986) Chap 1
Pierson (1991) pp 69–79
Rowbotham (1973a)
Williams (1989) Chap 3
Wilson (1983)

CHAPTER 4

Social-policy strategies

4.1 ALTERNATIVE SOCIAL-POLICY STRATEGIES

The three ideological perspectives each employ distinctive strategies for the delivery of social policies as shown in the table below.

Table 4.1 Left, centre and right social-policy strategies

	Left	**Centre**	**Right**
Mechanism	Universalism Free distribution	State organised provision	Individualism Markets Private ownership 'New wave' management
Role of state	Organised to benefit the recipients	To finance and deliver a limited range of services	To be reduced 'Enabling' role
Degree of universalism	Mainly universal	A combination of universal and selective services	Mainly residual, means-tested services
Status of recipients	Equal citizens	Entitled recipients Clients of professionals	Low 'pauper' status for recipients of cash
Examples covered	1. Decommodi- fication 2. Public ownership and democratic control 3. Positive discrimination 4. Empowerment	1. National Insurance 2. Universalism 3. Administrative reorganisation 4. Participation	1. Privatisation 2. Provider markets 3. Means-testing 4. Manageriali- sation

RELATED TOPICS

1.11 Right-wing approaches: general features
1.18 Reformist approaches: general features
1.23 Welfare pluralism

1.25 Radical approaches: general features
3.1 Theories of social-policy development

FURTHER READING
George and Wilding (1985)

Part 1 Right-wing strategies

4.2 PRIVATISATION

Privatisation reflects a strong belief on the right in the virtues of free markets and private ownership for the provision of all goods and services including those normally seen as part of social policy such as health care and education. In the area of social-policy, privatisation means putting assets in the hands of private owners. This can be achieved in a number of ways.

1. By directly transferring ownership from public to private hands.
2. By requiring agencies to seek tenders from the private sector for service delivery. This is know as 'compulsory competitive tendering' (CCT) and has been used in Britain for many NHS hospital ancillary services, such as laundry, since the early 1980s.
3. By requiring agencies responsible for delivering a service to purchase it from the private sector. In Britain under the NHS and Community Care Act 1990 local authorities have to purchase 85 per cent of community-care provision from private companies.
4. By allowing people to 'opt out' of state provision and buy the service from the private sector. This can be achieved by providing public services of a low standard in order to encourage private provision. Tax incentives have also been used to encourage this process. Private pensions were encouraged in this way by the 'opt-out' provisions of the Social Security Act 1988.

... privatisation can mean reduced government provision, reduced government finance and reduced government regulation, and that reduced government provision and finance usually means the transfer of responsibilities to non-statutory agencies. Easily the most common meaning attributed to privatisation, however, is the sale of public assets. (Johnson, 1990: 192)

In Britain, since 1979, significant areas of privatisation involving social services have been:

• the sale of council houses
• the extension of private health
• the growth of private pension provision

- increased private-sector involvement within the NHS
- the growth of the private sector in community care through requiring local authorities to purchase care from private providers
- the use of private capital in schooling through City Technology Colleges.

The state has attempted to ensure that adequate standards are met by the private providers. Detailed contracts in the form of 'service level agreements' have been used. Requirements may also be specified by legislation. Sometimes inspections are required.

RELATED TOPICS

1.17 Neo-liberalism
3.2 Overloaded government
3.3 Bureaucratic self-interest
5.7 Schooling: right-wing view
8.5 Great Britain: the old

FURTHER READING

Johnson (1990) pp 7–14 and 192–8
Le Grand and Robinson (1984) Chap 1
Papadakis and Taylor-Gooby (1987) Chap 1
Walker (1984)

4.3 PROVIDER MARKETS

A *provider market* (or 'quasi-market' or 'internal market') exists where the suppliers of a public service are subjected to market disciplines:

- suppliers have their revenues determined by the 'demand' for their services from 'consumers'
- successful operating units will get more clients (and more income) and expand
- unsuccessful units will contract or even close.

... 'quasi-' or 'internal markets' ... have been introduced into several areas of publicly provided services, like the health and education services in the United Kingdom. The intention here is to provide the conditions for a more 'productively efficient' provision of the services offered in these areas by making sure they are produced at the lowest price (or perhaps at a lower price than they are at present supplied). With this type of approach the attempt is to mirror some of the features of the 'external' market in the internal functioning of the organization. (Thompson et al., 1991: 8)

In a provider market the forces of supply and demand operate, but are restricted by law. For example, publicly owned hospitals are not at liberty to abandon treating patients and move into a completely new area of business. Provider markets are often also accompanied by *managerialisation* involving moves to encourage a more business-like approach. There is an emphasis on business methods and managerial skills for those making decisions. This will normally involve a system of delegated budgets with semi-independent operating units. These are run by boards which:

- are supposed to act like the Board of Directors of a private firm
- have wide powers, including paying and employing staff
- can contract for the services they require at the best price they can get.

RELATED TOPICS

1.17 Neo-liberalism (the new right)
3.3 Bureaucratic self-interest
4.5 Managerialisation
5.7 Schooling: right-wing view
8.4 Great Britain: health care

FURTHER READING

Le Grand and Robinson (1984)
Mullen (1991)

4.4 MEANS-TESTING AND SELECTIVITY

Means-testing is sometimes also referred to as *selectivity* and contrasted with *universalism*. The right generally favours means-testing in order to 'target' benefits where they are most needed. Systems for distributing income supplements using means tests are often known as 'social assistance' and contrasted with 'social insurance', which is another term for *National Insurance*.

Eligibility for benefits can also be targeted using other kinds of 'test'. For some benefits a 'work test' may be used. This is where applicants have to be willing to undertake specified work tasks to be eligible for a benefit. 'Workfare' is the modern name for this approach. Under the 1834 Poor Law, relief was dependent on the 'workhouse test' (see 1.12). Applicants had to agree to enter the workhouse and accept its rules before being given relief.

With a means test, eligibility for a benefit depends on having an income and/or wealth below a specified level. Means-testing is designed to:

- keep public expenditure down

- encourage thrift
- support the private provision of services.

A system of benefits largely based on means-testing can result in a 'poverty trap'. Workers receiving means-tested benefits cannot get much extra income from a pay increase, since this will mean they lose benefits. In Britain, low income-tax thresholds mean higher taxation and National Insurance contributions on the pay increase and the loss of other benefits such as free school meals. Low-paid workers may then be 'trapped' at an income level just above the poverty line.

A common problem with means-tested benefits is that in practice many of those eligible for do not claim them. This can be due to:

1. ignorance of the benefits available
2. the complexity of the procedures involved in claiming them
3. the invasion of privacy involved in having to disclose personal details
4. the stigmatisation of benefit recipients.

The fatal objection to a policy of extending selectivity is that it misconceives the nature of poverty and reinforces the condition it is supposed to alleviate. The policy assumes that poverty is an absolute condition, a lack of a minimum subsistence cash income, which requires little more than the diversion of a minute proportion of national income in an efficient manner to alleviate. It fosters hierarchical relationships of superiority and inferiority in society, diminishes rather than enhances the status of the poor, and has the effect of widening rather than of reducing social inequalities. Far from sensitively discriminating different kinds of need it lumps the unemployed, sick, widowed, aged and others into an undifferentiated and inevitably stigmatised category. (Townsend, 1970: 5–6)

The political implications of means-testing are complex. Means tests have tended to be associated with a right-wing approach through their use to reduce state expenditure. On the other hand, some means-tested modes of distribution may be viewed favourably on the left because, in principle, they can benefit the poor more than the rich, so leading to a more equal distribution of income. Schemes such as negative income tax would have this effect by making payments to those too poor to pay tax.

RELATED TOPICS

1.17 Neo-liberalism (the new right)
4.2 Privatisation
4.7 Universalism

FURTHER READING

Pratt (1997)
Titmuss (1968) Chap 10
Townsend (1970)
Townsend (1975)

4.5 MANAGERIALISATION

A neglected feature of the market-based social-policy reforms of the 1980s was *managerialisation*, or 'new managerialism', which involved giving an enhanced role to management. Managerialisation involves a more business-like approach, which puts the emphasis on efficiency and measures of performance rather than meeting 'needs'. It began with the recruitment of managers from business to introduce private-sector management methods.

> ... managerialism is the connecting thread linking markets, partnerships, an emphasis on customers and the recomposition of the labour force ... it seeks to introduce new orientations, remodels existing relations of power and affects how and where social policy choices are made. (Clarke et al., 1994: 3–4).

Managerialisation has often been accompanied by the rhetoric of 'new wave' management involving 'quality', customer care, 'empowerment' and giving subordinates a sense of 'ownership'. Managerialisation has involved a reduction of the power of professionals and its replacement with one of three alternatives.

1. The use of central direction to impose a pattern of service desired by the government such as a national curriculum imposed on schools in many states.
2. More power for local managements based on devolving control of budgets.
3. Increased consumer power from treating users of social services as customers (of a service industry) rather than clients (of professional experts). *Provider markets* are a means of doing this. In Britain the customers of some social services are now also given more information through hospital and school 'league tables' which rank service providers according to measures of the quality of their output.

RELATED TOPICS

4.3 Provider markets
4.8 Administrative reorganisation
4.9 Participation
5.7 Schooling: right-wing view

5.23 Professionalism: right-wing view

FURTHER READING

Clarke et al. (1994) Chap 1

Part 2 Reformist strategies

4.6 NATIONAL INSURANCE

National Insurance (NI) employs compulsory personal saving to provide a fund to supplement income when it is interrupted. It works by redistributing income within an income group – healthy workers support the sick, those in work support the unemployed. 'Social insurance' is another term for *National Insurance* and is often contrasted with systems for distributing income supplements using *means-testing*, which are often known as 'social assistance'.

NI was first used in Germany in the late nineteenth century and introduced in various other countries early in the twentieth century. In Britain, the 1911 National Insurance Act introduced means-tested health insurance and a scheme of unemployment insurance for workers in seven industries particularly subject to fluctuations in demand for labour. During the inter-war period the scope of the benefits provided and the proportion of workers covered gradually increased.

In Britain, the Beveridge Report of 1942 proposed a system based on a single weekly contribution which would finance a comprehensive range of benefits set at subsistence level. The scheme was implemented in 1948 and formed a central part of the welfare state. The benefits and contributions were set at a single rate applying to everyone. It excluded those unable to work such as the handicapped, and offered lesser benefits to women.

> ... even had the scheme been implemented fully it would not have abolished poverty in the post-war world ... Beveridge underestimated the extent of family poverty which was caused by low wages ... the plan did not advocate a comprehensive insurance policy for women or the disabled ... the subsistence principle was undermined by Beveridge's unwillingness either to set benefits high enough to cover all rent levels. (Field, 1981: 90)

Key features of the scheme were consistent with the values of capitalism.

1. The insurance principle would reinforce self-help.
2. Rules on the number of contributions necessary before benefits could be drawn would prevent abuse by malingerers.

3. Contributions from the employer and the state would symbolise a concern for employee welfare and contribute to a sense of citizenship.
4. Benefits set at subsistence level would keep the cost low, maintain work incentives and encourage the private provision of insurance.

RELATED TOPICS

1.13 Bismarckianism
1.19 The new liberalism
2.15 Citizenship: reformist view

FURTHER READING

Field et al. (1977) Chap 4
Field (1981) Chap 4
Gilbert (1966)
Kincaid (1973) Chap 3

4.7 UNIVERSALISM

Universalism is the name given to the principle that social benefits should be made available to everyone in an eligible category. It is often contrasted with the principal of *means-testing and selectivity* or targeting. Universal benefits avoid the poverty trap. A poverty trap occurs when benefit recipients are unable to improve their living standards by taking a job, since they lose means-tested benefits when they obtain an increased income.

Child allowances which are paid to all families with children regardless of their income are an example of a universal benefit. Citizens' income (see 4.10) is also based on the universalist principle. The British National Health Service, which is available free to all, is a prime example of a universal benefit. National Insurance benefits are also universal, although these have to be 'earned' by contributions.

Its proponents view universalism as avoiding the weaknesses of a selective approach. There are no means tests to humiliate and deter claimants. The lack of a means test also reduces administrative costs. Universalism is believed to foster social unity by creating a sense of equality of entitlement. Some authors see this as part of *citizenship*. Titmuss holds a distinctive view, which sees universalism as the background against which programmes of *positive discrimination* can be operated.

The real challenge resides in the question; what particular infrastructure of universalist services is needed in order to provide a framework of values and opportunity bases within and around which can be developed socially acceptable selective services aiming to discriminate positively, with the minimum risk of stigma, in favour of those whose needs are greatest? (Titmuss, 1968: 135)

RELATED TOPICS

2.15 Citizenship: reformist view
4.4 Means-testing and selectivity
4.6 National Insurance
4.10 Decommodification
4.12 Positive discrimination

FURTHER READING

Titmuss (1968) Chap 10

4.8 ADMINISTRATIVE REORGANISATION

Many reformist approaches assume that *administrative reorganisation* can lead to rationally designed organisations which will provide solutions to social problems.

... if social deprivations do exist, then the agencies are not properly fulfilling their tasks ... it is concluded that social deprivations can be resolved by identifying and remedying the faults within agencies. (Holman, 1978: 147)

The administrative deficiencies identified may include:

• inadequate planning
• unclear goals
• departmentalism
• administrative failure
• duplication of services
• overlapping or unclear responsibilities
• lack of inter-agency coordination
• failure of different professional groups to work together.

Administrative reorganisation uses a 'rational' approach to organisational design to improve the delivery of policy without increasing costs. This is a version of *technocracy* (see 3.4). But 'rational' organisational designs do not always work in the way anticipated on organisation charts. The process of reorganisation is often itself very costly:

1. many people seek to secure 'opportunistic' gains for themselves
2. informal networks which have helped organisations to run smoothly are damaged
3. Prolonged periods of uncertainty and chaos may ensue.

In Britain, major administrative reorganisations of social work and health care undertaken in the late 1960s and early 1970s failed to meet the aspirations of their proponents.

RELATED TOPICS

3.4 Democratic elitism and technocracy
4.5 Managerialisation

FURTHER READING

Brown (1975) Chap 2
Room (1979) pp 95–113

4.9 PARTICIPATION

In Britain, *participation* enjoyed a vogue in the late 1960s and early 1970s. This was partly a response to disillusion with local-authority slum-clearance policies. Older urban working-class housing was demolished and residents were re-housed in peripheral housing estates, often with substantial quantities of deck-access and high-rise accommodation. These policies were partly inspired by a 'modernist' vision of working-class housing based on the ideas of Le Corbusier. The new estates were seen to lack the community spirit of the older working-class areas they replaced.

Participation was an attempt to make decision-making in planning more responsive to local needs. The Skeffington Report, 'People and Planning', was the basis for the 1968 Planning Act. The act required participation in the planning process, including the use of a 'community forum' involving local groups.

In the Seebohm Report of 1968 on the reorganisation of social-work services, participation was identified as a means by which any stigma associated with the receipt of social benefits could be eliminated:

> ... the development of citizen participation should reduce the rigid distinction between givers and takers of social services, and the stigma which being a client has involved in the past. (Seebohm, 1968: para. 492)

Participation was also an element in other British social-policy reforms around this time.

1. In the 1974 reform of local government the Ministry of Local Government recommended the establishment of 'Neighbourhood Councils'.
2. Similar ideas lay behind the provision for Community Health Councils in the 1974 reorganisation of the health service.

3. Participation in local policing using community forums was also recommended in the Scarman Report on the riots of 1981.

In practice, participation can take a variety of forms. Some are token forms of participation, such as manipulation or 'therapy', others are more substantive and may involve informing, consultation, placating and even handing over a share of power. According to critics on the left, participation generally involves a form of managed and manipulated participation which does not represent a real shift of power.

RELATED TOPICS

2.12 Community: reformist view
4.13 Empowerment

FURTHER READING

Arnstein (1971)
Cockburn (1977) Chap 4
Hill and Bramley (1986) Chap 11

Part 3 Radical strategies

4.10 DECOMMODIFICATION

A commodity is something which is distributed through sale at a market price. In Marxism the process of commodification occurs when production is undertaken for profit and the goods and services produced become commodities for sale. *Decommodification* refers to the process by which services are distributed on the basis of a form of entitlement other than ability to pay.

Decommodification has been viewed as a defining feature of a radical social policy, which meets needs or distributes essential goods and services to those who require them. The principle is that access to the service should not depend on willingness and ability to pay. This entitlement might be based on people's own stated preferences or on an 'objective' or professional assessment of need. In some cases a token or standard payment might be employed.

The extent of decommodification can be seen as measure of the extent to which the values of capitalism have been rejected. In Britain, as in other countries, this varies in different areas of social provision.

- Education is largely decommodified but there is also a substantial private sector.
- Health care is largely decommodified although it not distributed strictly according to need. There is private health care, and this allows paying customers to have their needs met more fully and more rapidly.

• Income support is partly decommodified through state benefits such as pensions, child allowances and benefits for the unemployed, but there is also a massive private insurance sector.

Universal family allowances paid to all families with children are a means of partially decommodifying personal incomes. Another very radical form of decommodification would be a scheme for 'citizens' income', sometimes known as 'basic income'. Citizens' income involves:

... an unconditional regular weekly payment made to all adults. Its main purpose would be to reduce the extent of reliance on wage labour as the determinant of individual and household incomes. The existence of the basic income would also reduce the proportional inequality between the highest and the lowest personal and household incomes since it would represent a higher proportional addition to the funds available to low income recipients. (Breitenbach et al., 1990: 33)

This has been viewed as a means of simplifying the income support system and of providing the conditions under which everyone would be able to pursue the kind of life they preferred.

Authors such as Offe view the process of decommodification as exemplified by state welfare provision as 'contradictory', as it is needed to maintain social harmony but at the same time it undermines the workings of the capitalist economy.

... the limitations of the welfare state ... derive from fundamental contradictions ... the various branches of the welfare state are compelled to perform two incompatible functions vis-à-vis the economic subsystem: commodification and decommodification... the policy-making and administering activities of the welfare state are constrained and limited by the dynamics of the sphere of economic production ... the healthy functioning of this economic subsystem is a crucial condition of the 'mass loyalty' to the welfare state and, indirectly, the vital source of its revenues ... welfare state administrators must therefore be concerned with preserving the 'private' power and scope of these commodification processes. In sum, the welfare state is required to be a self-limiting state. (Offe, 1984: 14–15)

RELATED TOPICS

4.7 Universalism
5.24 Professionalism: reformist view

FURTHER READING

Breitenbach et al. (1990) pp 30–4

Jordan (1977) pp 149–64
Offe (1984) Introduction

4.11 PUBLIC OWNERSHIP AND DEMOCRATIC CONTROL

The methods by which social-service organisations are run and controlled is an issue of concern to many radicals. Many radicals argue that social services should not be delivered by hierarchical welfare bureaucracies or private-sector contractors.

1. There should be *public ownership* of the delivery organisation.
2. There should be *democratic control* with overall policy determined by elected representatives.
3. There should be *collective management* with day to day decisions influenced by employees and clients.

We must rethink the relationship between the citizen and State, be wary of providing benefits without also conferring clearly understood rights, and be suspicious of developing services that are not run by democratically elected or accountable bodies. Above all else we must measure progress not by the growth of bureaucracies or the increasing strength of professionals or para-professionals, but by output, both the number and quality of services provided to those requiring them, and by the increase in the standards, self esteem, dignity, power and liberty of ordinary people. (Wicks, 1987: 225)

The extent to which current social-policy provision in Britain is organised on this basis varies substantially from service to service. A few examples of this are given in Table 4.2.

An important implication for radicals is that the scope for organisational reform designed to radicalise service provision varies greatly across the social services, since some are currently much more radically organised than others.

RELATED TOPICS

1.26 Marxism: 1 Capital logic
1.27 Marxism: 2 Balance of social forces

FURTHER READING

Breitenbach et al. (1990) Chap 6
Deacon (1983) Introduction and pp 244–67
Wicks (1987) Chap 11

4.12 POSITIVE DISCRIMINATION

Positive discrimination, termed 'affirmative action' in the United States, is a strategy for pursuing equality based on the principle that

Table 4.2 Public ownership and democratic control in current British services

	Public ownership	Democratic control	Collective management
State-financed schooling	Mainly, but with some assisted places in fee paying schools	Some elected governors Local authority committee	Control by headteachers alone
State-financed hospital care	Mainly, but with some contracts with private hospitals	Appointed Community Health Councils Appointed NHS hospital trust boards	Some representation of professionals especially doctors
Social-service departments	Private-sector contractors provide much residential care	Local authority committee No elective control at local offices	Hierarchical management control
Social-security system	Full public ownership	Part of bureaucratic government department No local elective control	Hierarchical management control

services should not just be distributed equally but that the deprived should receive more than an equal share.

> ... we face the positive challenge of providing selective, high quality services for poor people over a large and complex range of welfare; of positively discriminating on a territorial group or 'rights' basis in favour of the poor, the handicapped, the deprived, the coloured, the homeless, and the social casualties of our society. Universalism is not, by itself alone, enough ... (Titmuss, 1968: 134)

Positive discrimination can be directed towards individuals. In the areas of race and gender positive discrimination may involve setting quotas for minority recruitment in employment or education.

Positive discrimination can also be directed towards areas. In Britain in the late 1960s, a number of area-based policy initiatives using the principle of positive discrimination were started. Areas were identified in which high levels of deprivation were present. Educational Priority Areas were established in some poor inner-

city areas and extra resources were channelled to the schools in
them. General Improvement Areas and Housing Action Areas
were also designated. The problems of the residents were viewed
as compounded by the general deprivation of the area in which they
lived. Some radicals saw this as a means of channelling resources
to the poor without using individual *means-testing*. The focus on
an area would, in principle, allow an integrated and comprehensive
approach involving a range of provision.

These policies operated as pilots and experiments rather than
as a general policy for the distribution of social-policy resources.
Critics of area-based positive-discrimination policies argued that
many deprived people did not live in deprived areas and that many
residents of deprived areas were not deprived.

RELATED TOPICS

2.13 Community: radical view
4.7 Universalism
4.13 Empowerment

FURTHER READING

Edwards (1987) Chaps 1 and 2
Jordan (1974) Chap 9

4.13 EMPOWERMENT

The term *empowerment* became popular in the 1990s across the
political spectrum. It is found in some versions of 'new wave'
management where it is seen as a means of increasing commitment
to the goals of organisations.

In its radical guise, the idea of empowerment emphasises that
policy should attempt to reduce or eliminate inequalities of power
and status. It identifies groups and categories which are
systematically disadvantaged. Empowerment involves helping
oppressed or passive groups to become aware of their rights and
of ways to enforce them.

It has become an important theme in *social work* and youthwork
training and practice. It rejects the traditional professional–client
relationship based on the passive receipt of, and compliance with
professional or expert treatment and advice. The clients are seen
as active agents who should be encouraged to 'challenge' oppressive
behaviour and to organise to pursue their demands.

The movement to counter domestic violence against women and
to provide women's refuges has been influenced by the idea of
empowerment. The idea has also had some influence on the
increased political consciousness of some previously 'invisible'

groups. It has played a part in the movements of the disabled and those with learning difficulties.

RELATED TOPICS

2.7 Gender: radical view
2.16 Citizenship: radical view
2.22 Race: radical view
3.10 New social movements
4.5 Managerialisation
5.25 Professionalism: radical view

CHAPTER 5

Social-policy issues

5.1 ISSUES IN SOCIAL POLICY

Social policy is at the centre of political disagreement and debate. Academic debates on social policy often focus on what are seen as politically charged issues. The arguments and ideas of academics who study and write about social policy often reflect these political divisions. Sometimes the academics, or their work, are themselves part of the debate.

The issues examined here have all been the subject of both political and academic controversy. The use of the three main perspectives developed in this book, along with an understanding of various schools of thought within them, can help us to make sense of many aspects of these controversies.

However, it should be remembered that there are other views on some of these issues which may start from different standpoints. In particular, various feminist viewpoints may adopt a different perspective and develop alternative concerns, and in places these are introduced.

The issues covered are:

1. the causes of crime
2. schooling
3. urban problems
4. social work
5. health and disease
6. professionalism.

RELATED TOPICS

2.1 Central concepts

FURTHER READING

Forder (1974)
Hill and Bramley (1986)

5.2 THE CAUSES OF CRIME: INTRODUCTION

Crime and how to deal with it has been an issue ever since organised government based on compulsory rules has existed. The response to crime always highlights the coercive nature of the state. Crime is an important feature of society. Crime is also an important and controversial issue in social science. Various schools of thought vie with each other to suggest explanations and solutions.

Some sociologists, such as Durkheim, have argued that crime is functional in that it can help society to function effectively. The response to crime allows members of society to express their outrage at a violation of social rules. In this process the rules governing society are publicly affirmed and clarified. Others view crime as a threat to society.

In recent years *feminism* has made an important contribution to the literature on crime. A major factor in understanding the pattern of crime is gender. Overall, the conviction rate for girls and women is much lower than that for boys and men. This may reflect differences in the patterns of social control experienced by males and females:

1. Girls tend to stay closer to home.
2. They are expected to undertake more household tasks.
3. They may be under a curfew more than men.
4. Higher standards of behaviour are often imposed on them.
5. The 'bedroom culture' for girls keeps them out of trouble.
6. Girls are more subject to parental control than boys.
7. Girls are generally less likely to meet others engaged in criminal behaviour.
8. They are excluded from crime by men.

During the post-war period, the proportion of women convicted for indictable offences against property, though not for violence, has risen. This may reflect women's greater role in wage labour and their exposure to the values of the market.

Consideration of crime and issues associated with the social response to it are increasingly seen as important in the study of social policy. It brings out clearly the divergent approaches offered by the different perspectives highlighted in this book.

1. The *right* sees crime as a result of human weakness, wickedness or lack of social control.
2. *Reformists* view crime as the product of poor socialisation or disorganised social conditions.
3. *Radicals* relate crime to capitalism and class.

RELATED TOPICS

2.6 Gender: reformist view
2.7 Gender: radical view
2.9 The family: reformist view
2.10 The family: radical view

FURTHER READING

Heidensohn (1987)
Young (1981)

5.3 THE CAUSES OF CRIME: RIGHT-WING VIEW

There are two approaches to dealing with crime on the right, the *conservative* and the *classical*.

Conservative social thought has always viewed crime as caused by moral weakness and lack of respect for morality and authority. The response to crime is retributive with a central place given to punishment. Punishment shows society's outrage at the violation of its laws. It is not designed to reform the criminal, although it might have a deterrent effect. A modern version of this view is that 'prison works', since it 'incapacitates' the offender.

> For the conservative, the causes of crime lie in the pursuit of individual gratification (usually incommensurate with effort), the undermining of traditional loyalties and the consequent unwillingness of the individual to accept discipline. (Young, 1981: 277)

The *classical* approach derives from the work of *liberal* reformers such as Beccaria and Bentham in the late eighteenth and early nineteenth century. They developed a set of criminological theories known as 'classicism', which assumed that crime involved the rational pursuit of self-interest. In order to prevent crime, circumstances needed to be such that potential criminals would calculate that it was not worth committing an offence. This required:

1. a high chance of criminals being apprehended and therefore necessitated an organised and efficient police force
2. laws based on the principle of 'proportionality', with punishments just sufficient to outweigh the expectation of gain
3. institutions for those people who offended because they were unable to regulate their behaviour, in which they would be remade or reformed as rational self-interested beings.

This classical perspective was influential in the first half of the nineteenth century when a modern police force, criminal law and prison system were being established in many capitalist states. With a rational system of laws, efficient policing and a prison system the problem of crime could be dealt with. Modern versions of this approach may be termed 'just deserts', 'neo-classical' or 'correctionalist'.

RELATED TOPICS

1.12 Supporting the market
1.17 Neo-liberalism (the new right)
2.2 The individual in society: right-wing view
2.17 Poverty: right-wing view

FURTHER READING

Eysenck (1977) Chap 9
Ignatieff (1978) Chap 1
Roshier (1989) Chaps 1 and 5
Wilson (1975) Chap 10

5.4 THE CAUSES OF CRIME: REFORMIST VIEW

Reformist views of the causes of crime are generally classified as 'positivist'. They are 'positivist' in the sense that they are based on the 'scientific' study of criminals. Crime is seen as caused by forces propelling the criminal rather than as a freely chosen form of behaviour. Because their offending behaviour is not freely chosen, criminals are not fully responsible for it. Punishment is therefore inappropriate and instead 'treatment' is normally required. Those who could not be treated might be segregated from society for the protection of others.

Reformist theories focus on three different ways in which crime can be caused:

1. The causes may be *social*, where social circumstances influence the likelihood of committing offences.

    In fact, if the aim is to tackle levels of crime in society, the whole process of police, courts, prisons, probation, is not the place to start ... Crime rates do not come ultimately from what happens or does not happen to criminals. They come from what is going on in society more generally, from housing policies, the state of the labour market, education, the level of affluence, the social and moral climate. (Stern, 1987: 265)

2. The causes may be *psychological* where people may have been born with, or acquired a personality susceptible to offending. In most modern versions of the reformist approach psychological or social-psychological causes are emphasised. Treatment takes the form of some kind of therapy or counselling such as youthwork, 'intermediate treatment', *social work* or probation.

3. The causes may be *biological*, where people may be genetically inclined towards crime. Until recently, psycho-surgery, such as removal of the frontal lobes, or castration was used in extreme

cases. Hormone therapies for some sex criminals are still used today.

This biological viewpoint is now usually associated with a right-wing approach but historically it had support from many reformers in the centre and on the left as the history of the *eugenics* movement shows.

RELATED TOPICS

1.16 Eugenics
2.9 The family: reformist view
5.16 Social work: reformist view

FURTHER READING

Roshier (1989) Chap 2
Stern (1987) Chap 13

5.5 THE CAUSES OF CRIME: RADICAL VIEW

The radical interpretation of the causes of crime in the *Marxist* tradition starts from the concepts of capitalism and class. Radicals claim the law will always be biased towards the interests of the dominant class, which will influence what is to count as crime. The dominant capitalist class may 'criminalise' activities which threaten its position – some forms of trade-union action and political protest may be restricted or banned. However, in order to remain legitimate, the law must also provide some general protection and rights for everyone.

> Definitions of serious crime are essentially ideological constructs. They do not refer to those behaviours which objectively and avoidably cause us the most harm, injury, and suffering. Instead they refer to only a sub-section of these behaviours, a sub-section which is more likely to be committed by young, poorly-educated males who are often unemployed, live in working-class impoverished neighbourhoods, and frequently belong to an ethnic minority. Crime and criminalization are therefore social control strategies. (Box, 1983: 13)

Capitalism promotes acquisitive and individualist values which may be a source of crime at various levels of society. Class influences the crimes that members of the different classes commit. Unemployment and social deprivation is a cause of working-class crime. Those controlling substantial economic resources may systematically undertake offences for gain. The 'crimes of the powerful', in the form of corporate crime and state crime, inflict serious damage on society though offenders are seldom apprehended or punished.

The enforcement of laws is also affected by class. The crimes of the lower classes are likely to be more strongly policed. Working-class offenders may often receive more severe penalties than those from higher classes.

An alternative radical viewpoint is what has been termed 'left realism'. This criticises the traditional Marxist view for failing to move beyond a critique of the influence of capital and class on criminal justice and the law. The left realists argue that, since the main victims of personal crimes are working-class people, a realistic left strategy must deal with this kind of crime. It must put the focus on victims and their protection. This has a great deal in common with the *communitarian* approach to crime.

> Left realism starts from the following assumptions: we need a police force because crime is a real problem. There is a lot of it and it harms the working-class community. Working-class crime is directed against working-class people. Vandalism, rape, mugging, burglary, etc., constitute just one more factor in the burdens that working-class people have to suffer. The issue is to get a police force that will deal properly with these problems. (Lea and Young, 1984: 259)

RELATED TOPICS

1.26 Marxism: 1 Capital logic
1.27 Marxism: 2 Balance of social forces
2.2 The individual in society: right-wing view
2.17 Poverty: right-wing view

FURTHER READING

Bonger (1969) Introduction
Box (1983) Chap 1
Lea and Young (1984) Chaps 7 and 8
Vold and Bernard (1986) Chap 16

5.6 SCHOOLING: INTRODUCTION

The establishment of state schooling is linked to industrialisation and the growth of democracy. School systems have many similarities.

- Schooling is normally compulsory and is controlled and largely financed by the state.
- Professional teachers are employed to instruct children.
- The attendance of children is normally a legal requirement.

School systems in advanced industrial societies also vary in a number of ways.

- The curriculum may be centrally determined or left to local or professional judgement.
- Teaching methods may vary from the authoritarian to those that are 'child centred'.
- The authority and influence exercised by children and parents in the school may vary.

The organisation of schooling will depend in part on the relative influence of the three perspectives discussed in this book.

1. The *right* is more concerned with the maintenance of social order and the effective transmission of dominant values.
2. *Reformists* see schooling as part of a strategy for the pursuit of the goal of equality of opportunity and economic efficiency.
3. *Radicals* may stress democratic control of the school and a curriculum designed to meet the needs of working-class students and the use of schooling to promote social solidarity.

FURTHER READING

Blackledge and Hunt (1985)

5.7 SCHOOLING: RIGHT-WING VIEW

The right has always been concerned that schooling should maintain social order, authority and hierarchy. Schools should transmit the knowledge and values of the dominant culture. *Conservative* thought has often proposed a differentiated system of education based on class.

1. In Britain the 'public schools' (private, fee-paying schools) were designed to educate those destined for positions of leadership in the state and the British Empire.
2. Grammar schools were to educate those destined for intermediate positions in the class structure.
3. The working class were schooled in 'elementary' and later 'secondary modern' schools to prepare them to occupy subordinate positions.

Right-wing critiques of *reformist* educational policies have focused on 'progressive teaching methods'. These include group work, child-centred education, lack of 'discipline' and what was seen as the radical political character of the progressive curriculum. Schooling has also been attacked for 'falling standards' caused by reformist policies.

A search for complete equality, combined with a vague Rousseautic belief that all men left unhampered are good, has brought the pressure for full secondary comprehensification for social ends, for non-streaming and the adoption of so-called 'progressive' and non-academic methods of teaching or non-teaching. This egalitarian movement [has been] driven forward by adult men and women with the sad simplicity of the militant students ... (Boyson, 1970: 57)

The debate over the national curriculum introduced in the late 1980s saw a challenge to the traditional approach to the teaching of British history. The left argued for more 'history from below', while the right wanted an approach stressing the role of monarchs and great men.

More recently, the right has attempted to restructure state education according to *liberal* principles. The 1988 Education Reform Act passed by the Conservative government was based on the *new-right* idea of a *provider market* in which schools have to compete. In this provider market:

1. Parental *choice* forces each school to compete for pupils and the income of the school depends on the number of pupils.
2. *Competition* between schools is intended to raise 'standards', since good schools will get more pupils (and more income) and expand and poor schools will contract or even close.
3. *Consumers* (i.e. parents) are given more information to allow informed choice, since schools have to publish the results from national tests of attainment.

Local Management of Schools (LMS) has been introduced in order to encourage a more business-like approach. Schools have a 'delegated budget' and are run by a Governing Body containing elected parents' representatives. This is equivalent to the Board of Directors of a private business, since it decides on staffing and can purchase services such as school meals or cleaning. Diversity is also encouraged by allowing schools to opt out of LEA control and become 'grant maintained' receiving funds directly from the government, and by the establishment of schools known as City Technology Colleges (CTCs). However, there is no choice for teachers or parents over what is taught, since the government now controls this through the National Curriculum Council. Teaching methods are also prescribed by the Office for Standards in Education (OFSTED), which undertakes regular inspections of schools.

RELATED TOPICS

1.12 Supporting the market

1.17 Neo-liberalism (the new right)
2.11 Community: right-wing view
4.2 Privatisation
4.3 Provider markets
4.5 Managerialisation

FURTHER READING

Boyson (1970) pp 1–14
Jencks et al. (1973) pp 64–83

5.8 SCHOOLING: REFORMIST VIEW

The *new liberalism* as a political theory developed two ideas which came to occupy a central place in social democratic thought. These were the ideas of *citizenship* and of 'equality of opportunity'. One of the main theorists of the new liberalism was Hobson:

> Liberalism is now formally committed to ... a new conception of the State in its relation to the individual life and to private enterprise. That conception is not Socialism ... though implying a considerable amount of increased public ownership and control of industry ... it appears as a fuller appreciation and realisation of individual liberty contained in the provision of equal opportunities for self-development ... it will justify itself by ... great enlargements of its liberative functions ... seeking to realise liberty for the individual citizen as 'equality of opportunity'. (Hobson, 1909: xx–xxii)

In Britain, one of the major reforms initiated during the Second World War was the 1944 Education Act under which secondary education was provided free of charge to all children. Subsequently most local authorities in Britain required pupils in their last year at primary school to sit an '11+' examination to decide what kind of secondary schooling they would receive. They would be allocated to a grammar or, sometimes, a technical school, or a secondary modern school. In principle, each of these types of schooling were meant to be equal in 'esteem'.

Many reformists believe that expenditure on education has strong links with economic growth. There was evidence that most working-class children went to secondary modern schools where their educational achievements were relatively low. Many reformists saw this as a waste of talent and as economically damaging, because it restricted the pool of abilities available to employers. It was also socially divisive, since it worked against equality of opportunity. Equality of opportunity was one of the arguments used to support the idea of comprehensive (non-selective) state secondary education. This was encouraged from the early 1960s, though the state sector of secondary education has continued to permit the retention of selection, and grammar schools remain in some areas.

Radical critics have claimed that comprehensive schooling alone would not be able significantly to raise working-class educational standards. These are chiefly the result of the social deprivation characteristic of working-class experience rather than the inadequacy of educational provision.

RELATED TOPICS

1.19 The new liberalism
1.21 Logic of industrialism
4.7 Universalism

FURTHER READING

Halsey (1979)
Williams (1981) Chap 11

5.9 SCHOOLING: RADICAL VIEW

Radicals have rejected the incorporation and encouragement of capitalist values in schooling. They point to a 'hidden curriculum' which familiarises children with a particular attitude to issues of power, hierarchy and conflict. They have criticised working-class schooling for being organised around the 'need' of the capitalist system for a docile and obedient manual workforce habituated to discipline and routine. In this view, education plays a major part in the 'reproduction' of the capitalist system. Schooling has also been described as part of the 'ideological state apparatus' designed to ensure ideological conformity rather than liberate the powers of the individual.

> Gramsci believed that schooling provided the means of transmitting a particular consciousness necessary to maintain a particular class rule. The way in which this is achieved is not a straightforward indoctrination of children; it is, rather, a saturation of consciousness by the meanings, values and practices which are already deeply embedded in the social structure in which we live. (Finch, 1984: 159)

Radical views on education often include the following:

1. A belief in a system of public education for all.
2. Support for high minimum standards of educational achievement for all.
3. A belief that the impact of adverse social conditions on the capacity to learn needs to be overcome.

4. Increased social equality has been portrayed as vital to educational improvement.
5. Support for a pupil-centred approach to teaching.

There is also a libertarian and progressive tradition in private education. Some radicals have rejected the state system altogether and supported 'free schools' based on progressive principles. Schools such as Summerhill – an independent boarding school run by A.S. Neill – were organised on libertarian lines with pupils choosing what and how to study. Illich takes this argument to its limits and proposes 'deschooling' society.

> The claim that a liberal society can be founded on the modern school is paradoxical. The safeguards of individual freedom are all cancelled in the dealings of a teacher with his pupil. When the schoolteacher fuses in his person the functions of judge, ideologue, and doctor, the fundamental style of society is perverted by the very process which should prepare life. A teacher who combines these three powers contributes to the warping of the child ... (Illich, 1973: 37–8)

RELATED TOPICS

1.26 Marxism: 1 Capital logic
1.27 Marxism: 2 Balance of social forces
1.29 Illich and anti-industrialism
4.12 Positive discrimination
4.13 Empowerment

FURTHER READING

Althusser (1971) pp 127–86
Blackledge and Hunt (1985) Chap 8
Bowles and Gintis (1976)
Finch (1984) Chap 6
Illich (1973) Chap 1
Salter and Tapper (1981) Chap 9
Sarup (1978) Chap 11

5.10 URBAN PROBLEMS: INTRODUCTION

Urban problems have been a feature of city life since the cities of antiquity first developed. The urban 'mob' under various designations has almost always been viewed with alarm by those in authority. With the development of capitalist industrial cities, urbanism has become a subject of study in its own right.

> ... urban sociology was premised on the assumption that the city was theoretically important in its own right, that certain social

phenomena were characteristic of and peculiar to cities, and that it was therefore possible and necessary to generate specific urban theories in order to explain urban phenomena. These assumptions ... were generally consistent with popular and governmental concerns regarding 'urban problems' (inner-city decay, street crime, black ghetto unrest, mental stress and so on) ... (Saunders, 1981: 250)

Urban problems in modern cities are often associated with inner-city social deprivation. As the city expands the middle classes move to peripheral suburban areas and poorer people move into the areas they have abandoned. The inner city contains low-quality housing including large older dwellings which have been subdivided into flats and poorer-quality owner-occupied housing. There may also be public-housing schemes, often comprising deck-access and high-rise housing. Inner cities may be characterised by:

- street crime, burglary and general 'incivilities' such as uncleared rubbish, graffiti and unrepaired street furniture
- a concentration of the most disadvantaged people, sometimes including members of ethnic minorities
- high levels of family breakdown
- a 'military' style of policing
- outbreaks of collective violence.

Since the major urban riots in the 1960s in the black ghettos of cities in the northern US, inner cities have been viewed in many Western societies as requiring special policy measures to contain the potential for disorder and social breakdown.

The view taken on urban problems will depend in part on the relative influence of the three perspectives discussed in this book.

1. The *right* is most concerned with the maintenance of social order.
2. *Reformists* are concerned with the role of the state in improving the conditions of urban life.
3. *Radicals* may stress how city life is structured by capital and by class conflict.

RELATED TOPICS

2.11 Community: right-wing view
2.12 Community: reformist view
2.13 Community: radical view

FURTHER READING

Cox and McKay (1979)
Lusha (1972)
Pahl (1970)
Saunders (1981) Chap 1

5.11 URBAN PROBLEMS: RIGHT-WING VIEW

The conservative view starts from the presumption that, in modern democracies, existing institutions are adequate to advance the interests of deprived groups within society ... Given this, collective violence is unnecessary to achieve group goals, and must reflect other factors. Individuals who indulge in violence are the unwitting dupes of power-hungry extremists ... or motivated by personal gain ... or find rioting entertaining ... or are acting on uncontrollable and irrational psychological impulses ... or are merely imitating the behaviour of others ... (Taylor, 1984: 25–6)

The cause of urban problems is seen to lie in the characteristics of the people who live in the areas. Urban problems are seen as caused by the spatial concentration of people who reject or who have never learnt to accept conventional social values. Their personal deficiencies are the cause of urban poverty, disorder and crime. In the late nineteenth century this section of the urban working class was depicted as a biologically distinct group consisting of a hereditary degenerate stratum bred in the conditions of slum life.

... devoid of joy they will tend to drink for excitement, they will go on deteriorating and as to their children the more of them grow up to manhood, the lower will be the average physique and the average morality of the coming generation ... (Alfred Marshall, quoted in Stedman Jones, 1971: 128, written in 1884)

Policy has often been designed to maintain the divisions between the 'respectable' working class and the 'residuum', the group at the base of the class structure. This provides a place above the bottom of the social status hierarchy for the respectable working class.

Modern right-wing social thought often describes this group as an underclass (see 2.17) which needs to be disciplined and contained. It is seen as a product of an over-generous welfare state and the breakdown of traditional values, and as perpetuating itself through a 'culture of poverty' sustained by a 'cycle of deprivation'. Right-wing views also often associate *race* with urban problems.

In recent years, in Britain, urban problems have also become associated with large public-housing estates built on the edges of cities, often termed 'outer estates'. These are also viewed as the territory of the underclass. Most consist of a mixture of semi-detached family dwellings along with some high-rise and deck-access accommodation. With the rise in unemployment in the 1980s many of these outer estates came to house large numbers of the poorest people. They often also have many older residents unable to move out into owner-occupied housing. The estates are an example of the 'residualisation' of council housing. Residualisation occurs when the clients of service are exclusively drawn from the lowest stratum of society; in Victorian language, the residuum. Some of these areas have now become a focus of a range of social problems:

- serious rioting involving unemployed male youth
- widespread unemployment
- poverty
- truancy
- large numbers of single-parent families
- high levels of street crime, burglary, vandalism and vehicle offences including car theft and joy-riding
- 'incivilities' such as unrepaired facilities, boarded-up dwellings and graffiti
- drug taking and solvent abuse.

Owing to sustained levels of high unemployment and the decline of a two-parent family structure many young men who would previously have married, settled down and got a steady job in their early 20s are not able to do so. This perpetuates and intensifies the social problems of these areas, which seem destined to last as long as employment prospects remain poor.

RELATED TOPICS

1.16 Eugenics
2.7 Gender: radical view
2.17 Poverty: right-wing view
2.20 Race: right-wing view

FURTHER READING

Banfield (1968) Chap 9
Clutterbuck (1978) Chap 17
Jordan (1974) Chap 1
Pearson (1975)

5.12 URBAN PROBLEMS: REFORMIST VIEW

In the reformist view the cause of urban problems is the operation of 'the urban system' which distributes 'life chances' unequally. Urban problems are generally seen as confined to particular areas, usually the inner city. Reformist approaches to analysing urban problems often view the city as the scene of a *pluralist* conflict over who exercises power and controls resources.

Social problems may arise because access to valued resources is controlled by 'gatekeepers' who impose their own systems of allocation. These gatekeepers are managers in both the public and the private sectors who control access to valued goods and services. These may include housing managers and building society officials. Reforms can be effected by bringing these gatekeeping processes under democratic control. Urban problems may also be tackled by policies which 'target' specific areas employing the principle of *positive discrimination* in the delivery of services such as housing and education.

The reformist perspective is also associated with the idea that urban problems result from the breakdown of *community*. The techniques of social and community work in the form of 'community development' can be employed for the recreation of a functioning community. The problems of those living in disadvantaged areas can be overcome by carefully managed intervention.

Marxist critics view the conception of urban problems as solvable by community-based policies as based on an illusion.

> ... community action is all too often defined as classless. In common usage it is a populist formulation, open to all classes, groups and interests. Where it is defined to exclude 'the middle class' it is nonetheless normally focused not on the working class as such but on 'the deprived', 'the poor' or even the 'poor-poor' ... it bites off what the Victorians called the residuum, the problem-fraction of the people, and distinguishes it from the 'real' working class. It ... rules out the reality of class struggle, in which huge and powerful forces are ranged against each other, not momentarily, but over centuries. It imposes blinkers which stop one working class group looking to another with similar problems as its natural ally and leads to a situation where groups in neighbourhood territories struggle in competition for the limited resources offered them ... (Cockburn, 1977: 160–1)

RELATED TOPICS

2.12 Community: reformist view
3.6 Pluralism
4.12 Positive discrimination

FURTHER READING

Benyon (1984) Chap 2
Glass (1989) Chap 13
Pahl (1975) Chap 13

5.13 URBAN PROBLEMS: RADICAL VIEW

In the radical view the cause of urban problems is the joint effect of the 'uneven development' of the capitalist economy and of class inequality and exploitation. The operation of the market for land and housing creates distinct areas within cities which reflect the inequalities in society. Material deprivation is concentrated among the inner-city working class. Older industrial cities often decline owing to the impact of more rapid economic and technological advance taking place elsewhere. Where there are new industrial jobs these tend to be found on the city periphery, while most new jobs in the city centre tend to involve poorly paid service-sector employment. City-centre industry declines, causing:

* irregular employment
* low wage levels
* high unemployment.

Housing problems result from the demolition of cheap housing owing to the expansion of the central business area and the development of new transport facilities such as urban motorways. Publicly provided facilities such as schools, leisure services and medical facilities are of poor quality. Inner cities contain a low-status population including the very poor and, often, migrant workers. The urban poor are likely to be stigmatised as an 'underclass' (see 2.17), thus helping to maintain a division between the 'respectable' and the 'rough' within the working class.

Collective violence in the form of rioting may break out in these areas. This is because the groups who live in these areas are unable to apply effective pressure for improvement owing to low levels of political organisation and consciousness.

... the growing frustrations of the inner-city communities have not been effectively channelled into the institutional patterns of political compromise which characterise a modern capitalist democracy ... The return of violence as a kind of politics of last resort leads us to suggest that the de-industrialisation characteristic of late capitalism is beginning to reproduce some of the social and political features of early capitalism, particularly the economic and political marginalisation of whole communities from the political process. (Lea and Young, 1982: 14)

RELATED TOPICS

1.26 Marxism: 1 Capital logic
1.27 Marxism: 2 Balance of social forces
2.19 Poverty: radical view
2.22 Race: radical view
3.10 New social movements

FURTHER READING

Benyon and Solomos (1988) Chap 20

Harrison (1983) Part 2
Harvey (1973) Chap 2
Lea and Young (1984) Chap 6

5.14 SOCIAL WORK: INTRODUCTION

Social work and social workers play a major role in welfare states. Social work is now dominated by reformist principles. However, it originated in procedures based on the precepts of nineteenth-century *liberalism*.

The origins of social work lie in the activities of the Charity Organization Society (COS) founded in 1869 to regulate the disposition of charitable funds to the poor. The COS originated the 'scientific' assessment of applicants for charitable support. Those who applied to the COS were interviewed in order to assess how they should be treated. The assessment was designed to allow the classification of the applicant as either 'deserving' or 'undeserving'. The undeserving were recommended for the workhouse (see 1.12), while the deserving were assisted through advice and occasional dispensations of cash. This individualised 'diagnosis' became the basic approach of casework. The COS was subsequently involved in establishing social-work training using a syllabus which reflected a strong attachment to a liberal 'laissez-faire' ideology emphasising personal deficiencies as a cause of poverty.

The social-work profession and social-work education greatly expanded as a result of the post-war welfare state as social work was given a statutory basis. When social-work training expanded in the 1950s it adopted a modified Freudian approach in which social problems were often viewed as the result of failures in 'maturation' or psycho-sexual development. This sustained the individualist ethos of the COS but gave it a new 'scientific' justification. The role of social worker now covers a wide range of functions.

> A social worker imparts information about rights, makes services available, helps to communicate needs to those in authority, and encourages action by the individual, family and group on their own behalf as well as on the behalf of the community. The advantage of this definition is that it suggests the role the social worker can play in the community whatever the type of social work or organizational attachment. (Sinfield, 1969: 11)

The view taken on social work will depend in part on the relative influence of the three perspectives discussed in this book.

1. The *right* is concerned with social order and with the elimination of a 'dependency culture'.
2. *Reformists* may emphasise supporting communities and families.
3. *Radicals* may stress the structural basis of individual problems and the empowerment of clients.

RELATED TOPICS

2.3 The individual in society: reformist view
2.17 Poverty: right-wing view

FURTHER READING

Dale and Foster (1986) Chap 5
Jones (1979)
Jordan and Parton (1983) Chap 1
Pearson (1975) Chap 5
Sullivan (1987) Chap 5

5.15 SOCIAL WORK: RIGHT-WING VIEW

The right continues to utilise the distinction between the 'deserving' and the 'undeserving' poor as the basis for social work. According to right-wing critics, modern social work operates on principles that worsen the problems it is supposed to deal with. This is echoed in populist criticisms of social workers, which sees them as motivated by left-wing views and as soft-hearted 'do-gooders'. The original principles of the COS are still supported.

> ... the only legitimate domain for philanthropists was deemed to be the large intermediate category, or what the COS called the 'deserving' and later, the 'helpable' poor. Moreover, if demoralisation was to be avoided, the charitable assistance offered had to be of a certain type and administered carefully. Merely dishing out soup or handing out doles as had been done in the past would do nothing, the COS claimed, for strengthening the character and social habits of this group. In fact such an approach would result in the pauperisation of the deserving poor given their already precarious grasp of the virtues of self-reliance.
> (Jones, 1979: 75)

Many social-work clients are seen as victims of the 'dependency culture' because the availability of state aid has rendered them incapable of making provision for themselves. The modern social-work profession is seen as having based itself on a *reformist* ideology, which undermines the sense of personal responsibility. Social work itself needs to be reformed in order to incorporate the principles of the 'enterprise' society.

The right also wishes to reorganise other welfare professions such as probation, which use a social-work approach. Attempts have recently been made by the right to reorganise probation training in Britain in line with the view that the probation service should primarily be responsible for supervising 'community punishments'.

RELATED TOPICS

1.12 Supporting the market
1.16 Eugenics
2.2 The individual in society: right-wing view

FURTHER READING

Anderson (1980) Chaps 1 and 3
Brewer and Lait (1980)
Pinker (1990)

5.16 SOCIAL WORK: REFORMIST VIEW

The reformist perspective generally views social work as playing a central role in the social services as a whole.

> Casework is an approach to a helping relationship which is based on compassion for people in trouble, sorrow, need, sickness and various other adversities. Properly applied, casework is a necessary condition for the humane and decent provision of certain services for people in various kinds of emotional distress, in crisis, suffering bereavement, trauma or despair ... Casework in this sense ... has very little to do with social control or the class war. (Jordan, 1974: 102)

Social work is a means by which forms of deprivation or impairment resulting from an absence or breakdown of 'normal' capabilities or relationships can be rectified. Those who are physically or mentally disabled and/or those dependent people without relatives to look after them, or with insufficient funds to purchase alternative care, should have care provided for them.

> ... the more liberal rehabilitative perspectives as epitomised by psychodynamics and social work emerged to exercise ... influence over the development of the post-war welfare state ... the struggle of the working class to implement a more vigorous social democratic politics ... was the decisive turning-point ... organized labour was demanding a change in the style of state welfare policy, moving away from the repressive and dehumanising style of policies such as the Poor Law. (Jones, 1983: 38)

The profession of social work and its organisation has been largely settled on reformist principles. In Britain, the unification of local-authority welfare services in 1970 was undertaken on the basis of the report of the Seebohm Committee of 1968. This proposed a new basis for social-work *professionalism*. This was to be founded on a system of 'generic' social work which rests on a core set of skills applicable to a wide range of social problems. Stress was also to be put on 'community development' and the provision of a 'community-based and family-oriented service'. There is also now more emphasis on knowledge of, and working with, the local community. Social work is normally now organised on a 'patch' system in which each social worker takes clients from a defined area.

RELATED TOPICS

2.9 The family: reformist view
2.12 Community: reformist view
4.8 Administrative reorganisation
4.9 Participation
5.24 Professionalism: reformist view

FURTHER READING

Barclay (1982) Chap 3
Seebohm (1968) Chap 7
Younghusband (1964) Chap 2

5.17 SOCIAL WORK: RADICAL VIEW

Radical critics argue that social work generally ignores the structural causes of *poverty* and deprivation. Radicals have criticised social work as an organised means of reconciling people to intolerable circumstances. The poor are persuaded to accept and adjust to their poverty by conforming to conventional social roles despite the oppressed situation this may leave them in. In this viewpoint, conventional social work is a form of social control.

> One of the truths of Marxism that we hold to is that capitalism contains within it the seeds of socialism ... any progressive movement in welfare work would need in the medium or long term to involve working people directly in it. The more that working people become involved in the construction and implementation of policy, in the actual experience of democracy in welfare, the more they build up a consciousness which reflects their ability to construct a social formation as a whole. (Bolger et al., 1981: 156)

Some libertarians have criticised the coercive powers over parents and children held by social workers. Feminists have argued that giving a priority to maintaining the family often requires women to stay in intolerable relationships.

A positive radical approach is based on opposing the oppressive circumstances in which clients find themselves. There are three main strategies involved.

1. *Empowerment* of clients so that they can resist oppression themselves.
2. Challenging behaviour which discriminates against working-class people and other oppressed and disadvantaged groups.
3. Encouraging collective action on the grounds that the problems are collective and the collective pursuit of solutions is therefore most likely to put effective pressure on the authorities to make improvements.

RELATED TOPICS

4.12 Positive discrimination
4.13 Empowerment

FURTHER READING

Bolger et al. (1981) Chaps 5 and 6
Corrigan and Leonard (1978) pp vi–xv
Langan and Lee (1989) Chap 1
Statham (1978) Chap 2

5.18 DEATH AND DISEASE: INTRODUCTION

Health is often defined as the absence of disease or illness. This definition reflects a 'curative' approach to ill-health based on the medical model, which sees improved medical services as the solution to health problems. An alternative account of ill-health puts much greater stress on social and environmental factors. In this view public-health measures and social reforms are seen as the key to better health.

In the past hundred years life expectancy has increased and the causes of ill-health have changed. In the industrialising capitalist states in the nineteenth century the major causes of death were tuberculosis (TB) and infective fevers such as typhus, typhoid, scarlet fever and diphtheria. Insanitary conditions, poverty and poor housing were major reasons for the prevalence of infections.

These diseases are no longer an important threat in most industrialised countries owing to improved housing, diet and, to a lesser extent vaccination and inoculation. The major causes of death today are cancers, heart disease and cerebrovascular conditions such as strokes.

In summary, the pattern of death and disease in the UK, in line with patterns in other industrialised societies, has changed during the century. The decline in infectious disease has led to increasing numbers surviving into middle and old age of each cohort of births. The largest single factor has been the greater survival rate of infants in the first year of life. The age structure of the population has changed so that there are large numbers of old and very elderly people, bringing a greater demand for medical and social services. (Allsop, 1984: 153)

In Britain, the Black Report of 1980 showed that class inequalities in health had increased over the previous 50 years. The explanations of the reasons for this is a political as well as a 'scientific' question.

The view taken on the causes of health problems and on what the state should do about them in part depends on the relative influence of the three perspectives discussed in this book.

1. The *right* is concerned with the role of choice of lifestyle as the main determinant of ill-health and sees changed lifestyles as the route to improved health.
2. *Reformists* stress a range of approaches based on a combination of conventional medicine, prevention and health education to improve health.
3. *Radicals* may stress the role played by the pursuit of profit and by class exploitation in causing ill-health and require a substantial reduction in the power of capital to improve health.

FURTHER READING

Allsop (1984) Chap 8
Townsend and Davidson (1980)

5.19 DEATH AND DISEASE: RIGHT-WING VIEW

The right-wing perspective puts the emphasis on 'individual choice' rather than broader social causes as the reason for ill-health. It is claimed that in advanced industrial societies, social conditions such as poor housing and workplace dangers are no longer a major threat to health. Working-class people suffer more illness because they choose to adopt riskier lifestyles.

1. They are more likely to damage their health through smoking and excessive drinking.
2. They choose to consume an unhealthy diet containing a great deal of fat.
3. They choose not make use of facilities for exercise and so suffer from lack of fitness.

Individuals bear the responsibility if they put their health at risk by choosing a dangerous occupation. Workplace accidents are seen as largely the result of idleness or apathy. Working-class childrearing practices do not put sufficient emphasis on personal responsibility for maintaining health.

Personal responsibility should be encouraged by making people pay for their health care, especially where ill-health results from their lifestyle. Services should be provided by the market, or, failing this, within a context in which public-sector agencies operate under market disciplines through a *provider market*.

Some on the right also believe that ill-health, and in particular those figures which appear to show a link between class and health, actually reflects genetic differences in which the genetically unfit fall to the bottom of the class structure.

> The occupational class structure is seen as a filter or sorter of human beings and one of the major bases of selection is health, that is, physical strength, vigour or agility. It is inferred that the Registrar General's class I has the lowest rate of premature mortality because it is made up of the strongest and most robust men and women in the population. Class V by contrast contains the weakest and most frail people ... low social worth as well as low economic reward ... play no causal role in the event of high mortality. (Townsend and Davidson, 1980: 112)

RELATED TOPICS

1.16 Eugenics
1.17 Neo-liberalism (the new right)
2.17 Poverty: right-wing view
4.2 Privatisation
4.3 Provider markets

FURTHER READING

Blaxter (1990)

5.20 DEATH AND DISEASE: REFORMIST VIEW

The reformist view generally accepts the idea that a key determinant of health is the quality of health provision and preventative measures rather than the nature of the social and physical environment. The main focus of the reformist approach has been on deficiencies in the organisation and administration of health services. Health-care problems have been seen as due to inadequate planning.

In Britain the *administrative reform* of the NHS in 1974 was designed to rectify this. This included an attempt to ensure that health-care provision was more equally distributed. A Resource Allocation Working Party (RAWP) was set up to move towards funding health provision across the country in line with health needs. Reformists have also called for more equity in provision with better care for relatively neglected groups such as the chronically sick, the mentally ill, the disabled and the old.

There is also concern over the balance between curative and preventative medicine. In the reformist perspective prevention has involved 'health education', which attempts to improve health by giving people more information about it. This assumes that many illnesses could be reduced by, for example, encouraging a reduction in smoking and drinking.

Radicals criticise this focus on individual behaviour and the belief that it can be changed by education because it fails to ask why people use tobacco and alcohol to deal with stress. It also gives insufficient emphasis to the social conditions and the commercial pressures which influence the lifestyles which people 'choose'.

> The pathologising of typical conduct ... according to some stereotypical perception of certain ways of life, we refer to as 'lifestylism' ... lifestylism can lead to a sense of moral failure and emotional inadequacy. Lifestylism is the realisation of the ideology of individualism ... (Rodmell and Watt, 1986: 4)

RELATED TOPICS

4.5 Managerialisation
4.8 Administrative reorganisation
5.24 Professionalism: reformist view

FURTHER READING

DHSS (1976) pp 38–43

5.21 DEATH AND DISEASE: RADICAL VIEW

The *Marxist* perspective asserts that many features of capitalism generate ill-health and premature death. Class is a major factor. Working-class people live shorter lives and suffer more from both chronic and acute diseases, and are less likely to go to a doctor when they are ill.

Ill-health is linked to the organisation of work in a capitalist society through:

- occupational disease
- extreme physical or climatic working conditions
- stress caused by rapid working, tedium, noise
- accidents at work.

The most obvious cause of class differences in morbidity and mortality will be the differential health risks of specific occupations. Certain groups of workers (often the lower paid) have more dangerous and unhealthy jobs than others ... Workers 'import' dangers from the workplace into the home, and clearly this will affect working-class families more often ...

The distribution of ill health in capitalist societies broadly follows the distribution of income. Those with lower incomes tend to have higher rates of morbidity and mortality, for a number of reasons. In a capitalist society income is a major determinant of the standard of housing individuals and families can obtain, of where they live, of their diet, and of their ability to remain warm and well-clothed. (Doyal, 1979: 25–6)

Fluctuations in the capitalist economy involving periodic high unemployment are associated with suicide and premature death. Capitalism also creates a number of environmental threats to health which most affect working-class people.

1. Poor housing conditions may involve damp, cold and overcrowding.
2. Lack of gardens and secure play space cause accidents to children.
3. Industrial processes which create localised air contamination are most likely to be found near working-class housing areas.
4. Traffic is often routed through working-class areas with vehicle-exhaust fumes causing asthma and the risk of brain damage in children through lead emissions.

Unhealthy lifestyles are often encouraged by intensive advertising and marketing. Many pre-cooked or prepared 'convenience foods' contain high levels of fat, contributing to obesity. The consumption of tobacco, which is heavily marketed, causes around 100,000 premature deaths in Britain each year.

Some radicals favour a strategy of 'health promotion'. This would involve compulsion and restrictions on the pursuit of profit where this damaged health.

An alternative *radical* viewpoint is developed by Illich, who argues that the modern medical profession as well as the operation of industrial society systematically damages health. He wants medicine to be reconstructed on a more human scale. He uses the term 'iatrogenic disease' to refer to ill-health caused by the activities of doctors.

The pain, dysfunction, disability, and anguish resulting from technical medical intervention now rival the morbidity due to traffic and industrial accidents and even war-related activities, and make the impact of medicine one of the most rapidly spreading epidemics of our time. (Illich, 1977b: 35)

RELATED TOPICS

1.26 Marxism: 1 Capital logic

1.27 Marxism: 2 Balance of social forces
1.29 Illich and anti-industrialism
4.11 Public ownership and democratic control
4.13 Empowerment

FURTHER READING

Doyal (1979) Chap 2
Illich (1977b) Chap 1
Kinnersley (1973)
Navarro (1976) Part IV
Thunhurst (1982) Chap 3

5.22 PROFESSIONALISM: INTRODUCTION

The term 'profession' is used to describe a particular kind of occupation. Professions play a major part in the delivery of social policies. The archetypes of the 'traditional' or 'old' professions are medicine and the legal professions, which possessed the following characteristics or traits.

1. A legal monopoly of the performance of the core tasks of the profession.
2. An extended period of higher education in the theory and practice of the profession.
3. The existence of a professional body controlling entry, supervising professional education and licensing accredited members.
4. The enforcement of the standards of the profession by a disciplinary body.
5. A code of professional ethics requiring members to put the interests of clients before any other consideration.
6. A high status and public acceptance of the expertise and authority of the profession.

'Professionalisation' is the process by which an occupation adopts the attributes of a profession. The development of state social-welfare provision has involved the growth of many 'new' or 'semi-' professions such as *social work* and teaching. These have some, but not all, of the attributes of the traditional professions. The process of professionalisation has also been associated with male dominance, since, as the status of a welfare occupation in which many women are employed is raised, it may come to be dominated by men.

There has been an ongoing debate about the conflict between professional and bureaucratic norms. This has particular relevance to the area of social policy, where professionals such as social workers or teachers are employed in an organisational setting.

Conflicts between professionals and managers are a common feature of social-service organisations. Indeed, these have intensified owing to the process of *managerialisation.*

The interpretation given to the professions depends in part on the relative influence of the three perspectives discussed in this book.

1. The *right* is split between a *conservative* approach, which supports the traditional ethos of the old professions, and a *neo-liberal* view, which sees professions as restrictive monopolies which require close regulation and subordination to management.
2. *Reformists* support professionalism as the guarantee of high-quality services.
3. *Radicals* stress the need to democratise professions and professional practice.

RELATED TOPICS

4.5 Managerialisation

FURTHER READING

Carr-Saunders and Wilson (1934)
Etzioni (1969) Chap 1
Forder (1974) Chap 7
Hearn (1985)
Hill and Bramley (1986) Chap 9
Wilding (1982) Chap 1

5.23 PROFESSIONALISM: RIGHT-WING VIEW

The right-wing view of professions is split between the traditional *conservative* view and the *neo-liberal* view.

1. *Conservatism* sees professions as providing the moral basis for disinterested and high-quality service. Professionalism is seen as a guarantee that important services are not dominated by the individualist values of personal profit-making.
2. *Neo-liberals* see the professions and semi-professions as riddled with restrictive practices and as using their claims to professional status as a mask for self-seeking. They are seen as having too much influence over the social services.

    ... perspectives of this kind on professional power give short shrift to those claims for professionalism which emphasise altruism and service ethics. They draw attention to the extent to which protection of the privileges of the profession also figure prominently in formal codes of conduct, and see concerns about malpractice as motivated by a desire to ensure that the professional monopoly remains unchallenged. (Hill and Bramley, 1986: 174–5)

The *new right* has a complex critique of professionalism:

- Long periods of professional education are considered a means of restricting entry.
- The use of technical language is seen as a way of concealing the simplicity of many professional activities from clients.
- Claims to status and authority are viewed as strategies for gaining control of organisations, such as schools and hospitals, where professionals are employed.
- Claims to maintain standards through the use of fixed fees and a ban on competitive advertising are viewed as no more than a strategy for exploiting users.

The *new right* believes that users should be seen as 'customers' rather than as 'clients' and given greater control. In Britain, the attempt to reorganise schooling and medical care using *provider markets* is partly designed to elevate the power of management and reduce that of the professions. In some cases the legal monopoly held by a profession has been abolished.

RELATED TOPICS

1.17 Neo-liberalism (the new right)
4.3 Provider markets
4.5 Managerialisation
5.7 Schooling: right-wing view

FURTHER READING

Friedson (1970) Chap 1
Parsons (1964)

5.24 PROFESSIONALISM: REFORMIST VIEW

Reformists see professional occupations as central to the operation of the welfare state. The process of professionalisation is encouraged in order to enhance standards of service. Control by professionals is seen as necessary to ensure that high standards govern services, though there is some recognition that this can lead to problems.

Doctors, teachers and social workers do have knowledge and skills which are useful to society. They do promote ideals such as improved health, cultural and educational values, and social concern for the disadvantaged. Enhancing their power and authority helps to spread the use of these skills and to ensure that the values receive more adequate expression in society. But it also promotes their own personal interests, and it is often very difficult for outsiders as well as the professionals themselves to distinguish clearly when self-interest is taking preference over ideals in their advocacy of a particular course. (Forder, 1974: 121–2)

The growth of the welfare state has led to the expansion of the 'welfare professions'. In three of the social services, education, health services and the personal social services, the work of professionals is central. As well as teachers, nurses and social workers, there are several professions supplementary to medicine such as speech therapy, radiography and occupational therapy.

Professional delivery is seen as a guarantee that needs will be met, since the values of professionalism are consonant with the reformist approach to welfare. Both professionalism and the *reformist* approach emphasise that primacy must be given to the needs of clients.

RELATED TOPICS

1.20 Fabianism
1.21 Logic of industrialism
3.5 Social betterment
5.16 Social work: reformist view

FURTHER READING

Seebohm (1968) Chap 18

5.25 PROFESSIONALISM: RADICAL VIEW

The Marxist view of professionalism is that professional values and practice have been too closely tied to maintaining the interests of capitalism and the capitalist class. The traditional professions such as medicine, law, architecture and accountancy originally developed to provide high-quality services to business and the well off. Radicals believe that capitalist interests have distorted professional activity and undermined the principle of putting the interests of the client at the forefront.

Professions gain power and influence as experts who are technically and politically useful to governments. Their use, and the granting of power to them, is legitimated by the technocratic rationality [see 3.4] which is part of the ideology of advanced industrial society. (Wilding, 1982: 17)

The dominant tradition of professionalism has excluded the clients from any control over how they are dealt with. In recent years, the elitist traditions of the old professions have been challenged. Many radicals argue for increased involvement of clients in professional decision-making.

> ... people often enter public employment ... with at least some commitment to service. Yet the very nature of this work prevents them from coming close to the ideal conception of their jobs. Large classes or huge caseloads and inadequate resources combine with the uncertainties of method and unpredictability of clients to defeat their aspirations as service workers. (Lipsky, 1980: xii)

Some radicals argue that professional standards cannot be maintained in the face of the pressures generated by heavy workloads and management demands. Radicals also criticise the remoteness of professional practice from working-class life. For example, in the area of legal services they may propose making professionals more accessible through the use of neighbourhood law centres.

Feminists have also criticised the traditional professions for ignoring the interests of women. Medicine especially has been strongly criticised for neglecting women's specific needs.

Those *radicals* who follow the approach of Illich view professionalism as a form of *technocracy* (see 3.4) and would like to dispense with it altogether. They also wish to democratise what is now professional knowledge and practice.

> ... we should at least understand the political impact of the disabling nature of professionalised definitions of need and remedy. Professionalised services communicate a world view that defines our lives and our societies as a series of technical problems. This technical definition is masked by symbols of care and love that obscure the economic interests of the servicers and the disabling characteristics of their practices. The sum of these disabling characteristics is an ideology that converts citizens to clients, communities to deficient individuals ... (Illich et al., 1977: 90)

RELATED TOPICS

1.29 Illich and anti-industrialism
3.4 Democratic elitism and technocracy
4.13 Empowerment
5.9 Schooling: radical view
5.17 Social work: radical view

FURTHER READING

Doyal (1979) Chap 6
Illich et al. (1977) pp 11–40

CHAPTER 6

Social intervention and vulnerable groups in Britain

6.1 SOCIAL STATUS AND SOCIAL INTERVENTION

Some groups are singled out for special treatment because of what is seen as their vulnerability or because they are viewed as a threat, or sometimes both. This chapter deals with parentless and deviant children, the old and the mentally disabled (slow learners). Members of these groups share a common 'status' in that the law may specify:

- the definition and classification of the characteristics defining group membership
- the nature of appropriate professional intervention
- standards of treatment
- restrictions on civil rights.

Where members of these groups are not attached to people such as relatives who are able to care for them, they may become the responsibility of the state. The state may define its responsibility as:

- directly providing care
- requiring others to undertake care
- encouraging or assisting others to undertake care.

In Britain, these state responsibilities date back to the Elizabethan period and the breakdown of feudalism. The growing social and geographical mobility of an emerging capitalist society increased the numbers of dependent people who were not cared for by local charity or religious bodies. They became the responsibility of the parish poor-law authorities. This system remained locally controlled over the next two centuries and operated with considerable variation from place to place. A uniform national system was established in 1834. As a result of the attempt to abolish cash payments through the Poor Law (Amendment) Act 1834 many children, old, sick, disabled and insane people found their way into workhouses. These formed the core of the long-term workhouse population.

Each of these vulnerable groups has a low status in relation to the dominant *liberal* values of economic independence, personal competence and participation in wage labour. In addition, they may suffer the stigma of abnormality through their distance from what are seen as normal lifestyles. This status degradation reduces barriers to their maltreatment in the form of:

- subjection to the power of others
- material exploitation
- physical and mental abuse.

Legislation has often contributed to this degradation through the establishment of systems of classification which depict those classified as having a distinct legal status to which normal rights are not attached. For example, old people and pauper children in the poor-law workhouses (see 1.12) and 'mental defectives' held in subnormality hospitals under the 1913 Mental Deficiency Act have all been denied normal rights of citizenship.

Reformists have often tried to improve conditions for these groups by abolishing the labels of degraded status such as the terms 'subnormal', 'defective' or 'pauper'. However, given the material reality of the degraded status the stigma soon comes to be attached to whatever new term is invented. In recent years radicals have made attempts to raise the status of these groups through policies designed to lead to their *empowerment*. Whether these will succeed remains to be seen.

RELATED TOPICS

1.16 Eugenics
2.15 Citizenship: reformist view
2.21 Race: reformist view
2.24 Social needs and problems: reformist view
4.13 Empowerment

FURTHER READING

Alcock and Harris (1982) Chap 2

6.2 CHILDREN: SOCIAL STATUS AND RIGHTS

The most fundamental feature of state policy on children generally involves enforcing the obligation on parents to care for them. This obligation is often linked to the legal regulation of marriage. The breakdown of marriage and separation or divorce may involve legal decisions on the custody of children and the assignment of responsibility for caring for them or paying for their upbringing.

In Britain, in the nineteenth century, state concern with children was focused on their future status as citizens and workers. The Education Act of 1870 established a system of 'rational' schooling designed largely to adapt working-class children to the requirements of capitalist wage labour by habituating them to obedience and providing them with the rudiments of literacy and numeracy.

Schooling is now central to policy on children. Legal controls exist to enforce compulsory schooling. Compulsory schooling lasts for twelve years and plays a major part in defining for children what is expected of them. In Britain, in the radical conditions fostered by the Second World War free schooling for all was provided. Under the 1944 Education Act schooling was to be child centred and to be adjusted to the 'ages, abilities, and aptitudes' of the children. Physical welfare was also emphasised. LEAs were required to provide dental and medical inspection and treatment, school meals and free transport for those travelling over a certain distance.

The state may act to protect children. In the mid-nineteenth century Factory Acts were brought in to regulate hours of work and promote the safety and protection of women and children in factories. In the early twentieth century policy developed towards the welfare of children based on their future role as workers and soldiers. In the aftermath of the Boer War, when a large proportion of those from industrial cities who had volunteered to fight were found to be physically unfit, the government established a Committee on Physical Deterioration. This reported in 1904 and recommended the provision of meals and medical inspections for school children. The physical welfare of school children was advanced by the Education (Provision of Meals) Act 1906, which allowed LEAs to provide meals. By 1912, about 30 per cent were doing so. Medical inspection in schools was introduced in 1907. These reforms formed a central part of the programme of the *new liberalism*.

A major element in policy towards children in the twentieth century has involved state support for the *family*. The right of mothers and children to an independent income lay behind the campaign for family allowances in the inter-war years. The Family Allowances Act was passed in 1944. This was a *universalist* measure which gave an allowance for each child in the family after the first. It was also a significant step towards the *decommodification* of wages.

Children and young people in Britain today experience a number of serious problems because of the social status of their parents, or because they are not protected, or because they get themselves into difficulties:

- The proportion of children on social support rose from 7 per cent in 1979 to 26 per cent in 1991.
- The number of homeless families with children and pregnant mothers rose by 82 per cent between 1979 and 1994.
- Teenage births for girls aged 11–14 rose from 7.9 per 100,000 in 1979 to 10.8 per 100,000 in 1993.
- Up to 360,000 primary schoolchildren are bullied at least once a week.

In an audit of the position of children in Britain in 1994 the UN voiced serious concerns about:

1. the number of children living in poverty in Britain
2. benefit cuts
3. the rising number of teenage pregnancies
4. the reappearance of children begging and sleeping on the streets.

The UN report:

- welcomed the 1989 Children Act
- supported initiatives on bullying in schools, cot deaths and sexual abuse of children
- called for legislation in Britain to ban corporal punishment in private schools and to outlaw 'chastisement' of children at home.

The idea of children having rights is now an important factor in debates about how to deal with them. There is a UN Convention on the Rights of the Child (see 9.5). In Britain, the Children's Society has identified six basic rights. All children should:

- have a good start in life
- be protected
- have somewhere to live
- have enough money to live on
- be treated fairly
- be listened to.

In many countries civil rights in terms of sexual activity, property ownership, political participation and rights to consume certain products such as alcohol and tobacco are subject to special restrictions based on age. These measures are claimed to protect children, but in the view of some critics they also serve to disempower them.

RELATED TOPICS

FURTHER READING

Alcock and Harris (1982) Chap 5
Hall et al. (1975) Chap 9

6.3 PARENTLESS AND ABUSED CHILDREN

Children without adults to care for them have often been put in the charge of the state or of institutions licensed by the state. In Britain, in the Victorian period, these children might find themselves in the workhouse (see 1.12) or in orphanages. Many were sent out to work by being assigned to employers as 'pauper apprentices'. They were treated as indentured labourers and put under the full control of their employers. Concern about the treatment of children was reflected in the establishment of the National Society for the Prevention of Cruelty to Children (NSPCC) in 1884. An Act was subsequently passed in 1889 providing legal protection for children.

A proprietorial attitude to children in state care continued well into the twentieth century. In Britain in the mid-1940s, in the aftermath of the war, there were large numbers of parentless children; some were orphans and some had been abandoned by parents unable to look after them. Some of these were sent to Australia, housed in institutions and denied any information about their own background and made available for adoption.

In Britain, since the Children Act of 1933, the distinction between children involved in crime (the 'depraved') and those unable to receive parental care (the 'deprived') has not been seen as a basis for differential treatment and children and young people in both categories have often been housed together in local-authority children's homes.

Under the 1933 Act, the ill-treatment and neglect of children first became criminal offences. The responsibility of the state for caring for children was reformed through the Children Act of 1948, which was for long held up as a model of progressive care. It required the individualised treatment of children based on an assessment of individual circumstances. The Act required local authorities to establish a children's department to provide residential accommodation and to regulate adoption and fostering. Local authorities were required by law to investigate cases of cruelty or neglect. They had a duty to take neglected children into care but social-work ideology and practice at this time emphasised family support rather than children's rights. Conditions in many children's homes were poor or worse and many children brought up in this way suffered abuse of various kinds. In recent years the extent of the physical and sexual abuse in children's homes has begun to become clear. The Utting report of 1997 has called for greater central government regulation and supervision of children's homes.

The 1980 Child Care Act established a voluntary basis for taking children into care though children can still be compulsorily removed from parents who are assessed as being 'unfit'. The Children Act of 1989 was avowedly designed to solve the problems of inadequate child protection and poor treatment in children's homes. A children's rights officer represents a child who is pursuing a complaint against a local authority, and provides information and support to young people over decisions about their care.

Child abuse has now become a major issue and child-protection work is now an important element in social work. Abuse may involve:

- physical abuse
- sexual abuse
- emotional abuse
- neglect.

Both physical and sexual abuse have been the subject of considerable controversy. Concern with physical abuse has also become part of the debate about child rearing and the role of physical punishment. Sexual abuse has been the scene of major disputes about its extent and about the possible existence of satanic abuse. Of an estimated 300,000 children considered 'in need' in England every year, about 160,000 are investigated and 25,000 are placed on local child-protection registers because of concern for their well-being. *Reformists* view the impact of the 1989 Act as a major advance for children. However, for some *radicals* the Act could be viewed as allowing individuals, often social workers, to be held responsible when child care goes wrong in conditions where material and other pressures made it very likely that it will.

RELATED TOPICS

1.12 Supporting the market
2.9 The family: reformist view
5.16 Social work: reformist view

FURTHER READING

Jack and Stepney (1995)
Moore (1993) pp 245–57

6.4 OFFENDING CHILDREN

Childhood is a problematic status for legal systems which base their approach to dealing with offenders on the assumption that offending is behaviour for which people can be held personally responsible. Debates have often centred around the extent to which adult standards, rights and obligations can be imposed on children and at what age.

In the nineteenth century the criminal behaviour of young people was identified as an issue requiring an institutional solution. Reformatory schools were set up under the Youthful Offenders Act of 1854. These schools were normally run by voluntary societies with approval by the Home Office. This was the first step in the process of separating children from the adult system of criminal justice. This continued when juvenile courts were established by the Children Act of 1908. The growth of child psychiatry in the early twentieth century helped establish a 'welfare' model for defining the problems of young people.

There has been a continuing debate between proponents of a legalistic 'due-process' approach, who wish to use the law to control delinquency, and proponents of a 'welfarist' approach, who wish to use social work. Policy on child offenders has often veered between attribution of full responsibility for their acts to a 'welfare' model, which views juvenile crime as a reflection of underlying maltreatment or social deprivation. The shifting status of deviant children is evident in relation to laws governing criminal responsibility. The welfarist approach became influential in juvenile crime in the Children and Young Persons Act 1933 which made 'the welfare of the child' a legal requirement. Until 1933, it was stipulated that no child under 7 could be held responsible for a crime. After 1933 this age was raised to 10. For offenders who were under 14 it still had to be proved that they knew that what they were doing was wrong. Welfarism was taken further in the Children and Young Persons Act 1969, which allowed social workers, not magistrates, to decide on the fate of juvenile offenders.

While children today are often portrayed as defenceless victims, some highly publicised cases of violence by young children have raised the issue of some children as being a serious threat to society. The age of criminal responsibility has again become a matter of controversy and is to be lowered to 10.

RELATED TOPICS

5.4 The causes of crime: reformist view

FURTHER READING

Bolger et al. (1981) Chap 4

6.5 THE OLD: SOCIAL STATUS

In most Western capitalist societies old people constitute a distinctive and growing group:

- their lifestyle is restricted
- they are largely excluded from the world of work
- many activities are closed to them for economic reasons
- they lack financial resources
- they have above average requirements for health care.

Ageism is common. Older people often do not have a positive image. Negative stereotypes abound and old people can justifiably claim that in many areas they are treated unfairly.

> ... the dependency of the elderly has been 'structured' by long-term economic and social policies: elderly people are perceived and treated as more dependent than they are or need to be by the state, and this outcome has been fostered by the rapidly developing institutions of retirement, income maintenance, residential and domiciliary care ... ageism has been and is being institutionalised in modern society. (Townsend, 1986: 15)

In Britain, a major part in determining the status of dependent old people was the legacy of the workhouse (see 1.12). Up until the middle of the twentieth century the workhouse was the last place of refuge for the elderly poor. It was feared as a place where you might go to die under a belittling and mean regime. Though conditions in some were more generous, the experience was one that people sought desperately to avoid. While the Poor Laws and the workhouses were officially abolished by the National Assistance Act of 1948, the buildings, the staff and often the institutional regimes lived on.

There are differing views on how to account for the position of old people in our society. Some authors believe that the old are not discriminated against. They see old age as a gradual process of voluntary withdrawal from life. *Radical* critics of this view argue that the reduced social participation of old people is more likely to result from their deliberate exclusion from normal social and economic opportunities rather than from choice.

> In our society the purpose of life in old age is often unclear. The way this period is described in social policy often underlines the experience. Old age is seen as a 'problem', with the elderly viewed as dependants; worse still, they are often described as a non-productive burden upon the economy. (Phillipson, 1982: 166)

Radicals go on to argue that the distinctive treatment of old people occurs because they do not have a permanent place in the labour force. They form part of the reserve army of labour (see 2.7). They are called on to work only when labour is in short supply. In these periods they are likely to be viewed favourably. When there are not enough jobs to go round, the old may be pushed out of the workforce through redundancy or schemes for early retirement.

RELATED TOPICS

2.18 Poverty: reformist view
9.22 Old age

FURTHER READING

Crowther (1978)
Phillipson (1982) Chap 2
Phillipson and Walker (1986)
Tinker (1984) Part 1
Walker (1987)

6.6 THE OLD: LIVING STANDARDS

Old people differ substantially in terms of their incomes. The inequalities of social class are magnified after retirement since those who had high earnings when in employment tend to have disproportionately high pensions. A high proportion of old people experience *poverty*. The level of state pensions has never been high enough to ensure subsistence at current standards. Since 1981 the spending power of the standard state pension has been fixed, allowing the living standards of those dependent on it to fall further behind average incomes (see 8.5).

... the combination of increases in the demand for benefits and services, caused mainly by demographic changes, and ideological opposition to increasing expenditure on the welfare state ... lies behind ... cuts in public expenditure ... the crisis experienced by the welfare state in recent years has had an immediate and, in some cases, pernicious impact on older people (Phillipson and Walker, 1986: 1)

Since the 1960s the old have been largely excluded from the right to hold a job. 'Retirement' in the sense of a final and permanent withdrawal from the labour force is now the normal situation for the old. Before the Second World War the majority of men over 65 years old still worked. Even by 1951, the proportion of men over 65 still in work was 31 per cent. During the relative labour shortages of the 1950s little attempt was made to discourage older workers from finding employment. However, unemployment began to increase substantially in the mid-1960s and older workers were disproportionately affected. From 1967, their rate of unemployment has been rising above the average for all workers and their prospects for part-time work have almost disappeared. State policy has accelerated this withdrawal from the labour force through:

1. the Redundancy Payments Act 1965, which increased inducements to older workers to leave their jobs
2. the encouragement of additional provision of severance pay for redundant workers
3. early retirement schemes, especially in the state sector

4. the use of the 'earnings rule' for those over pension age though which pensioners returning to work had their earnings over a certain limit deducted from their pensions.

Since the end of the long boom in the mid-1970s, employment prospects for old people have generally deteriorated further. Schemes for 'early retirement' and 'enhanced' or 'voluntary' redundancy have become common for those in work aged 50 or over.

Some special provision is made for the old including concessionary fares on public transport and admission to some entertainment facilities at a reduced price. However, many old people have a sense of uselessness resulting from exclusion from the labour market. They suffer poverty, poor housing, inadequate heating, social isolation, a limited diet, ill-health and lead very restricted lives with few treats or luxuries.

RELATED TOPICS

2.18 Poverty: reformist view
4.6 National Insurance
8.5 Great Britain: the old

FURTHER READING

Kincaid (1973) Chap 7

6.7 THE OLD: HEALTH AND SOCIAL CARE

Extensive welfare provision is made for the old. About 20 per cent of all referrals to area offices of local-authority social-services departments involve people over 75 years of age. In recent years, however, the provision of domiciliary services has been cut back and charges are sometimes made for home helps. Some 35 per cent of all expenditure on health and welfare goes on the old, and members of this group occupy a majority of all non-maternity hospital beds. Many old people benefit from the high standard of medical care available for accident cases and acute episodes or conditions. However, those suffering from conditions unamenable to effective medical intervention receive less favourable treatment. Geriatric medicine is a low-status specialism with few 'merit awards' (individualised additional payments) for doctors and little opportunity for private practice. Medical research into the problems of the old is also relatively under-developed.

Many old people are unable fully to care for themselves or suffer disabling long-term illness. These were formerly often cared for in the geriatric wards of general hospitals. Since the mid-1980s a policy of moving old people out of free long-term NHS care into the means-tested care of local authorities has been pursued. The 1989 White Paper, 'Caring for People' and the NHS and Community Care Act 1990 which followed it reaffirmed the government's commitment to promoting care in the community for older people and those with mental illness, disabilities or learning difficulties, preferably in their family home. It recommended a change in the role of local-authority social-services departments from that of service providers to that of 'enabling agencies' operating on the principle of *welfare pluralism*. Their job is to assess need, plan services and promote consumer choice among a range of public, private and voluntary organisations. Statutory support is provided for *privatisation* with local authorities having to spend 85 per cent of the funds available on private residential and nursing homes.

In recent years the concept of elder abuse has been developed as a recognition of the physical, psychological, financial and sexual abuse that old people are subject to in both domestic and institutional settings. The Social Services Inspectorate produced *No Longer Afraid* as a set of guidelines on elder abuse in 1993. Elderly people also suffer discrimination in the health service according to the Royal College of Physicians. Discrimination can be explicit where units have age limits for certain treatments. There is also often an implicit assumption that the old should be at the back of the queue because they have less time to live.

RELATED TOPICS

1.23 Welfare pluralism
4.2 Privatisation
4.5 Managerialisation

FURTHER READING

Biggs (1996)
Moore (1993) Chap 11
Tinker (1984) Chap 6

6.8 MENTAL DISABILITY

The mentally disabled pose a *social problem* because they are usually unable to survive without assistance in a society based on paid work as the normal source of income. Radicals argue that rapid social change during the period of early capitalist industrialism was a major factor in creating this 'problem'. The separation of work and home brought about by the industrial revolution and the growth of factory employment meant that dependent relatives, including the mentally disabled:

• were now harder to look after
• were more likely to be excluded from work

- could make less contribution to the economic survival of the family they belonged to
- became more likely to end up in the workhouse (see 1.12).

In the latter half of the nineteenth century in many capitalist societies social problems were often seen as concentrated amongst those referred to as the 'feeble-minded'. They were often viewed as a threat to economic and social progress. Feeble-mindedness was seen as hereditary, and it was widely held that those suffering from it should be identified, classified and segregated through institutionalisation.

In Britain, a major reform designed to reduce social problems was the 1913 Mental Deficiency Act (see 1.16), which was strongly influenced by the ideas of the Eugenics Society, which itself had strong support from many supporters of *Fabianism* and from those active in the *new liberalism*. Under this act, local authorities had to establish a Mental Deficiency Committee and employ an Executive Officer to classify defectives. Feeble-minded mothers of illegitimate children, feeble-minded minors, vagrants, habitual drunkards, criminals, imbeciles and idiots of any age could be compulsorily detained in institutions. For most of the twentieth century this act provided the basis for the treatment of the mentally disabled. However, the categories provided for in the act allowed it to be used to incarcerate many social deviants such as unmarried mothers. Even in the 1990s there were still women held in long-stay mental institutions whose only offence had been to get pregnant whilst unmarried.

The Mental Health Act of 1959 put the control of the treatment of those with mental disorders in the hands of the medical profession. The act refers to four types of mental disorder: mental illness, subnormality, severe subnormality and psychopathic disorder, though without defining them. Admission to institutions is generally 'voluntary' though compulsory detention and retention is possible. Compulsory admission for treatment or for observations (for a month) can be secured without a court appearance by certification by two doctors. Emergency admission can be secured by application from a social worker or a relative along with a doctor. This is the most widely used method by which people end up being involuntarily admitted to mental institutions.

For much of this century the mentally disabled remained hidden from view in long-stay subnormality hospitals. In the 1960s the poor conditions in these hospitals began to become public knowledge. This knowledge was incorporated into the general critique of institutionalism that was developing at this time. Those with mental disabilities are now covered by the National Health Service and Community Care Act of 1990. This requires local authorities and the health service to provide 'appropriate' community care for those who are discharged from institutions. The vogue for community care has led to the closing of many hospital and the release of former patients into 'the community'. The quality of community care provided for former patients is not consistent:

- it varies from place to place
- in many areas little or no extra funds have been provided
- some have been housed with private landlords who have gained control over their lives and finances
- some may live in sheltered accommodation and have access to day centres
- employment opportunities are limited
- incomes are low and poverty is the norm
- public acceptance is low.

The mentally disabled suffer from the cultural legacy of over a century of exclusion, institutionalism and negative evaluation, based on their inability to survive without assistance in the social environment of the capitalist economic system. The lack of provision of opportunities for employment, family life and political participation, along with social rejection, which these reinforce, maintains the position of this group at the extreme margin of society.

> Medicine – its institutions, personnel, concepts, and modes of explaining behaviour – has been the main instrument for excluding mentally handicapped people from society ... the medical profession has sanctioned this rejection by producing a whole way of thinking that justifies it. To categorise mentally handicapped people as 'defective' or 'subnormal' is to describe them entirely in terms of their supposed pathology, what is wrong with them. Such descriptions effectively mask other aspects of their social existence, or even deny them one at all. (Ryan and Thomas, 1980: 15)

With the development of knowledge of genetics demand for pre-natal genetic diagnosis sometimes followed by abortion is likely to grow. This may further contribute to the degradation of the status of the mentally disabled.

RELATED TOPICS

1.16 Eugenics
1.19 The new liberalism
2.17 Poverty: right-wing view
2.25 Social needs and problems: radical view

FURTHER READING

Moore (1993) pp 297–306
Ryan and Thomas (1980)

CHAPTER 7

The diversity of welfare states

7.1 INTRODUCTION

In this chapter a wide range of welfare states are examined in order to illustrate the diversity of welfare provision. The states covered differ in various ways which affect the form of their welfare services. The most obvious difference concerns the type of political regime, and associated with this, the type of economic system which this sustains. The majority of the welfare states we shall examine can be broadly classified as right-wing, reformist or radical.

The *right-wing* welfare states are Japan, the Asian Tigers and Germany.

The *reformist* welfare states are Sweden, the Netherlands and Austria.

The *radical* welfare states are Cuba and China.

We shall also look at two other welfare systems which influence a number of states:

1. The transitional welfare state systems of the former USSR and the emerging states of the new Eastern Europe, which are undergoing a shift from the radical Soviet model.
2. The principles of Islamic social policy, which play a part in welfare provision in a number of states where Islamic values and movements are influential.

Economically the states examined in this chapter differ in terms of:

- their dominant pattern of ownership
- their level of development
- their economic dynamism.

The states also differ culturally in ways which affect their welfare provision. Particularly important are the different dominant religious traditions, which include Catholicism, Protestantism, Confucianism and Islam.

The social policies of these welfare states also differs along a range of dimensions.

1. They vary in the emphasis given to egalitarian policies involving vertical redistribution.
2. They differ in terms of whether they make extensive use of *National Insurance* or *means-testing*.

3. They diverge in terms of the extent to which policy aims to create *gender* equality.
4. They differ in the priority given to supporting economic development rather than meeting welfare needs.

RELATED TOPICS

1.11 Right-wing approaches: general features
1.18 Reformist approaches: general features
1.25 Radical approaches: general features
4.4 Means-testing and selectivity
4.6 National Insurance

FURTHER READING

Deacon et al. (1997) Section 2.6
Esping-Andersen (1990) Chap 1
Ginsburg (1992) Chap 1

7.2 JAPAN

Extensive principles of welfare provision were written into the post-war constitution of Japan.

> The Constitution enunciates, explicitly, the concept of the people's right to social security and social welfare and the state's obligation to guarantee that right ... the idea of a state-guaranteed right to substance soon became popular: it became the welfare ideology of the people. (Takahashi and Someya, 1985: 13)

Since Japan was restored to sovereignty in 1952 the main party has been the Liberal Democratic Party, which has a conservative centre-right approach. The Liberal Democrats have generally formed the government, though from 1994 to 1996, while the Liberal Democrats held the most seats, a three-party coalition with a socialist Prime Minister was in office for the first time. The Liberal Democrats returned to power after the election of 1996.

Support for the parties of the left has been relatively low and working-class organisations such as independent trade unions are weak. *New social movements* opposing nuclear power and campaigning on environmental issues have become active in recent years.

Japanese society differs from the advanced capitalist states of western Europe and North America in a number of ways:

1. There is a strong collectivist ethic where group loyalties are strong and Western individualism is weak.

2. There is a high level of social consensus based on loyalty to the state and obedience to authority dating back to the tradition of imperial rule and what is sometimes called the 'emperor system'.
3. Political power and the perceived role of the state has a strong element of *paternalism*, which is reflected in social policy.

The organisation of work is partly based on the system of lifetime employment and paternalistic authority. The lifetime workers receive a range of social benefits from employers in addition to a wage. Firms also employ workers on a short-term basis and these are often women, immigrants or retired workers. This system is supplemented by a pool of casual labourers who are viewed as social outcasts. Inequalities of income from work are less than in Western capitalist states. Working hours are very long and only a fifth of workers get two free days at weekends and nine or more days' annual holiday.

A great deal of caring is left to women and families. *Family* relationships are often based on a traditional ethic involving the submission of women and arranged marriages, which account for about 25 per cent of the total. This is reinforced by the long hours which many men work thus leaving housework and child-rearing to their wives. There has been an Equal Opportunity Employment Act since 1986, but women still occupy a subordinate position.

There was some welfare legislation before 1945 including limited schemes for health insurance set up in 1922 and pensions insurance in 1941. Under the post-war occupation by the US unemployment insurance was set up in 1947. Means-tested social assistance began in 1950 under the Livelihood Protection Act. There was a National Pensions Law in 1959 setting up a means-tested benefit.

Means-tested child allowances were first introduced in 1972. In the 1970s pensions were available from schemes run by employers and the state though with the lower paid getting very low benefits. In 1985 the schemes were consolidated and, in addition, women were given pensions in their own right. Well-paid and securely employed workers are eligible for generous benefits of about 60 per cent of incomes.

National health insurance was first set up in 1958 and by the 1970s some insurance coverage for both medical bills and subsistence was available for most workers. Medical care is generally state financed but mainly privately provided, though a third of hospital beds are in the public sector. Under an act of 1982 the elderly pay a small charge for health care. Japan has very high levels of life expectancy and a growing population of old people. There are very high levels of hospitalisation of the old because of a lack of alternative forms of care. From 1999 a compulsory scheme of insurance for long-term care in old age will operate. This is designed to reduce the use of hospitals by the old. Everyone over 40 will pay a monthly contribution. Half of the total costs will come from taxes rather than contributions.

Race is an issue in Japan. There are large minorities of Korean and Chinese background who have been subjected to harsh aliens laws. There is a strong belief that they should assimilate and adopt Japanese names and values. There is also a minority of indigenous people, the Ainu, who are largely restricted to the northern island of Hokkaido. The Burakumin minority are the remnants of the lowest caste in the traditional caste system. The caste system survives in many rural areas in a concern with ancestry and in ensuring that the family is not 'polluted' with untouchable blood.

In the 1970s the government aimed to establish a Western-style welfare state though this aim was abandoned in the 1980s. By the late 1970s Japan had a broad welfare system though with minimal benefits. Overall expenditure on social policy is low compared with European levels. The Japanese welfare system does not guarantee a subsistence minimum standard of living. Social assistance is not an effective means of combating poverty, since benefits are set at about half the lowest earnings levels. Only about 1 per cent of the population receive social assistance, although this is far less than the number of those who are eligible. There are numerous vulnerable groups such as the old, those not in lifetime employment, women and members of minorities.

RELATED TOPICS

1.15 Conservative paternalism
2.8 The family: right-wing view
2.20 Race: right-wing view
3.10 New social movements
4.4 Means-testing and selectivity
9.15 Race

FURTHER READING

Gould (1993) Part 1
Maruo (1986)
Takahashi and Someya (1985)

7.3 THE ASIAN TIGERS

The rapidly growing economies of South-East Asia are known as Asian Tigers. In the last two decades this group of countries including Hong Kong (a Special Administrative Region of China from July 1997), South Korea, Singapore and Taiwan have had annual economic growth rates of up to 10 per cent, though in the 1990s this began to slow. In late 1997 many of the Tigers experienced a collapse of currency values and share prices, leading to financial instability and company failure. The IMF has intervened with massive support including credits of $55 billion for South Korea. This crisis is likely to lead to lower growth rates. Living standards can be high; both Singapore and Hong Kong have a per capita income higher than that of the UK. In each of these states except Hong Kong, protection of domestic markets, subsidies for exports and non-tariff controls on imports along with state support or sponsorship for growth industries have been widely used. This approach has been described as 'developmental authoritarianism'.

In 1993, the World Bank produced a report on *The East Asian Miracle* which viewed social policy as a tool of economic growth.

> The study drew a distinction between desirable market-friendly and other, undesirable, interventions. Market-friendly interventions ... remedied generic failures in markets ... market-friendly policies ... were confined to support for human-capital formation (health and education), openness to information flows (technology inflows from abroad), and export promotion ... (Lal, 1996: 5)

Apart from Hong Kong, where there has been support for a pluralist political system, the dominant political ideologies of the Asian Tigers are distinctive, with both Western *liberalism* and communism viewed as alien creeds. The governments of these states tend to be authoritarian and *paternalist* even where the constitution is democratic. A tradition of repressive anti-communism dating from the cold war years is sustained in state antagonism to any domestic radicalism. There is also support for conformism, obedience and loyalty reinforced by a punitive system of justice sometimes employing corporal and capital punishment, promoting a respectable and conformist lifestyle.

Some commentators believe the Confucian ethic plays a similar role to that ascribed by Max Weber to the Protestant ethic in the establishment of Western capitalism, by promoting personal qualities favourable to capital accumulation. These include frugality, self-discipline and industriousness.

Governments have taken to promoting 'Asian values' as an integrative device. The approach to social policy is linked to Confucian ideas of:

- concern for the misfortune of others
- reliance on family support
- voluntary effort
- self-help.

Social policies have been influenced by those Western states which historically have had a major role in a particular society. The US exercised an influence in Taiwan and South Korea and the UK did the same in Hong Kong, which remained a British colony until 1997.

Hours of work are long and hard work is promoted as an official virtue. Working conditions are often poor and industrial disease and accidents are widespread. Apart from in Hong Kong, trade-union organisation is weak and is often subject to state harassment.

While inequalities have increased, economic growth has been accompanied by improved social indicators. Infant mortality rates have fallen and schooling is widely available. Unemployment is likely to be low – in Taiwan in 1992 it was 1.5 per cent. However, major social problems have been created by the rapid pace of industrialisation and urbanisation. These include:

- serious air and water pollution
- inadequate sanitation
- shanty towns
- widespread squatting
- lack of a social infrastructure.

Housing is in short supply, housing clearance for industrial redevelopment is common and many workers are housed in company dormitories. In Hong Kong state provision of housing has developed owing to land shortages, and housing provision is beginning elsewhere to relieve the pressure in rapidly growing cities.

Opportunities for women have improved though women's wages remain well below those of men. The employment of young women at low wage rates is common. Traditional *family* structures often impose considerable caring obligations on women.

Limited schemes of social insurance based on payments by workers and employers are widely found but benefits are restricted to workers. Deviant groups such as unmarried mothers may receive little or no state support. In Hong Kong only a third of those living in poverty receive social assistance.

Race and ethnicity is a factor. There are usually significant Chinese, Indian and other minorities. These may not be given equal treatment and they can also pose problems for national integration. There may also be large numbers of illegal immigrants who face *poverty* and exploitation without legal protection.

Where there are schemes of social assistance they tend to be inadequate. The range of needs covered is limited, many of those eligible fail to receive them and the value of benefits is low. Publicly provided health care is beginning to develop and insurance-based schemes are being established in Taiwan and South Korea. Overall social expenditure is starting to expand facilitated by the expansion of the tax base owing to economic growth.

RELATED TOPICS

1.11 Right-wing approaches: general features
1.15 Conservative paternalism
4.4 Means-testing and selectivity
9.8 International Monetary Fund

FURTHER READING

McLaughlin (1993a)
World Bank (1993)

7.4 GERMANY

The Federal Republic of West Germany was set up in 1949 following the Second World War after a period of government by the Allied Occupation Forces. A pluralist democratic constitution was established with a federal structure vesting considerable powers in the states. The constitution includes a requirement for the state to meet basic social rights, which are laid out in a social code based on the European Social Charter.

State social policies began in the late nineteenth century when unemployment and sickness insurance was established by Bismarck. The social policies of the Nazi era were based on racial purity, family support and a traditional role for women. Authoritarian conservatism combined with a degree of *paternalism* has been influential in the development of social policy.

The two major parties are the Christian Democrats and the Social Democrats. The Social Democrats have a radical past but have embraced *reformism* since the late 1950s. The Christian Democrats are strongly influenced by Catholic *corporatism* (see 8.7). The centrist Free Democrats and the Green Party also play a significant role.

The organising principle of the Christian Democratic post-war policy was the 'social-market economy'. This doctrine differs from *new right* approaches in that the state accepts the role of maintaining employment and redistributing income as well as stabilising the currency and guaranteeing property rights.

> ... since the establishment of the modern German state in 1871, there has always been a positive emphasis on social policy ... to ensure social cohesion and well-being. In the Basic Law this is embodied in the concept of the social state ... whereby the state's general commitment to providing income and employment security is complemented by an emphasis on the obligations of private associations or groups (above all employers and trade unions), families and individuals to support themselves. There is no question of any commitment to equalising welfare

outcomes, or even of an unambiguous welfare safety net ...
Policies in West Germany ... are governed by group-specific
compulsory insurance systems based firmly on occupational
status and income-related contribution principles. (Ginsburg,
1992: 68)

The Catholic principle of 'subsidiarity' in which care should be
provided by those closest to the recipient is influential. This places
an obligation on close relatives to support those unable to provide
for themselves. This increases the dependence of the young and
old on their relatives.

Social insurance is provided for the unemployed, sick and old.
Unemployment benefit is time limited and depends on the
contributions record supplemented by means-tested
unemployment relief. Sickness benefit is paid by employers for six
weeks and then from health insurance, which also pays for
treatment and medical bills.

The pension is wage related and normally amounts to about 75
per cent of the recipient's former net income. The retirement age
is variable, depending on the length of contributions.

The federal system of public assistance is administered by
municipalities and provided on a test of need. Under a separate
scheme compensation is provided for 'victims' such as injured
workers and early retirers. Social assistance benefit levels are
relatively generous and with associated means-tested benefits they
normally amount to about 50 per cent of average earnings. They
are set by an Association for Public and Private Relief representing
a range of voluntary bodies such as trade unions and the Red
Cross. A form of 'workfare' exists in that those on assistance can
be drafted into public-works projects. Personal social services and
institutional care are provided by local authorities or private welfare
bodies in receipt of public funds.

Health care is organised on the basis of social insurance covering
over 90 per cent of the population. It is administered by private
insurance funds operating under state regulation. Most doctors
work in private practice but about half the hospital provision is in
the public sector.

The constitution gives special protection to marriage and the
family with provision for equal treatment for children of unmarried
parents. Child benefits, child tax allowances and a year's worth of
pension rights are given to the parent who raises a child at home.

Most housing is rented and subsidies are provided to occupants
at a level designed to ensure that people do not have to move from
their accustomed area of residence. Rising rents and higher
unemployment have increased the social assistance budget since
the mid-1970s.

Germany has made extensive use of migrant labour through the *Gastarbeiter* ('guestworker') system. This has involved importing workers from states in southern Europe. The number of foreign workers reached around 4.5 million in the 1980s. These workers have been subject to exploitation and racism, and have limited social and political rights. Many have now become permanent residents, but they occupy a vulnerable position at the bottom of the social hierarchy.

The reunification of East and West Germany in 1990 increased the size of the country and changed the nature of social problems. Economic problems have resulted from the collapse of former state industries leading to a fall of around 40 per cent in the value of output in the former East Germany. Extensive programmes of youth training and early retirement have been instituted. The difficulties of integrating the former East German population have caused problems of social exclusion and discrimination against 'Easterners'. Social dislocation in the East has resulted from the breakdown of the comprehensive communist welfare system. Women have been particularly affected because of the high proportion of working women in the former East Germany. However, in comparison with other EU states Germany has a relatively low proportion of the population living in poverty, 11 per cent against the EU average of 17 per cent.

RELATED TOPICS

1.13 Bismarckianism
1.15 Conservative paternalism
2.22 Race: radical view
3.8 Welfare corporatism
3.10 New social movements
7.10 The former USSR and the new Eastern Europe
9.6 The European Union
9.15 Race

FURTHER READING

Clasen and Freeman (1994) Chap 1
Ginsburg (1992) Chap 3
Grunberger (1974) Chaps 15–17
Wilson (1993)
Zapf (1986)

7.5 SWEDEN

A relatively comprehensive welfare state developed in Sweden before the Second World War. The similarity of the welfare provision made in the neighbouring countries of Norway, Finland

and Denmark has given rise to the concept of 'Nordic' or 'Scandinavian' welfare states. In Scandinavia the peasantry was never reduced to serfdom and its political influence reduced the degree of political ascendancy of the capitalist class in the nineteenth century.

> Industrialisation ... was accompanied by a great deal of hardship and poverty. In rapid response three popular movements arose – the labour movement, the temperance movement and the free church movement. Most of their members came from the lower strata of society ... The establishment of the Social Democratic Workers' Party in 1899, the federation of manual workers' trade unions in 1898, and the Swedish Co-operative Union and Wholesale Society in 1899 ensured the working class of a high degree of political representation and industrial muscle in the early decades of the century. (Gould, 1988: 18)

At the start of the twentieth century Sweden was a relatively poor country. Working-class demands and middle-class benevolence led to the growth of *Bismarckian* social legislation. In 1913 Old Age and Invalidity Insurance was established, followed by a limited scheme of unemployment benefits in 1914.

Following the end of the First World War a fully democratic voting system was in place and in 1932 the Social Democrats took power and remained in government until 1976. They governed through *corporatist* agreements made with the Trade Union Federation and the Employers' Confederation.

The welfare state in its developed form dates from the late 1940s. Public expenditure grew throughout the post-war period and is financed by relatively high tax rates. There is a corporatist political system in which both labour and capital are represented by well organised and powerful bodies which negotiate wages and conditions for the majority of workers. The focus of policy on unemployment has been on job creation and training rather than on benefit provision.

Social insurance is centrally controlled and administered by voluntary insurance funds. Eligibility for unemployment benefit depends on contributions, work records, availability for work and willingness to take work offered. Those ineligible for unemployment insurance benefit may be eligible for social assistance if they have a record of having worked for five months in the previous year. Policy towards those in need is based on the principle that they should be enabled to live as normal a life as possible. Social assistance is provided by local authorities.

Universal flat-rate pensions were established in 1948. An earnings-related pension supplement was added in 1960. A disability pension is available to those with a reduced capacity to work of 50 per cent or more.

Child allowances were introduced in 1948 and are paid for all children under the age of 16 with extra for larger families. Services for child care are highly developed, enabling a very high percentage of women with young children to work. Maternity leave is relatively generous, covering 90 per cent of income for 270 days.

Compulsory health insurance dates from 1955. Health provision is jointly shared between central and local authorities. Hospital care is generally free and family doctor care and sick pay for the employed are paid for by insurance.

In some respects the welfare system has become somewhat more redistributive in the last few decades, largely owing to increased spending on the old, while unemployment has been relatively low by European standards. Sweden has been seriously affected by the economic problems which have occurred throughout the West since the early 1970s, but the welfare state has not been seriously cut.

> Welfare policies in Sweden have contributed to substantial improvements in living standards. The number of people experiencing multiple deprivation has declined. But, despite this, welfare problems still remain unevenly distributed in society ... The vulnerable groups are women, the aged, and the working class. A widening of the gap between the incomes of the bulk of the population and the minority at the base of society has been conspicuous. The Swedish welfare state, as an 'attempt to synthesise capitalism and socialism', has predictably been criticised from both the political right and from the left ... Marxists have alleged that its 'reformism' has merely buttressed capitalism; it has created working-class dependency and passivity while leaving the social structure and economy untouched. From the radical right the all-caring society has been criticised for developing social-security servitude and dependency on the state. (Digby, 1989: 14)

Sweden has a comprehensive welfare system based on the *reformist* model. A distinctive feature is the degree of compulsion exercised against those who may be deemed to require help but will not accept it voluntarily. These may include drug users and those who will not support themselves. Eugenic policies were pursued in Sweden from 1935 until 1976. More than 160,000 people, 90 per cent of them women, were sterilised for reasons of racial impurity, lifestyle or mental capacity. Sweden remains the archetype of a comprehensive *Keynesian welfare state* based on social-democratic principles and organised through corporatist institutions.

RELATED TOPICS

1.13 Bismarckianism
1.16 Eugenics
1.18 Reformist approaches: general features
1.22 Keynesian welfare state
3.8 Welfare corporatism

FURTHER READING

Digby (1989) Chap 2
Ginsburg (1992) Chap 2
Ginsburg (1993)
Gould (1993) Part 3
Olsson (1990)

7.6 THE NETHERLANDS

Both capitalism and a poor law designed to maintain work incentives developed early in the Netherlands. Until the mid-nineteenth century poor relief was undertaken solely by the church and even after 1854 the state could only intervene if the church or private benevolence was failing. Insurance for industrial injuries began in 1901. It was extended to invalidity and old age in 1919 and to sickness in 1930. Family allowances were introduced in 1941.

Over most of the post-war period the Netherlands has been governed by centre-right coalitions with strong confessional influence, though from 1973 to 1977 the Social Democrats were in power. The parties differ on the role of social insurance with the Social Democrats favouring a *universal* system and Conservative and confessional parties a system restricted to workers.

Until the late 1960s Dutch society was segmented or 'pillarised' into vertical groupings based on Catholic, Protestant and socialist bodies. Each had their own parties, trade unions and newspapers. The dominance of church organisations has been eroded though they still have a strong presence in the Cabinet. In 1976, the Catholic and socialist trade unions merged.

Means-tested pensions were provided from 1947 for all over-65s and are now set at about two-thirds of the average wage. The poor law was in force until the General Public Assistance Act of 1963 which gave the state the major role. Means-tested social assistance under the General Public Assistance Act 1963 is specifically designed to cover 'basic needs' with benefit levels related to average earnings. Since 1967 there has been a comprehensive scheme of flat-rate insurance compensation for any incapacity preventing work. Health care is based on compulsory health insurance and a means-tested scheme under the General Medical Expenses Act.

During the period of the long boom the welfare system was extended and consolidated in line with constitutionally defined principles of 'self-realisation' and 'equality of rights'. However, from the mid-1970s, in response to deteriorating economic conditions, social expenditure rose and some benefits were reduced in value. Social-expenditure financing was shifted to cut business contributions and increase those of households. In the 1980s, the purchasing power of pensions declined and many pensioners are now worse off. Unemployment benefits are earnings related and since 1987 their duration has been linked to the recipients' contributions and employment record. The benefit levels are relatively high by European standards.

Since the Second World War two general (ideological) options dominated the Dutch welfare system, a Bismarckian and a Beveridgean one. The Bismarckian option stressed the 'subsidiarity' and the principle of 'sovereignty in own circle': social policy should appeal to the own responsibility of people and social organizations; and only in case they fail, the state has the moral right, and even duty to intervene. The Beveridgean option asserted programmes for the whole population and pointed at safeguarding from want for all citizens and some degree of income redistribution, mainly financed through taxation and administered by state institutions ... since the economic crisis [there has been] a more selective system, in which the state only guarantees a minimal level of security and the above-minimal section is privatised. (Roebroek, 1989: 185–6)

The Dutch system mainly rests on income transfers with relatively little direct state provision for personal social services. The system overall, and in particular pensions, involves a substantial degree of redistribution. However, 13 per cent of families live below the official poverty line with many of these having a single parent.

While the dominant role in government has been played by the centre right, social-democratic influence has been strong reflecting the generally *reformist* culture of the Netherlands. Since 1989, the Social Democrats have been the dominant partners in successive coalition governments.

RELATED TOPICS

1.13 Bismarckianism
1.18 Reformist approaches: general features
4.6 National Insurance

FURTHER READING

Roebroek (1989)

7.7 AUSTRIA

Austria was created on the break-up of the Austro-Hungarian Empire in 1919. In the early 1930s Vienna became something of a showcase for advanced social democratic reforms in various areas, including housing. After 15 years of democratic government there was a civil war in 1934 followed by a semi-fascist regime with a strong Catholic conservative influence. In 1938, Austria was merged with Nazi Germany. It became an independent state again in 1947 following a period of control by the Allied armies of occupation. Austria now has a federal constitution with nine provinces. Despite these constitutional changes some elements of Austrian social policy such as war pensions have a long and continuous history, owing to the *Bismarckian* legacy.

From 1948 to 1966 Austria was governed by a coalition of the (Catholic) People's Party and the Social Democrats. Government was undertaken using a *corporatist* 'social partnership' (see 3.8) to build a policy consensus. The partnership is based on commitment to full employment and a market economy operating alongside an effective system of social welfare. This corporatist approach also reduces overt political conflict and settles most major issues through top-level negotiation rather than public debate. From 1971 to 1983 there was a Social Democratic government. Since 1987 there has again been a Social Democrat and People's Party coalition with an emphasis on 'modernisation', meaning EU membership, privatisation and labour flexibility.

Economic growth was rapid during the long boom and Austria moved from being a predominantly agricultural society to one based on modern industry. The main direction of policy is to use tax revenues to maintain a high level of employment and to finance welfare services while keeping the costs at a manageable level. The proportion of GDP going to social expenditure continued to increase until the mid-1960s, when it stabilised. Following the economic dislocation in the 1970s after the oil price rises, Austria was successful in developing policies to retain full employment and control inflation.

> ... it is recognised that if social policy objectives such as full employment and social welfare are to be achieved, economic issues must be addressed ... the interdependence of and the relationship, including the trade-off between economic wages and social welfare, wages and inflation, and inflation and unemployment, forms the basis of the general policy approach. (Mishra, 1990: 52)

Social security insurance is organised centrally. Insurance is provided for accidents, sickness and pensions, with contributions from employers and employees and a state addition of 20 per cent. Unemployment insurance is provided by the federal government and covers about 60 per cent of previous earnings for up to 30 weeks.

Around 99 per cent of Austrians are covered by health insurance though members of some occupations have to pay a share of the costs. Family doctors operate under contract to the health insurance authorities.

Separate bodies administer the six pension schemes which cater for different occupational groups. The value of pensions is relatively high and can reach 80 per cent of earnings for lower-paid workers.

Means-tested social assistance is a local responsibility and has its origins in the poor laws. Social assistance is available for those unable to 'secure the needs of life'. The recipients are mainly old people with inadequate pensions, the disabled and the unemployed who have run out of benefit. Those needing care in nursing homes are not covered by the health service but social aid provided by the provinces is available.

Support for families with children is available in the form of family allowances, maternity benefits and maternity leave for working women. In 1977, child tax allowances were abolished and child allowances were increased along with enhanced benefits for single mothers.

In the 1980s, unemployment increased though by less than the European norm. As economic conditions worsened the government reduced some family benefits, failed to uprate others to compensate for inflation, and increased pension insurance contributions by 1 per cent. Large-scale cuts in social services were avoided, though the numbers in *poverty* grew due to rising unemployment, increased family breakdown and more single parent families.

Economic problems and the inability to agree on a budget eventually led to the collapse of the coalition in late 1995 accompanied by the resurgence of the far-right populist Freedom Movement. However, in the election of 1996 the Social Democrats gained an unexpected victory and the Freedom Movement did less well than many had expected.

RELATED TOPICS

1.13 Bismarckianism
1.22 Keynesian welfare state
3.8 Welfare corporatism
4.6 National Insurance

FURTHER READING

Busch et al. (1986)
Friedman et al. (1987) Chap 7
Mishra (1990) Chap 3

7.8 CUBA

From the early twentieth century a range of social policies were developed, including numerous schemes of tax-subsidised social security catering for particular occupations. This system remained fragmented and inegalitarian giving the best-paid occupations the best provision. From 1934, maternity insurance was available for employed women. Some health care was also available through voluntary bodies and cooperatives but the poorest people had little access to this.

The Cuban revolution took place in 1959. At this time Cuba was a relatively under-developed capitalist state with a low level of industrial development. The Cuban government later formed an alliance with the USSR. Cuba then became heavily subsidised by the USSR to the extent of about 20 per cent of GDP through generous pricing of imports and exports and direct aid. It then began to pursue a *radical* programme of social and economic reforms based on the principles of Soviet Marxism. Policy was based on collective ownership and egalitarianism.

In 1963, the framework for a universal pension and health-care scheme was established and by 1983 it covered all occupational groups. The pension funds for all salaried workers and public-sector employees along with maternity insurance funds were nationalised.

A 10 per cent payment for social security is made by employers though in total this only covers around half the total cost. From 1979, all social security was run by the State Committee of Labour and Social Security (CETSS). Local Organs of People's Power (OPPs) administer some welfare benefits and disability pensions. Unemployment insurance and family allowances are not provided in Cuba.

In the 1960s private health-care facilities and the pharmaceutical industry were nationalised and doctors were required to renounce private practice. Health services are centrally run and the standard of medical care is high though there are some regional variations. Mortality rates are the lowest in Latin America. Levels of school attendance and participation in higher education are high. The retirement ages are 60 for men and 55 for women with five years less for those involved in arduous work.

Among the most notable improvements are: the creation of a national health system of universal scope which protects the entire resident population; the expansion of coverage of the pension programme from 63 per cent to 93 per cent; the unification and standardisation of the pension programme which eliminated its extreme inequalities; the integration of the health system ... in terms of health services and levels, Cuba ranks ...

first in life expectancy and in having the lowest infant mortality rate ... (Mesa-Largo and Roca, 1992: 71–2)

The Cuban economy suffers from a lack of growth opportunities through the economic embargo imposed by the US which makes the development of international economic links in the American sphere of influence very difficult. In the 1980s, unemployment and inflation increased and the real value of benefits was cut in 1986 by a series of austerity measures. In response, attempts have been made to move surplus labour to agriculture and construction though this has only had a limited impact. Following the collapse of Soviet Communism Cuba is experiencing further major economic problems.

RELATED TOPICS

1.25 Radical approaches: general features
4.10 Decommodification
4.11 Public ownership and democratic control
7.10 The former USSR and the new Eastern Europe

FURTHER READING

Deacon (1983) pp 115–23 and 170–5
Mesa-Largo and Roca (1992)

7.9 CHINA

Since 1949 China has been governed by the Communist Party, seeking to establish a society built on socialist principles. Since the revolution many changes have taken place in the social-welfare system reflecting changing Communist Party doctrines and strategies. Most of the Chinese population of 1.1 billion is rural and lives in 'communes' which have a wide range of administrative functions, many covering social policy.

The values of the Chinese welfare system partly draw on Confucian principles of family obligation and mutual aid. There is a right and duty to work and the work ethic is strongly supported.

Welfare support is provided in a way that neither inhibits economic development nor frustrates the consolidation of socialism by fostering a sense of welfare dependency which would corrupt both revolutionary zeal and the desire to work ... It has allowed a continuance of low income policy, thereby maximising investment rates by providing low income earners with welfare support on the basis of need. (Dixon, 1985: 57)

Social policy is largely based on ensuring income from employment is available rather than on redistribution. It is intended to reinforce work incentives and to prevent people becoming dependent on benefits. Policy is selective with support only provided to those on low incomes who are in need.

Until 1958, social policy developed piecemeal with a wide range of occupational benefits being administered by trade unions. The bodies responsible for providing services changed frequently in the period from 1956 to 1976. Employers were made responsible for providing services such as health care and nurseries. Urban residents' committees also had some local welfare responsibilities.

In 1965, a labour-insurance programme was brought in covering all workers in state enterprises. Unemployment insurance and free medical treatment for sick and injured workers in state enterprises is available but benefits for workers in collectives depend on profitability.

There has been economic growth of around 8.5 per cent since the early 1970s. After the death of Mao in 1976 a policy of modernisation was pursued. Towards the mid-1980s serious economic problems developed with unemployment at over 5 per cent and inflation at over 15 per cent. In response a move towards marketisation was instituted within the state-run industrial sector:

- enterprise autonomy was increased
- some private enterprise was permitted
- a freer labour market was introduced.

The welfare system depends on locally provided assistance centred on the family, the workplace and the neighbourhood. Some groups such as the mentally and physically disabled are expected to receive family care, though relief will be given if this is not available. Low-paid workers and low-income families can seek relief from a local source such as a street-welfare committee.

The provision of benefits is uneven especially for those who have not been in regular work. Those disabled at work receive better treatment than those whose disability has other causes. Only women covered by labour insurance receive maternity benefits.

Since the late 1970s family support has been subordinated to the policy to reduce population growth. Chinese social policy employs authoritarian methods to control family size. In many areas support is only provided for families with one child. The arrival of further children leads to a loss of a range of benefit entitlements.

The retirement age is 60 for men and 55 for women but only about 20 per cent of old people are eligible for a pension. Old people are often cared for in a family setting with the collective or local community acting as a back up.

In the late 1980s China established a number of Special Economic Zones in which foreign companies may operate with few restrictions. These are situated along the coast and are a means of building up exports and of importing Western technology. Annual growth rates in these areas have sometimes reached 30 per cent and incomes have risen well above the norm for the rest of China. In these zones social-policy requirements are relaxed and those who live and work in them are less protected than residents of ordinary areas.

China is now characterised by rapid economic change, particularly in the Special Economic Zones, rising expectations amongst the populations, and national and international pressures for political reform. All this suggests that major changes in social policy will take place over the coming years.

RELATED TOPICS

1.17 Neo-liberalism (the new right)
4.4 Means-testing and selectivity
4.6 National Insurance
4.10 Decommodification
7.3 The Asian Tigers
9.16 Population

FURTHER READING

Deacon (1983) pp 98–115 and 161–70
Dixon (1985)

7.10 THE FORMER USSR AND THE NEW EASTERN EUROPE

The social policy of the USSR was the model for the Soviet bloc, although the extent to which it was fully adopted varied. Social policy in the USSR was based on egalitarian principles designed to ensure a guaranteed minimum standard of living to all. Some groups such as party members had privileged access to extra economic benefits through special shops and leisure facilities.

> The social welfare system is uniform all over the country. No forms of social insurance, education, health care, or social assistance exist outside those provided by the state ... social welfare policy is implemented either directly by specialised state agencies, or by trade unions acting in strict relations with state administration and political authorities. (Wiktorow, 1992: 193)

The system of administered prices played a key role as a determinant of living standards. Many items of ordinary expenditure were *decommodified*. Prices of necessities such as basic foods, basic clothing, fuel, public transport and housing were all kept low so that those on low incomes could afford them.

State control of employment was central to the welfare system. Full employment was a priority, though this often involved 'concealed unemployment'. The wages of manual workers were relatively high. Facilities enabling women to work were made available through an extensive system of nurseries and creches for the children of working parents. Because the welfare system was occupationally based, groups outside the workforce such as the disabled, widows and single parents were not well covered.

Welfare provision also involved the direct provision of a range of services:

- Medical services were free and often based on the workplace giving occupational health and disease a high priority.
- Education was provided free.
- Benefits for sickness and old age were relatively high, though the unemployed were not eligible for any payment.

Since the collapse of communism in 1989 the imposition of market economies has had similar effects in the USSR and its successor states, Poland, Hungary, Czechoslovakia and Bulgaria, in what is now often called the 'new Eastern Europe'. Proponents of a rapid process of marketisation have portrayed it as 'shock therapy' which may initially be painful but which will eventually be beneficial. This process has been encouraged by international agencies such as the *World Bank* and the *International Monetary Fund*. The privileged access to facilities accorded to party elites has been ended. The economic impact of shock therapy has been severe:

- Many existing enterprises have proved unable to survive competition and have closed.
- The end of subsidised employment has left many without jobs and unemployment has increased to 10 per cent or more.
- Inflation has risen, government spending has been cut and poverty has increased.
- Many health facilities provided by employers have been municipalised or privatised.
- Living standards have fallen by around 30 per cent in many of these countries, with the poor being the worst affected.
- Some services have partially collapsed, though attempts have been made to preserve medical and educational provision.
- The right of women to return to a job after childbirth is being restricted or abolished and many child-care facilities have closed.
- Housing subsidies are being phased out and selective housing benefits are replacing them.
- Price subsidies for basic goods have been cut or abolished.

- Attempts have been made to replace state-funded benefits with schemes based on insurance.
- In education, religious bodies are now being encouraged to play a part in what were purely secular systems.

Political divisions are emerging between those who adopt a fully *liberal* free-market philosophy and those who support a more social *reformist* approach. There are signs of a resurgence of a fairly radical strand of reformism through the increased electoral support in some states for reconstructed versions of the former communist parties. Social dislocation has also led to racism, the emergence of authoritarian nationalism and an extreme form of anarchic liberalism which supports minimal state-welfare intervention.

RELATED TOPICS

1.17 Neo-liberalism (the new right)
4.2 Privatisation
4.10 Decommodification
9.7 World Bank
9.8 International Monetary Fund

FURTHER READING

Deacon (1983) Chap 3
Deacon and Szalai (1990) Chap 1
Deacon et al. (1997) Section 2.7
Dixon and Kim (1985)
Manning (1982)
Manning (1984)
Mishra (1977) Chap 7
Wiktorow (1992)

7.11 ISLAMIC SOCIAL POLICY

There has been a considerable neglect of the role of Islamic thought and beliefs in the literature on social policy. Islam has become an important political force in the modern world. Islam has undergone a revival with the increased significance of Islamic fundamentalism and the resurgence of support for strict adherence to Islamic principles. Powerful Islamic political movements are challenging for power in many states such as Algeria. A number of large states such as Indonesia have substantial Islamic populations.

Some of the states where Islam is influential have based their social policies and sometimes their entire constitutions on Islamic principles. Iran is a prime example. Many other states with Muslim majorities, such as Kuwait and Pakistan, explicitly incorporate Islamic ideas in their constitutions.

The Islamic states tend be relatively under-developed with a low level of industrialisation, a small urban sector and a large rural population. While they may be influenced by Islamic ideas and Islamic political movements, a range of other factors also exercise an important influence on their social policies. These factors include:

- the power of domestic Islamic political movements relative to secular political parties
- the degree of fundamentalism of the Islamic political movement
- the character of the national Islamic tradition and its degree of uniformity or diversity
- the level of urbanisation and the significance of secular urban culture
- the level of development and the available material resources
- the degree of power exercised by a traditional elite and the level of its attachment to 'modernising' values
- the level of dependence on international agencies such as the IMF
- status as an ex-colony and the nature of any influence exercised by the former colonial power.

Given the substantial variation amongst those states where Islamic influence is strong, it would be wrong to expect a high degree of uniformity of social policies amongst them. However, Islam does contribute some distinctive ideas to social policy. The first is *zakat* which refers to the principle that a Muslim is expected to donate a certain proportion of his wealth to the poor and those in need such as the aged and the sick. Islam also enjoins 'cooperation for common good', which implies a willingness to support *paternalism* involving collective provision with contributions from all members of the community.

> The Koranic exhortations of fraternity, co-operation and solidarity among Moslems promote the cohesion of its adherents and a mutual aid system based on justice and charity. The achievement of Islamic economic justice requires the forbidding of interest-bearing loans (called riba) and the paying of an alms-tax (or zakat), which is considered one of the principal obligations of Islam. (Hammoud, 1987: 98)

Islamic beliefs also include a range of other ideas which contribute to a distinctive social ethic:

1. there is support for consideration and respect for the *old*
2. there is support for a traditional *family* structure with a high degree of respect for parents by children
3. there is emphasis on a subordinate place for *women* within the family and a distinctive and subordinate social role generally

4. there is support for obligations to kin in the extended family
5. there is support for the idea that there should be a high degree of security and that the state should guarantee a minimum standard of living
6. there is support for a system of civil and criminal justice based on the *shariah* (Islamic law).

Islam is not easily classified within the normal terms of the left–right political spectrum, since this secular and materially based typology does not readily incorporate spiritual values. Islam itself does not appear to have a strong consonance with the values of either the left or the right. Islamic policies both in theory and in practice appear able to coexist with both a free-market economy and one with a high level of state ownership.

A dividing line amongst the states strongly influenced by Islam which is important to social policy, concerns the attitude taken by those in control of the state to modernisation or traditionalism. Some of the more fundamentalist movements such as the Taliban in Afghanistan wish to obliterate all signs of what they identify as modernism. Other states with a strong Islamic influence such as Saudi Arabia wish to modernise under elite control, whilst maintaining significant features of Islamic traditionalism such as a subordinate role for women and an Islamic system of law.

The most evident social-policy issue raised in Islamic states concerns the position of women. Some versions of Islamic fundamentalism are used to support policies which maintain a range of gender divisions. Women may be subject to differential treatment in various ways:

- they may be denied access to some forms of education
- they may be excluded from some or all forms of paid employment
- the law may enforce their domestic subordination
- they may fail to be given legal protection from physical violence
- their rights to own property may be limited
- they may be denied political rights such as the right to vote or otherwise participate in politics.

RELATED TOPICS

1.15 Conservative paternalism
2.5 Gender: right-wing view
2.8 The family: right-wing view
9.14 Gender

FURTHER READING

Dixon (1987) pp 163–77
Hammoud (1987)

CHAPTER 8

The developed Anglophone welfare states

8.1 INTRODUCTION

This chapter examines major features of the developed Anglophone (English-speaking) welfare states of Great Britain, Ireland, the US, Canada, Australia and New Zealand. For each state there is a description of key features of the general historical, social, economic, political and ideological background to the development of social policy. The following areas of policy are then briefly examined:

1. poverty
2. health care
3. the old
4. race.

Apart from Britain, these countries share a number of features.

- They are linked by a common language and a common past as British colonies.
- With the partial exception of Ireland, none has a feudal background or a residual pre-capitalist aristocracy.
- Each was extensively settled by British people.
- An indigenous population resided in each prior to British colonisation and was excluded from power by British rule.
- In each case the traditions of the British Poor Laws played a part in the development of social policy.
- Each country now has a pluralist democratic political structure.

Along with these common elements there are important differences which are linked to the widely different patterns of social policy found in them.

1. The process of industrialisation shows major variations, with Britain industrialising earliest. The current levels of economic development differ, with the US having been for many decades at the centre of the world capitalist economy and Ireland having had until recently a relatively undeveloped economy, though it is now growing very fast.

2. Democracy and statehood developed relatively peacefully in these states, apart from in the US and Ireland, which both experienced civil wars.

3. The party structures are very different, though in most cases there is some kind of division between the major parties which is based on their degree of support for and opposition to the *liberal* values of capitalism.

4. Social democratic *reformism* has played a major role in Australia, New Zealand and Britain but less so in Canada, the US and Ireland.

5. *Liberal* individualism has been a major force in the US though a more egalitarian individualism is found in Australia and New Zealand. In Britain individualism has been tempered by *conservative paternalism*.

6. The values of the right are influential in each but there are national differences. There is a strong pro-business culture in the US and a traditional Catholic *conservatism* is influential in Ireland. A combination of *liberalism* and *conservatism* is evident in Britain.

7. The states vary in the degree to which the development of social policy was affected by major national emergencies such as war and economic depression.

8. The constitutions vary from federal to unitary systems. The federal states often have significant regional variations in social policy.

9. The role and importance of ethnic divisions varies – the US has the legacy of the slave-owning plantation economy of the South and Canada has a bilingual society with a large French minority. Some states have residual populations of indigenous people.

10. The countries differ in the role played in their development by migration. Ireland has lost millions through emigration, in contrast to the other ex-colonies whose populations have expanded through migration.

11. The role played by religious beliefs and organisations varies substantially, with both the US and Ireland having a strong religious influence, while Australia, New Zealand and increasingly, Great Britain are largely secular societies.

RELATED TOPICS

1.6 Esping-Andersen: welfare regimes

FURTHER READING

Cochrane (1993a)
Ginsburg (1992) Chap 1
Mishra (1990)

8.2 GREAT BRITAIN: BACKGROUND

The legacy of the Poor Law (Amendment) Act of 1834 has played a major role in the British welfare state. The Act established the use of the workhouse (see 1.12) for the poor and the old and established the principle of 'less eligibility', which kept benefit levels below the lowest wages.

> The main thrust of the 1834 Act had been the workhouse test, whereby indoor relief (i.e. in the workhouse) for the able-bodied poor would be so distasteful that independent labour would be preferred to welfare dependence. (Digby, 1989: 33)

A major impetus for the development of the welfare state came from *new liberalism*. This lay behind the Liberal government reforms in the period 1906–14 before the First World War, which established old-age pensions, *National Insurance* for sickness and unemployment, and a programme of child health and welfare.

The major social-policy initiative during the inter-war period was the establishment of public housing although social provision generally expanded across the range of services. Policy towards the unemployed shifted continuously with governments trying both to restrict expenditure on benefits and to prevent opposition to benefit cuts from threatening social order.

The second major formative period was the Second World War, which produced a general radicalisation and a desire for social reform organised around the idea of a welfare state.

1. Radical sentiments grew because of the breakdown of the social values and assumptions of pre-war Britain.
2. Social discontinuities were widespread with the end of mass unemployment, the experience of the blitz, the evacuation of school children and the arrival of prosperous US troops.
3. Political changes included the major role played by the Labour Party in the wartime coalition and the enhanced role of trade unions at government level and in the workplace.

Government policy during the war shifted dramatically from the largely *liberal* laissez-faire policies of the 1930s.

1. There was widespread and effective economic planning including the adoption of Keynesianism in the 1942 budget.
2. The Beveridge Report of 1942 (see 4.6) proposed a welfare state based on *universalism*.
3. The report also called for a comprehensive system of *National Insurance* along with family allowances, full employment and a National Health Service (NHS).
4. A major educational reform and a universal system of family allowances were put in place in 1944 before the end of the war.

The reform proposals of the war years for a comprehensive social-security system and the NHS were enacted by the Labour government of 1945–50. The *reformist* principles of the welfare state continued to dominate social policy under both Conservative and Labour governments. Until the 1970s social-policy expenditure grew and the welfare professions expanded across the range of provision.

In 1974, a *corporatist* 'social contract' was agreed between the Labour government and the trade unions in which social reforms were to be conditional on wage restraint, but in the late 1970s this broke down and welfare budgets were cut. In the turbulent economic conditions of the mid-1970s inflation and unemployment rose.

In the 1980s, after the imposition of highly restrictive *neo-liberal* monetarist policies, unemployment grew and benefit levels and entitlements were reduced. Increased use was made of 'targeting', employing *means-testing. Provider markets* were widely employed, especially in the reform of education and health services. Poverty increased and some areas of the welfare state were drastically cut, particularly state housing provision through the sale of council houses.

Universal benefits such as free education, family allowances and free health care have proved politically impossible to abolish and difficult to cut. Overall welfare spending has been maintained though the budget has been restructured because of the large increase in the numbers of unemployed and big cuts in housing expenditure. Following the Labour Party election victory in 1997 it is likely that *communitarian* ideas will play a larger role in policy than previously.

RELATED TOPICS

FURTHER READING

Bryson (1992) pp 77–88
Marwick (1968) Chap 6
Mishra (1990) Chap 2

8.3 GREAT BRITAIN: POVERTY

The welfare state reforms based on the proposals of the Beveridge report of 1942 (see 4.6) were designed to abolish *poverty*. A comprehensive *National Insurance* scheme operated from 1948 and there was *means-tested* national assistance for those not covered by National Insurance. These reforms had a major impact on the extent of poverty. Research by Rowntree in 1952 showed that less than 2 per cent of people in York lived in poverty compared with 31 per cent in 1936. Poverty was substantially reduced during the post-war period, though it was periodically 're-discovered' by academics researching into living standards. Throughout the 1950s and 1960s unemployment and poverty remained relatively low.

The benefit system came under serious strain when unemployment underwent a substantial and permanent increase from the mid 1970s. *Neo-liberal* principles and rhetoric increasingly came to influence social policy in the late 1970s and 1980s especially after the election of a Conservative government in 1979.

> The moral fibre of our people has been weakened. A State which does for its citizens what they can do for themselves is an evil State; and a State which removes all choice and responsibility from its people and makes them like broiler hens will create the irresponsible society. In such an irresponsible society no one cares, no one saves, no one bothers – why should they when the State spends all its energies taking money from the energetic, successful and thrifty to give to the idle, the failures and the feckless? (Boyson, 1971: 6)

In the UK benefits were made taxable and earnings-related supplements were abolished in 1982 almost halving the value of benefits to an unemployed worker on average earnings. Means-tested Supplementary Benefits were replaced by Family Credit and a 'Social Fund' providing loans for the poor. These changes along with regressive taxation, the growth of part-time work and increased unemployment all increased *poverty* in the UK in the 1980s. During this period the benefits of growth, and revenues from the privatisation of publicly owned industries and from North Sea oil were used to finance tax cuts rather than to increase social expenditure. These tax cuts along with the high levels of unemployment substantially increased income inequalities.

Persistent poverty now seems most to affect large and single-parent families, the unemployed, the long-term sick, the disabled and old people reliant on the state pension. According to an EU report in 1993, levels of inequality in the UK were well above the European average. The EU Cohesion Report of 1996 showed that 17 per cent of households in the UK lived in poverty, where this was defined as a household income less than 50 per cent of the average.

The Labour government elected in 1997 plans to tackle unemployment with a scheme designed to take 250,000 young people aged 18–25 off the dole and to put more than half the long-term unemployed into subsidised jobs or training. This will be done with a New Deal programme costing £3.5 billion. Participants will be presented with four options:

1. a private-sector job with a wage for which the employer gets a £60 per week subsidy
2. work with a voluntary organisation
3. work with an environmental task force
4. full-time education or training.

There will be sanctions for the under-25s who refuse to take part in the programme, involving total or partial benefit withdrawal.

RELATED TOPICS

1.17 Neo-liberalism (the new right)
2.17 Poverty: right-wing view
2.18 Poverty: reformist view
4.4 Means-testing and selectivity
4.6 National Insurance

FURTHER READING

Moore (1993) Chap 3

8.4 GREAT BRITAIN: HEALTH CARE

Publicly provided hospital care began in the nineteenth century when many poor-law workhouses (see 1.12) established infirmaries for sick paupers. From 1911, hospitals for victims of infectious diseases were built by local authorities and poor-law infirmaries continued to expand. State-funded family doctor care also began for insured workers under the 1911 National Insurance Act. Throughout the inter-war period the numbers of workers (but not their families) covered by health insurance grew.

The National Health Service Act of 1946 nationalised hospitals and brought in free, universal health care covering family doctors, hospitals and dental care for everyone. The extent to which the establishment of the NHS was a revolutionary change is debatable.

With the major exceptions of the new form of hospital management for the former local authority hospitals and, outstandingly, the provision of free treatment, few changes had been made in the health and welfare system. Hospital medicine and its senior practitioners retained their dominant status and influence. No effective system of health service planning was established. The existing pattern of priorities, which emphasised acute medicine at the expense of preventive provision and care for the chronically sick, was maintained. (Burden and Campbell, 1985: 159)

Expenditure on health increased throughout the post-war period as medical technology advanced and new specialisms and health *professions* developed. The control and planning of services was unchanged from 1948 to 1974, when the *administrative reorganisation* of the NHS took place.

A major change took place in the 1980s when business methods and compulsory competitive tendering were introduced into the hospital sector. From 1988 public-sector health-care provision was reorganised using a *provider market* following the proposals in the government White Paper 'Working for Patients'. Many hospitals have applied for 'trust' (i.e. independent) status and operate in part as separate businesses supplying hospital services under contract to District Health Authorities (DHAs) and 'fundholding' GPs. A widespread two-tier system is now developing as private provision expands leaving those able to pay with access to better services.

A new approach based on managerialist principles was the 'Health of the Nation' policy established in 1992. It set 29 targets to reduce the number of deaths from major causes of ill-health. The new Labour government elected in 1997 believes that this policy failed to look at the underlying reasons for ill-health. Its new strategy will involve the departments of health, environment and transport, education, trade and agriculture, and will take into account poverty, poor housing, ethnic minority status, pollution and poor education.

RELATED TOPICS

4.2 Privatisation
4.3 Provider markets
4.5 Managerialisation
4.8 Administrative reorganisation
5.24 Professionalism: reformist view

FURTHER READING

Allsop (1984) Chap 11
Moore (1993) Chap 5

8.5 GREAT BRITAIN: THE OLD

The proportion of over-65s in the population is likely to increase from 14 per cent in 1995 to 19 per cent in 2020. Whether this constitutes an accelerating crisis in welfare provision which can only be met by cuts and private provision is a matter of political debate.

At the beginning of the century there was little provision for the elderly apart from the Poor Law, charities and almshouses. Since then the state has played a major role at a national level, particularly in the provision of pensions and health services. At a local level authorities have taken on wide responsibilities for housing and a range of domiciliary services to keep people in their own homes. (Tinker, 1981: 32)

Pensions were originally introduced on a non-contributory means-tested basis in 1908. In 1925 pensions were brought into the *National Insurance* system and eligibility was based on the contributions record of the participant. Universal flat-rate state pensions were introduced in 1948. A small earnings-related element was introduced in the state pension scheme in 1966. An attempt was made to produce a state-run system of earnings-related pensions with the State Earnings Related Pension Scheme (SERPS) set up in 1975.

While Britain has a universal basic pension for everyone this is set below the *poverty* line and since 1981 it has is only been uprated in line with prices, so its spending power never increases. Many middle-class people, and some workers, especially those in the public sector, have tax-subsidised occupational pensions.

In the 1980s the government tried to move to a system based more on private pensions through the encouragement of 'personal pensions' (i.e. personally owned and individualised pension plans). This scheme led to widespread 'mis-selling' in which large numbers of people were persuaded to opt out of SERPS or their occupational schemes and purchase personal pensions which left them worse off.

The government has encouraged the growing private insurance sector by allowing employees to contract out of the state scheme if they belong to an approved private superannuation scheme. In Britain the Labour government elected in 1997 is planning to retain the flat-rate state pension but to supplement this with a state-sponsored private pension for all those not currently covered by occupational pension schemes.

Older people have also been adversely affected by cuts in health and social-care budgets. Since the early 1990s many old people have had to pay from around £8,000 to £15,000 annually if they require long-term nursing care. This care is now only provided free if they possess capital, including housing, worth less than £8,000. Many have been forced to sell their houses, which are usually their only substantial asset, to pay for care.

In 1996, a White Paper, 'A New Partnership for Care in Old Age', proposed that old people could be encouraged to take out insurance to cover care costs for a fixed period. In return they would be exempted from handing over all their assets if they required care for longer than the period that their insurance paid for. In 1997 the government announced that a Royal Commission would examine the financing of care for the elderly.

An issue under debate in 1997 is whether to revert to *universalist* principles by reinstating the system by which the flat-rate pension increased in value in line with average earnings so as to provide recipients with a standard of living that improves over time. If this is not done it has been estimated that by 2030 the flat-rate pension will be worth just 9 per cent of average earnings.

RELATED TOPICS

4.2 Privatisation
4.6 National Insurance
4.7 Universalism
6.5 The old: social status
6.6 The old: living standards
6.7 The old: health and social care

FURTHER READING

Moore (1993) Chap 11
Tinker (1981) Part 1 and Chap 4

8.6 GREAT BRITAIN: RACE

Racism has deep and strong roots in British history going back to the slave trade, colonialism and imperialism. The acquisition of colonies and the subjugation of their populations provided a basis for sentiments of national superiority and racism. In England there is also a long tradition of anti-Irish racism, which originated in the centuries of British colonial domination of Ireland and was given a strong boost by the degraded status of Irish migrant labourers in Victorian Britain.

The jingoism which was developed in the popular press in the last quarter of the nineteenth century integrated a number of ideological themes into a coherent 'national' ideology. These included:

- racism
- a general contempt for foreigners
- the glorification of military power under aristocratic leadership
- nationalism
- a cult of military heroism.

In the boom years of the late 1940s and 1950s large-scale Commonwealth immigration was encouraged in conditions of labour shortage. At street level, racism was common and in 1957 there were major race riots. When the labour shortage eased, policy shifted towards restrictions on immigration, starting with the Commonwealth Immigrants Act 1962. There have subsequently been further restrictions on immigration and on the eligibility of Commonwealth subjects to become British citizens.

Race relations were to be improved by *reformist* policies in order to counter discrimination and prejudice. The Race Relations Acts of 1965, 1968 and 1976 established the Community Relations Council and the Commission for Racial Equality.

Inner-city policies have been used to try to defuse the potential for disorder created by spatially concentrated ethnic minorities. Black people living in inner-city areas have been subject to distinctive patterns of policing. There is evidence of harassment, passport raids in search of illegal immigrants and crackdowns on leisure activities. In the 1970s there were complaints of excessive use of 'sus': stopping and searching and sometimes arresting black people on the grounds that they were 'suspected persons' who were likely to commit an offence.

There was widespread urban violence in 1981. Following these riots, the Scarman inquiry took place and the report it produced led to some changes in policing. Scarman proposed that racism should be a disciplinary offence in the police, although the government rejected this. Later, statutory force was given to the proposal for the establishment of 'community liaison committees' in which police would have to argue out policies with local representatives.

Most black immigrant workers have occupied low-paid jobs and have often been occupationally and industrially segregated. The black population has been viewed through a complex and changing ideological lens. Initially depicted as making a welcome economic contribution in a period of labour shortage, taking jobs that otherwise would not be filled, the image has gradually shifted both towards 'taking our jobs' and 'scrounging', and to the view of the white population being 'swamped' and suffering a major threat to physical security through the growth of 'street crime' and 'mugging'.

... the problem is very different from that suggested by politicians and the media. First, it is a problem of racism: our attention should not be primarily focused on the migrants and their culture (their religion, mode of dress, diet, etc.), but on the reaction to them of employers, the state, the trade unions, and the working class ... Second, labour migrations can only occur in the form that they do because labour power is only another commodity, to be bought and sold on the market. Capitalists never want people, only their capacity to labour ... the second dimension of the problem in Britain is that it is a capitalist society. (Miles and Phizacklea, 1984: 19)

While the race-relations legislation has inhibited the public expression of overtly racist statements, at least by those in positions of authority, official endorsement of racism in a 'coded' form, such as in the selective presentation of crime statistics, or in statements concerning the operation of the immigration and citizenship laws, has been widespread. Radicals argue that these problems of black people stem from 'institutional racism'. In 1997, a report from the UN Committee on the Elimination of Racial Discrimination (CERD) on Britain:

- condemned high black unemployment
- condemned the under-representation of ethnic minorities in politics, the army and the police
- criticised the large number of black children expelled from schools
- expressed 'serious concern' about the British government's race-relations policies
- said the asylum and immigration regulations would lead to racism.

RELATED TOPICS

1.18 Reformist approaches: general features
2.20 Race: right-wing view
2.21 Race: reformist view
2.22 Race: radical view
5.13 Urban problems: radical view

FURTHER READING

Barker (1980)
Solomos (1989) Chap 4

8.7 IRELAND: BACKGROUND

Ireland was a British possession from the sixteenth century, though British rule had been subject to continuing opposition. The state of Ireland, or Eire, as it exists within its present borders, was established in 1922. In that year the island of Ireland was 'partitioned'. Six northerly counties were combined as Northern Ireland, which remained in British hands. The remainder of the island made up the new state of Eire.

Ireland has a large rural population and is less urbanised than many EU states, with the urban population concentrated in Dublin though there are a few other large towns. Irish social policy rests on the legacy of British colonial rule which imposed the Poor Law, the pensions scheme of 1908 and the National Insurance Act of 1911.

Irish social policy has been most strongly influenced by Catholic *corporatism* based on Catholic social teaching. The principles of this doctrine were written into the constitution adopted in 1937 in which fundamental principles of social policy are specified. Article 45 of the Constitution is headed 'Directive Principles of Social Policy'. This article condemns excesses of wealth and poverty, encourages the provision of social provision through occupational associations and promotes widespread land ownership as the basis for economic security. The ideology behind this is consonant with the values of small-scale rural enterprise, the traditional family, and a shared religion. In common with some features of *conservative paternalist* social thought and in contrast to *liberalism*, Catholic corporatism:

- views the family rather than the individual as the basic unit of society
- prefers local and religious welfare institutions to those run by the state
- sees these as constituting an integrative network which is the basis of an 'organic' social solidarity
- supports widespread property ownership and the pre-capitalist idea of a 'just wage'.

... socio-professional groups organize themselves into corporations and collaborate in decision making, and ... the independence of the family and voluntary organizations from the state is guaranteed. This Catholic corporatist organization ensures ... that all voices are heard and that institutionalised dialogue is geared towards producing class harmony. (Peillon, 1982: 96)

The church has opposed increased direct state intervention and sought financial support for voluntary welfare provision organised through religious bodies. In the education system two-thirds of secondary schools are run by religious bodies. Unmarried mothers used to be dealt with in mother and baby homes run by the church. Most hospitals are run by religious bodies.

The main political division between Fianna Fáil and Fine Gael is a legacy of the civil war of 1923 and the two parties adopt similar centre-right policies on most domestic issues. There is also a *neo-liberal* Progressive Democrat Party and a *reformist* Labour Party.

The historical factors influencing the development of social policy in Ireland are distinctive:

1. The Irish industrial working class was small and weak and social democratic reformism has had little influence on social

policy, though in Dublin working-class radicalism linked to militant trade unionism has sometimes been a strong force.

2. Following the leftward shift in the church resulting from Vatican II there has been more ecclesiastical support for social reform.

3. In contrast to the UK, the world wars were not an important factor in social-policy development.

In 1933, an Unemployment Assistance Act provided *means-tested* benefits for the workless. In 1942, a scheme of unemployment insurance for those laid off due to bad weather was brought in. A universal system of child benefits was set up in 1944 for the third and subsequent children, and became payable for all children in 1963. Social-policy expenditure remained low in the 1950s but grew from the early 1960s. A scheme to provide benefits to smallholders was established in 1966, reflecting the importance of rural society in Ireland.

A compulsory *National Insurance* scheme for all employees was established in 1974, giving income-linked benefits mainly for unemployment and disability. Means-tested social-assistance benefits are available for the sick, the unemployed smallholders and the old. In 1974, a National Economic and Social Council was formed and a report on a national social policy was commissioned, which identified areas of inequality which should be the subject of social intervention.

Gender has been a central issue in Irish social policy. The 1937 constitution defined women's role within the *family* and banned divorce. Contraception was made very hard to obtain. Married women were refused employment in the civil service while working women who had a baby often lost their jobs.

The position of women began to change radically from the 1960s as women's employment increased though it is still lower than elsewhere. The National Commission on the Status of Women in 1969 called for improved rights for women. Under pressure from the *European Union*, women's entitlements to social-security benefits were brought more closely into line with those of men. In 1981, the marriage bar was ended, equal employment policies were brought in, a maternity allowance was introduced and social assistance was made available to unsupported women. A referendum in 1983 inserted a 'pro-life' clause in the constitution and another in 1986 defeated a proposal to allow divorce. In 1991, Ireland obtained written protection for its constitutional ban on abortion in the Maastricht Treaty. Following the decision of the Irish High court in 1992 to prevent a young rape victim from going to Britain for an abortion there was a massive public campaign. The Supreme Court lifted the ban and ruled that Irish women could travel to another EU state for an abortion if the life of the mother was threatened.

The issue of women and their social and legal status has helped to lessen the influence of the Catholic Church. Following the election of a reformist female president in 1990, the government announced an attempt to modernise legislation on divorce. In 1993, the government fell after revelations about its complicity in protecting a priest wanted for child abuse. In 1995, a referendum produced a majority in favour of legalising divorce and a divorce law was enacted in 1996.

Membership of the EU and the social changes associated with industrialisation and urbanisation have helped to produce a shift to a more secular approach to policy. Ireland has received large grants from the EU Regional and Social Funds. Irish politics now shows signs of developing a pattern closer to that commonly found in European states. In 1989–90 the Haughey government proposed a *corporatist* approach to social policy in its Programme for Economic and Social Progress (PESP).

In recent years the *reformist* Irish Labour Party has made considerable political headway and in 1992 it formed a coalition with Fianna Fáil. In 1994, Labour was again in a coalition government, this time with Fine Gael and the Democratic Left. In the election of 1997 Fianna Fáil defeated the Fine Gael coalition. Both the Labour Party and Progressive Democrats ended up with reduced numbers of seats. Fianna Fáil formed a minority government with support from the Progressive Democrats.

Ireland now appears to be close to completing the transition from a backward Catholic corporatist state to a prosperous modern secular welfare state. In 1996, income per head was above the EU average and also greater than that in the UK.

RELATED TOPICS

2.6 Gender: reformist view
2.7 Gender: radical view
2.8 The family: right-wing view
3.8 Welfare corporatism
4.2 Privatisation
4.4 Means-testing and selectivity
9.6 The European Union

FURTHER READING

Cahery et al. (1992)
Curry (1980)
Higgins (1981) pp 76–86
McLaughlin (1993b)

8.8 IRELAND: POVERTY

By European standards Ireland, until the last decade, could be viewed as relatively under-developed with a low level of industrialisation and generally low living standards. After very slow growth during the 1950s the Irish government sought to encourage inward investment as a growth strategy. Taxation of property owners and corporations was cut back with a reduction of marginal tax rates. Farmers and the self-employed pay little income tax but wage earners are heavily taxed under PAYE.

In 1971, at least 24 per cent of the population were estimated to live in poverty. The main groups involved were single-parent families, large families, the unemployed and farming households. Escape from poverty was difficult because the education system provided few opportunities for working-class children.

A large part in supporting incomes was played by the expansion of state employment. Insurance schemes for invalidity and retirement were introduced in the 1970s. A national minimum income was set up using a Home Assistance scheme. In 1977, a Supplementary Welfare Allowance for the poor was established and benefits were raised above subsistence level for the first time.

> ... financial poverty in Ireland and other dimensions of social deprivation, are directly linked to social class position, with families of manual workers far more likely to be poor, probably with inferior housing, a greater likelihood of unemployment and very little likelihood of their children attaining an education and occupational level far above their own. (Joyce and McCashin, 1982: 91)

In the 1980s, eligibility for benefits for the unemployed was reduced in an attempt to hold down public spending. Poverty is still widespread. In 1987, unemployment reached 18.9 per cent and a *corporatist* national programme of wage restraint was instituted. This involved agreement between employers, employees and government with support for 'enterprise' and labour 'flexibility'.

Since that time growth has accelerated leading some to compare Ireland with the rapidly growing economies of South-East Asia by referring to it as the 'Celtic Tiger'. This rapid growth has been associated with a widening gap between rich and poor, a continued high level of long-term unemployment and severe pockets of both urban and rural deprivation. Poverty levels remained above the EU average in 1993. Whether these higher levels of growth can be sustained and will lead to generally improved employment prospects and to decreases in poverty and inequality is not yet clear.

RELATED TOPICS
2.18 Poverty: reformist view
3.8 Welfare corporatism
4.4 Means-testing and selectivity

FURTHER READING
Joyce and McCashin (1982) Chap 8
Powell (1992) pp 289–99

8.9 IRELAND: HEALTH CARE

Ireland does not have a free health service though policies are designed to prevent lack of funds from preventing anyone from obtaining health care. Free health provision in Ireland has a relatively narrow scope by European standards. Medical facilities are substantially privately owned, though many of these are not owned by private commercial institutions but establishments run by religious bodies.

> ... provision of a free national health service has never been an objective of state policy. Only medical card holders are entitled to free services which effectively means only social welfare recipients and their dependants have access to comprehensive health care. The rest of the population is encouraged to insure themselves under the state-regulated Voluntary Health Insurance Scheme. The Church still has a considerable role to play in the provision of health care. Approximately half of hospital beds in Ireland are provided by the non-state sector. (McLaughlin, 1993b: 220)

Until the 1970 Health Act the poor could obtain free family doctor services at what had formerly been a local poor-law dispensary. Since 1972, they can attend the surgery of a doctor of their choice. Access to free health care largely depends on income:

1. About 40 per cent of the population obtain free health services through a *means test*. Welfare recipients and their families are given a medical card which entitles them to free health provision.
2. The 45 per cent of middle-income earners pay a 1 per cent tax levy up to an income ceiling and obtain free hospital services.
3. The remaining 15 per cent of well-off people get free hospital accommodation but pay doctors' fees. A Voluntary Health Insurance Board was set up in 1957 to enable this group to purchase health insurance.

RELATED TOPICS
4.4 Means-testing and selectivity

FURTHER READING

Powell (1992) pp 307–11

8.10 IRELAND: THE OLD

In 1908, while Ireland was still part of Great Britain, the British *means-tested* pension scheme was established. This formed the basis of the provision of state income support for the old. Family care and religious charitable assistance were heavily relied on.

There are regional variations in the numbers of old people. Some of the more remote rural areas have a high proportion because of the migration of younger people. A contributory pension scheme for the over-70s was established in 1961 and the pension age was progressively reduced, reaching 65 in 1970. Means-tested pensions are still available for those who are ineligible for the contributory pension or whose pension is too low. Pensioners with no other income are also given a General Medical Service Card, which entitles them to free medical care.

Institutional care and some domiciliary services for the old are generally provided by religious charities. Around two-thirds of pensioners also receive benefits in kind including TV licences and an electricity allowance.

> The risk of poverty is above average in households where the head is aged sixty-five or over. Approximately a third of all poor households were headed by someone of sixty-five or more. (Joyce and McCashin, 1982: 16)

RELATED TOPICS

4.4 Means-testing and selectivity
6.5 The old: social status

8.11 IRELAND: RACE

Ireland does not have major problems with ethnic minorities associated with immigration. The main issue relating to 'race' now involves citizenship, national identity and the question of the national borders. The national conflict is between Irish nationalism and the unionism of Protestant Northern Ireland.

> The main stems of nationalism and unionism in Ireland share some common historical roots. They also have much in common so far as social philosophy is concerned ... Aside from a few specific questions like divorce, abortion and contraception, they share strongly conservative attitudes on many social issues: opposition to secularism and support for clerical influence in

education; resistance to the growth of a strong political labour movement; and general support for the social and political values of rural and small town society over those of the city. (Hepburn, 1980: 7)

The partition of the country in 1922 and the maintenance of the British control of the 'six counties' of Northern Ireland as part of the UK is opposed by many people on both sides of the Irish border. The issue underlying the foundation of the two major Irish political parties was whether or not to agree to the partition of Ireland in an agreement made with Britain in 1922.

As part of the process of establishing Irish national identity following independence, attempts were made to safeguard the traditional language and culture, since this was largely destroyed during the period of British rule. The *Gaeltacht* are areas designated as Irish speaking. Gaelic is also taught to all schoolchildren.

Another race issue involves gypsies and travellers who have a very low status in Ireland and are often treated in a racist fashion. Their living conditions are poor and few facilities are provided for them. Education levels and life expectancy are very low.

RELATED TOPICS

2.20 Race: right-wing view
2.21 Race: reformist view
2.22 Race: radical view

8.12 AUSTRALIA: BACKGROUND

The Commonwealth of Australia was formed in 1901 on the basis of universal suffrage though with aboriginal people excluded. Australian values date from the colonial era and combine individualism with egalitarianism. Colonial labour shortages along with an economy based on wage labour rather than small property ownership favoured the emergence of working class organisations. Trade unionism and the Labour Party were significant forces from the late nineteenth century.

A degree of social provision was established early with a scheme of wage regulation in 1907 based on the principle of a wage sufficient for a family with three children 'living in a civilised community'. A pensions scheme was set up in 1909 based on residence and racial criteria. The first Labour majority government was formed in 1910. Maternity allowances were established in 1912, though with racial exclusions.

Further reforms were undertaken during the Second World War. Child endowment benefits and widows pensions were introduced in 1941 and a National Welfare Fund in 1943. This was followed by the Unemployment and Sickness Benefits Act of 1944. Extra benefits for service veterans and their families are provided under the 'repatriation' system.

Social security is run at federal level while other social policies such as education, health and housing are run by the states though often funded by the centre. Conflict between states and the centre occurs, especially during times of recession or when they are controlled by different parties.

Social benefits for pensions, old age, unemployment and sickness are flat rate and are all based on *means-testing* of income and assets rather than *National Insurance*. The only universal benefits are family allowances. Nearly all social expenditure apart from Medicare is financed by general taxation. Personal taxation is relatively high but there are no social insurance contributions. Fiscal welfare in the form of tax reliefs is used to encourage home ownership and occupational pensions.

> The Australian social security system evolved alongside a strong wages policy and protectionism. Australia was an early starter in many areas of welfare and did not introduce later new thinking in social security policy because it already had a workable system and because change was difficult in a federal system. Consequently it is unique in providing flat-rate, means-tested, social security payments financed out of general revenue. (McCallum, 1989: 40–2)

The Labour Party has generally been responsible for initiating social policy reforms. The first post-war Labour government since 1949 was in power from 1972 to 1975. It planned to abolish means tests and to establish a national health service. The succeeding Conservative government of Fraser, 1975–83, followed a *neo-liberal* policy of cutting expenditure and the Labour welfare reforms of the early 1970s were reversed.

Labour was re-elected in 1983 and pursued a *corporatist* policy based on an 'Accord' with the trade unions involving economic expansion aided by wage restraint. *Neo-liberal* economic policies of deregulation and privatisation were pursued. Youth unemployment rose substantially and economic inequalities generally increased. Under the accord Labour won three successive elections, maintained industrial peace and controlled unemployment. However, Labour lost in 1996 and a Liberal–National Party coalition government took power.

Australia has been described as an example of social corporatism in which a welfare state is sustained by a moderate reformist government gaining power and implementing policy through corporatist arrangements. The Australian welfare state developed piecemeal and is mainly organised around selectivist principles with a relatively low level of welfare expenditure. Australia has been termed a 'wage-earners' welfare state, since the strength of the labour movement has led to reforms involving working conditions, wages and benefits for ex-workers rather than social provision aimed at helping everyone in need.

RELATED TOPICS

1.17 Neo-liberalism (the new right)
3.8 Welfare corporatism
4.2 Privatisation
4.4 Means-testing and selectivity
9.15 Race

FURTHER READING

Bryson (1992) pp 89–98
Carson and Kerr (1995)
Castles (1985) Chap 2
Jones (1992) Chap 1
McCallum (1989)
Mishra (1990) Chap 4
Rodgers (1979) pp 150–60

8.13 AUSTRALIA: POVERTY

From the end of the Second World War until the mid-1970s Australia had full employment and relatively low levels of income inequality. Following the economic dislocations of the early 1970s an Australian Government Commission into Poverty in 1975 recommended a more planned approach to dealing with poverty. However, since then, unemployment has remained high and poverty has increased, especially amongst those unemployed for long periods. Benefits have not been uprated in line with inflation and their real value fell in the 1980s. The main costs of benefit cuts in the 1980s fell on those outside the workforce, leading critics to suggest that the corporatist 'Accord' had marginalised the poor, unemployed and single parents who are not represented in the bargaining process. This criticism is consistent with the view that Australia is a 'wage-earners' welfare state'.

> ... the costs of the breakdown of the system are borne by the unemployed, the aged, single parents and those, in general, not in the workforce ... (McCallum, 1989: 42)

Unemployment and inability to work because of child-care commitments or age are now the main causes of poverty. The proportion of single-parent households has been rising, causing more problems of family poverty. Over half of the children in these families had an income below the poverty line in the early 1980s. Family Income Supplement was introduced and means-tested children's benefits were raised in 1983, but the relative incomes of single-parent families did rise in the 1980s.

Poverty persists due to the high level of unemployment and 20 per cent of children are in families with income below the official poverty line. The UN Human Development Index for 1992 showed that Australia had the third-highest score for inequality amongst 53 industrialised states. The extensive use of means-tested benefits creates a 'poverty trap' (see 4.7). In 1995, a report entitled 'Working Nation' suggested that benefits should only be partially withdrawn from recipients who subsequently obtained employment in order to eliminate the poverty trap for the unemployed.

RELATED TOPICS

1.17 Neo-liberalism (the new right)
2.17 Poverty: right-wing view
2.18 Poverty: reformist view
3.8 Welfare corporatism
4.4 Means-testing and selectivity

FURTHER READING

McCallum (1989)
Mishra (1990) Chap 4

8.14 AUSTRALIA: HEALTH CARE

Until 1975 health care was provided by private insurance with free treatment for the poor largely in public hospitals. A universal system of health insurance was established in 1975 with the Medibank programme.

> By the mid 1970s, Australia had a national health scheme, similar to the Canadian system, which has continued into the 1980s ... Australian pay an income tax surcharge that entitles them to basic hospital and medical services. (Jones, 1992: 200)

Since 1983 Medicare has been provided for a payment of 1.25 per cent extra income tax. This provides a comprehensive system of basic medical services. Some 85 per cent of the cost of a scheduled medical fee is paid, or where the government is billed, the patient pays nothing. Free hospital care is available but private hospital insurance is widely used to obtain better service.

RELATED TOPICS

4.4 Means-testing and selectivity
4.6 National Insurance

FURTHER READING

Jones (1992) Chap 10

8.15 AUSTRALIA: THE OLD

There has been a means-tested old-age benefit in Australia since 1909. The state pension is the main income source for two-thirds of old people. The pensionable age for women is 60 and for men is 65, though war veterans are given more favourable terms. Index-linked pensions are provided on a means and assets test along with a ten-year residence requirement. Benefit levels are relatively low at 25 per cent of average earnings and many pensioners have incomes below the poverty line.

Occupational pensions are largely financed through tax reliefs but only about 10 per cent of the elderly rely principally on these. A state superannuation scheme has been a major development resulting from the *corporatist* approach of the Accord and now covers nearly 90 per cent of the workforce. Employers are required to make a substantial contribution and trade unions are heavily involved in the administration of superannuation.

Means-tested residential care for the elderly is publicly funded. It is principally provided by the private sector along with some by voluntary bodies, with about a fifth operated in the public sector. The elderly population is set to grow substantially over the next 20 years as those born in the baby boom years of the 1950s and 1960s retire. Policy towards the old is relatively selective and benefits the poor much more than middle- and high-income groups.

> ... the Australian system is probably more generous to the aged workers who have had low earnings than is the US system. In contrast the Australian system gives far less to those at the middle-income levels than do US and other social insurance systems. (Caves and Krause, 1984: 362)

RELATED TOPICS

3.8 Welfare corporatism
4.4 Means-testing and selectivity
6.5 The old: social status

FURTHER READING

Caves and Krause (1984)
Jones (1992) Chap 7
Kinnear and Graycar (1983)

8.16 AUSTRALIA: RACE

Australia has a long tradition of racism alongside its (white) egalitarianism. Until 1966, immigration was controlled on the basis of a 'white Australia' policy which operated with trade union support. In that year the policy was relaxed although not completely abolished.

Historically, the process of European settlement displaced indigenous Aboriginal peoples from their ancestral lands. The Aboriginal population has gone from about 750,000 in 1788 to 100,000 in 1900 and 180,000 in 1991. Up until the 1960s an assimilationist policy was pursued in which some Aboriginal children were forcibly taken from their families and brought up with white children. Aboriginal Australians were excluded from normal social participation until 1967, when a referendum gave them full citizenship. The destruction of their traditional economy and way of life has left many dependent on the welfare state.

The Department of Immigration and Ethnic Affairs and the Department of Aboriginal Affairs deal with policies on race. There is special expenditure on housing, education, unemployment, health and legal aid. Aboriginal people are disadvantaged on most measures of deprivation including housing, education, income and incarceration. Housing is particularly bad with a low rate of home ownership and many living in shanty dwellings. The health record is also very poor.

> Australian Aborigines have life expectancies substantially lower than those of the overall Australian population ... [they] may comprise a significant proportion of the Australian underclass [see 2.17], even though they are remarkably scattered and often live in non-metropolitan areas. (Jones, 1992: 100)

The question of Aboriginal rights has been forced on to the political agenda in the 1980s. A major issue concerns Aboriginal claims to up to 40 per cent of land owned by the government and held under pastoral leaseholds. The government proposed to transfer ownership of this land to the leaseholders, thus eliminating the Aboriginal claim. This issue is unresolved at the time of writing. Since the end of the 'white-Australia' policy, policies on race have gradually shifted towards a *reformist* stance encouraging ethnic pluralism. Australia generally has moved towards multi-culturalism with the changing pattern of immigration. In 1994 a Racial Hatred Act was passed to prevent public expressions of racism. However, racism remains a strong feature of Australian culture.

Attempts to resolve Aboriginal issues have involved a Reconciliation Commission which was meeting in early 1997 in order to deal with a range of contentious issues involving the rights of Aboriginal Australians. However, at the same time the populist One Nation movement led by Pauline Hanson, with anti-Aboriginal, anti-Asian and anti-free-trade policies, gained considerable political prominence.

RELATED TOPICS

2.20 Race: right-wing view
2.21 Race: reformist view
2.22 Race: radical view
4.13 Empowerment
9.15 Race

8.17 NEW ZEALAND: BACKGROUND

New Zealand was formerly part of the British Empire. Unlike Australia it is a unitary state. It pursued progressive policies early in its history. Women were first given the vote in 1893. Since 1936, power has alternated between the Labour Party and the National Party. The two parties are not strongly divided ideologically and similar social policy measures have been supported by both.

Social policy reforms date from the introduction of *means-tested* old-age pensions in 1898. This was followed by widows pensions in 1911. Means-tested family allowances were introduced in 1927 though only for the third and subsequent children. In the aftermath of the depression Labour established the basis of the welfare state. A comprehensive system of social security was set up in 1938 with means-tested benefits for sickness and unemployment and a small universal pension for the over-65s. Family allowances were made a *universal* benefit payable for all children in 1946. Social policy is organised from the centre by the Department of Social Welfare.

> The New Zealand social security system is unusual in its reliance upon flat rates of benefit which are financed through general taxation ... this reflects the continuing strategy of organized labour since the turn of the century to focus narrowly on wages and working conditions. The social security system represents the safety net beneath that wage system. (Uttley, 1989: 195)

The only exception to the flat-rate benefit system is the earnings-related scheme for compensation for all kinds of accidental injury and associated medical costs. This is financed by levies on employers, car owners and the self-employed. This is a novel scheme which provides compensation on the basis of need rather than restricting it only to those able successfully to sue for negligence.

Benefits act as a safety net rather than an enhancement of the living standards of all and as in Australia insurance schemes have not been widely used. The labour movement has generally supported social improvement through policies on wages and workers' rights rather than social benefits. For this reason New Zealand, like Australia, has been described as a 'wage-earners' welfare state'.

A Labour government was elected in 1984. While it had a radical non-nuclear foreign policy it continued to pursue strongly *neo-liberal* monetarist economic polices. This has involved economic liberalisation, cuts in public spending, deregulation and a shift from direct to indirect taxation. Inflation has remained high and unemployment grew for much of the period since 1984. Since the election of 1990 the National Party has continued similar policies.

RELATED TOPICS

1.11 Right-wing approaches: general features
1.17 Neo-liberalism (the new right)
4.4 Means-testing and selectivity

FURTHER READING

Carson and Kerr (1988)
Castles (1985) Chap 2
Jack (1986)
Rudd (1993)
Uttley (1989)

8.18 NEW ZEALAND: POVERTY

In New Zealand policies on poverty have focused on families with children. In 1972, child tax allowances were abolished and child allowances were increased thus benefiting poorer and larger families. Single-parent families get a Domestic Purposes Benefit (DPB), introduced in 1973, and an additional child-benefit supplement for the first child. In 1975, around 25 per cent of children still lived in poverty.

The increase in unemployment, the slowdown in growth in the 1980s and the rising numbers of single-parent families have increased poverty. From 1984, Family Care was paid as a supplement to low-wage families with children. This was replaced by Family Support in 1986, which gives a means-tested family allowance to all families, whether they are earning or on benefit. Family Support is based on a guaranteed minimum family income linked to family size. The value of this benefit in relation to average earnings fell in the late 1980s. The old and the unemployed rely on means-tested benefits which are set at a bare subsistence level.

As economic problems increased from the mid-1980s *neo-liberal* policies were undertaken. Charges for public services were increased, subsidies to public utilities were reduced, leading to price increases for basic necessities, and poverty grew. By 1983, a third of all children lived in poverty. According the UN Human Development Index, in 1992, New Zealand had the second-highest score for inequality amongst 53 industrialised states.

RELATED TOPICS

1.17 Neo-liberalism (the new right)
2.17 Poverty: right-wing view
2.18 Poverty: reformist view
4.4 Means-testing and selectivity

FURTHER READING

Uttley (1989) pp 212–21

8.19 NEW ZEALAND: HEALTH CARE

The New Zealand health system involves a mixture of free, subsidised and purchased provision. Those buying private health insurance obtain tax subsidies. Free hospital care was first provided under the Social Security Act of 1938. Part payment for General Medical Services (GMS) involving family doctor fees was provided from 1941. From that time there has been a piecemeal establishment of free services for various patient groups. GMS benefits were increased for social security recipients in 1969 and for children in 1974.

> Medical insurance has grown dramatically in New Zealand over the past 25 years, with over one third of the population currently insured with private funds. Much of this growth can be attributed to the unwillingness of the welfare state to deliver non-acute hospital care at a zero price, to provide for choice of surgeon, or to maintain the share of fees for primary care paid by patients. (Woodfield, 1989: 127)

In effect, there is a differentiated service with better care for those able to pay. Those in most need of medical care do not necessarily receive it, since medical services are generally of a lower standard in poorer areas.

RELATED TOPICS

4.4 Means-testing and selectivity
4.6 National Insurance

FURTHER READING
Easton (1980) Chap 8

8.20 NEW ZEALAND: THE OLD

Means-tested pensions for those over 65 were established in 1898 based on residence and race. The 1938 Social Security Act gave a means-tested benefit at 60 and a small universal benefit at 65.

In 1975, a compulsory National Superannuation Scheme with earnings-related benefits financed by employer and employee contributions was brought in by Labour. In 1976, the National Party made this a taxed universal payment for all over-60s, paying 80 per cent of the after-tax average wage.

> ... the introduction of National Superannuation [involved] a generous, universal old age pension for all New Zealanders from the age of 60 years with the married rate being indexed to 80 per cent of the average wage. The large number of beneficiaries of this scheme (approximately 22 per cent of all voters) has led both the major political parties to guarantee to keep the scheme intact. (Jack, 1986: 168)

Tax reliefs now encourage private provision for old age, though occupational pensions are most commonly received by government employees. Medical services and care for the old are provided by Hospital Boards. Residential care is mainly provided by voluntary bodies run by religious organisations, though there are also private nursing homes and some state provision. Institutional care is overused owing to the lack of alternative forms of provision.

RELATED TOPICS
4.4 Means-testing and selectivity
6.5 The old: social status

FURTHER READING
Easton (1980) Chap 4
Uttley (1989) pp 200–6

8.21 NEW ZEALAND: RACE

New Zealand, in common with many other white-dominated ex-colonies, has a minority population of indigenous people. New Zealand has a population of 3.7 million people. About 9 per cent of the population are Maori, with another 3 per cent from Pacific islands and other minorities making up about 2 per cent.

Until the early 1950s the Maori population was overwhelmingly rural, though now Maoris are mainly urban dwellers often in the poorest accommodation. Maori people are disadvantaged in terms of health, mortality, educational achievement, home ownership, income and unemployment. Unemployment rates are high – 14 per cent for Maoris against 5 per cent for the whole population in 1985 – and much higher amongst the young. Social benefits are not freely available to members of ethnic minorities. A one-year residency requirement means that some Pacific islanders are not eligible for benefits.

The Department of Maori Affairs has, over the last decade, moved towards a developmental approach rather than one based on individual pathology. Emphasis on economic development for Maori people has been regarded as central to this approach. The government has allocated funding for a Maori Enterprise Development Scheme in which funds will be allocated from the Board of Maori Affairs to local level committees, usually based on tribal affiliation, for use in promoting employment ... (Uttley, 1989: 215)

In the 1970s Maoris began a challenge to existing welfare institutions and to demand more local control over services. The issue of race remains a source of unresolved tension in New Zealand.

RELATED TOPICS

2.20 Race: right-wing view
2.21 Race: reformist view
4.13 Empowerment
9.15 Race

FURTHER READING

Uttley (1989)

8.22 UNITED STATES: BACKGROUND

The US was founded in 1776 with a constitution based on *liberal* principles of government. There is shared responsibility between federal government and states, though conflicts occur because of centralising tendencies opposed by a strong tradition of states' rights.

The Democratic and Republican parties are not strongly divided by ideology. Both generally support right-wing values though the left of the Democratic Party supports *reformism* in the New Deal tradition. Liberalism and pragmatism have been major influences on political values in the US. The lack of a mass working-class political party has meant that socialist values have had little national influence. Individualism is a strong theme in culture and the ideas of Social Darwinism have also been influential. The right is powerful and has recently been reinforced by the advance of Christian fundamentalism.

The Elizabethan Poor Law based on parish responsibility formed part of the legacy of British rule and some local social welfare provision was established during the eighteenth and nineteenth centuries. From the last quarter of the nineteenth century, the Charity Organization Society (see 5.14) became influential in many cities.

The inter-war depression involved industrial unemployment and rural depopulation and decline. The 'New Deal', which began after the election of Roosevelt in 1933, was a key moment in the development of American social policy. The social policies of the New Deal were explicitly based on the principle of 'social security'. Support for the New Deal came from a coalition of industrial workers, poor southern whites, urban blacks and reformists (known in the US as 'liberals').

> Franklin Roosevelt's Message to Congress in June 1934, with its concept of social security, marked a watershed in American social policy. He stated, 'Among our objectives I place the security of the men, women and children of the nation first ... People ... want some safeguard against misfortunes which cannot be wholly eliminated in this man-made world of ours.' Enactment of insurance based unemployment and pension schemes followed in the Social Security Act of 1935, which was to form the basis for subsequent social legislation in the decades ahead. (Digby, 1989: 16)

The New Deal involved major shifts in policy:

- There was an increase in federal spending largely financed by government borrowing rather than taxation.
- A National Housing Act was passed in 1934 to promote house building.
- The Social Security Act of 1935 established statutory earnings related *national insurance* benefits for the unemployed and for old age, with a means-tested addition for the elderly poor. It is financed by employers and employees contributions but without a contribution from the state. The subsequent extension of this scheme to cover other groups has produced the system known as OASDHI (Old Age, Survivors, Disability and Health Insurance).

- Aid for Families with Dependent Children (AFDC) began as a federal benefit for mothers and children in the 1935 Act and is the main *means-tested* welfare benefit.

The next major period of reform was the 1960s. The Democratic administration led by President Johnson launched the Great Society programme and the 'war on poverty'. These involved major reforms of social policy:

1. The 1964 Civil Rights Act was designed to establish voting rights for blacks, many of whom had been excluded from electoral rolls.
2. In 1964 the Food Stamp Act provided means-tested vouchers for food purchase for the poor.
3. The Economic Opportunity Act of 1964 set up the 'poverty programme'.
4. The Demonstration Cities and Metropolitan Development Act 1966 channelled funds to deprived urban areas.

There are federal insurance programmes for old age and hospital insurance, and income support schemes for old age, disability and veterans. Employers and the private sector play a major role. Occupational welfare in the form of tax-subsidised benefits are provided through occupational schemes for pensions and other benefits.

In the US there are no universal schemes for sickness or family allowances and means-tested benefits are used extensively. General (Social) Assistance is available as a means-tested social benefit in some states. Means-tested public housing built with federal support is available especially in large cities. The use of means tests expanded in the 1970s with the development of Medicaid and the growing expenditure on AFDC and Food Stamps. Around a third of all services are run by private or voluntary-sector organisations and these have grown in importance with federal budget cuts, decentralisation and the use of contracting rather than direct provision.

The Unemployment Compensation programme is financed by a payroll tax with eligibility conditions that vary from state to state. 'Workfare' programmes, in which benefits are available on condition of participating in designated work schemes, are now becoming more common.

Reaganism supported reductions in welfare in 1981 when disability and retirement benefits were cut and benefits were raised less than wage levels. The only universal benefit cut substantially was for the unemployed though there were also tightened eligibility rules for means-tested programmes such as such as Food Stamps and AFDC. In the 1980s, there was a move back towards giving the states responsibility for welfare through the Social Services Block Grant Act. This reassertion of the powers of the states has often been accompanied by a rhetoric of opposition to the federal bureaucracy.

President Clinton, a Democrat, took office in 1992 with some moderate *reformist* plans including a proposal for a wide-ranging reform of health care, which have proved difficult to implement owing to congressional opposition. In the 1995 congressional elections the Republicans won a Senate majority on the platform of a 'contract with America' involving an attack on the 'dependency culture'. They proposed to abolish Food Stamps and free school meals, saving $21 billion. Funds for welfare would be dispensed by the states with federally determined cash limits. The Republicans planned to rein in future welfare spending plans by legislation setting limits on public spending and requiring the national budget to be balanced. The Clinton presidency pursed policies of welfare cuts though it resisted the more extreme demands from the Republican right. In 1996, an act was passed which shifted the main responsibility for welfare benefits from the federal government to the states, thus paving the way for cuts in welfare benefits in many parts of the country.

Clinton was re-elected in 1996. The economy is currently booming with a high growth rate and lowered unemployment. An extension of the compulsory period of schooling from 12 to 14 years is planned along with two years' vocational post-school study for all. The re-election of a Democratic President has reduced the influence of the extreme right. However, the Democrats have adopted some of the budgetary and welfare polices previously espoused by the Republican Party. Social policies therefore generally seem set to remain in the centre-right area of the political spectrum though with some elements of *communitarianism*.

RELATED TOPICS

1.16 Eugenics
1.17 Neo-liberalism (the new right)
1.24 Communitarianism
2.17 Poverty: right-wing view
3.3 Bureaucratic self-interest
3.4 Democratic elitism and technocracy
4.4 Means-testing and selectivity
4.6 National Insurance
5.15 Social work: right-wing view

FURTHER READING

Bryson (1992) pp 99–105
Glazer (1986)

Mishra (1990) Chap 2
Piven and Cloward (1982) Chap 1

8.23 UNITED STATES: POVERTY

The 1960s War on Poverty had a considerable effect and reduced the numbers in poverty by half, though in the late 1960s disillusion with welfare spending grew and a shift to the right was evident in the election of the Republican, Nixon, as President. In the 1980s, in the US unemployment rose less than in the UK because of the huge budget deficit and the high levels of military spending, which helped to create jobs.

The long-term unemployed who have used up or lack entitlement to unemployment benefit are not eligible for a means-tested allowance. The numbers of the unemployed receiving benefit fell from 75 per cent in 1975 to 25 per cent in 1984. The continuing 'welfare backlash' intensified and budget cuts were concentrated on services for the poor, increasing income inequalities. Compulsory workfare was operating in 20 states by 1984 and took a variety of forms, involving job search, training and work experience as well as work itself. Women with no children under six in families receiving AFDC have to take part in a workfare scheme called the Work Incentive Programme (WIN) designed to encourage them into paid work.

> Given the anti-welfare ethos in the USA, workfare has attracted increased support; it has been seen as a way out of long-term welfare dependency providing a half-way house to economic independence. There have been growing anxieties in Reaganite America over the alleged existence of an 'underclass' [see 2.17] of Blacks and Hispanics who were permanent recipients of welfare. These fears have fuelled recent moves to stiffen and extend workfare provisions. AFDC recipients were seen as a prime target for workfare ... (Digby, 1989: 19)

According to the UN Human Development Index, in 1992, the US had the seventh-highest score for inequality amongst 53 industrialised states. Around 32 per cent of the poor are non-white with blacks being three times as likely as whites to be poor. Poverty is the US is 'feminised' owing to low female wage rates, high levels of economic non-participation and large numbers of single-parent families. One in four families with children now have a single parent. Single-parent families make up around half of all poor families.

In 1996, further changes to the welfare laws were prescribed which are likely to further reduce the living standards of those without incomes from employment:

- a two-year limit for the continuous receipt of benefits
- a five-year limit over the lifetime of the recipient
- no benefits without a demonstration of availability for work.

RELATED TOPICS

2.17 Poverty: right-wing view
4.4 Means-testing and selectivity
8.26 United States: race

FURTHER READING

Ginsburg (1992) pp 103–13
Higgins (1978) pp 28–36
Joe and Rogers (1985) Chap 2

8.24 UNITED STATES: HEALTH CARE

There are huge inequalities in the provision of health care and the degree of *universalism* of health provision is very low compared with other advanced industrial countries.

> ... mortality and morbidity in the US can ... be explained in terms of social class. Even if we take income and occupation as indicators of class ... using age standardised figures, we find far more mortality and morbidity among the working class than among the corporate and upper-middle classes. (Navarro, 1976: 85)

The cost of medical care is now over 10 per cent of GNP compared with under 5 per cent in 1950. Around 60 per cent of health-care expenditure is privately financed. The proportion of hospitals operating as private businesses has now risen to about 30 per cent.

Medicaid is the main *means-tested* health benefit and this is available for children in families receiving AFDC. Eligibility is linked to AFDC, which was cut in the 1980s. The system varies from state to state though the standard of medical care provided is generally set at a basic level and many people in *poverty* fail to qualify. In the US, health insurance in the form of Medicare is only provided for those over 65. Medicare is organised in two parts:

1. Part A was set up in 1965 and restructured in 1973 as a universal scheme to provide hospital care by making payments to compensate private health providers.
2. Part B Medicare is a voluntary scheme for family doctor care in which participants pay a monthly fee.

The Clinton Democratic administration tried to institute a comprehensive reform of health care but it failed to get it through Congress in its original form. A substantial and increasing number of people now lack health-care insurance coverage and only about 40 per cent are fully covered.

RELATED TOPICS

4.2 Privatisation
4.4 Means-testing and selectivity
4.6 National Insurance

FURTHER READING

Ginsburg (1992) pp 127–35
Navarro (1976) pp 82–99

8.25 UNITED STATES: THE OLD

Means-tested assistance was provided for the old under the Social Security Act of 1935 as part of the New Deal though the amounts of benefit were to be set by individual states. Under the federal pensions scheme insured workers aged 65–69 get an index-linked, wage-related, means-tested monthly grant with a dependants allowance for those eligible. At aged 70 the pension for insured workers is provided without a means test. There is also a *means-tested* Supplemental Security Income (SSI), which is designed to establish a national minimum income for all old people.

Old people are a group of some political importance with a long tradition of political participation. In the 1930s the Townsend movement promoted the interests of the old in national politics and became highly influential.

> Prior to the Second World War ... benefits were a form of social insurance, based on a notion of subsistence ... middle-class workers ... were able to organize for change as a part of their contracts of employment ensuring a system of occupational pensions. This effectively divided retirees into two groups: the poor, living on social security, on the one hand; and those who received social security in addition to their occupational pensions ... Since the middle-class elderly had access to occupational pensions, they were in effect removed from the political struggle to improve the state pension. (Hendricks and Calasanti, 1986: 254)

Since 1965 the health care of old people has been covered by Medicare. This is a scheme of universal health insurance for the old. The proportion of old people is rising fast and will grow from 11 per cent in 1983 to 21 per cent in 2030. Old people are the group that is most favoured by social policy in the US in terms of the level and coverage of benefits available. However, the living standards of old people still largely reflect their class position. The second

Clinton administration which took office in 1997 has proposed to try to develop a 'bi-partisan' policy on the old in partnership with the Republican Party.

RELATED TOPICS

4.4 Means-testing and selectivity
4.7 Universalism
6.5 The old: social status

FURTHER READING

Hendricks and Calasanti (1986)

8.26 UNITED STATES: RACE

As in other colonies extensively settled by whites, indigenous peoples were persecuted and subjugated. America was formed as a multi-ethnic but white 'melting pot' in the nineteenth century when population expansion was mainly due to immigration. Throughout this process, and despite the abolition of slavery following the civil war, black Americans remained socially and often legally oppressed.

The non-white population is 12 per cent black, 6 per cent Hispanic and 2 per cent 'other' including American Indians and Asians. The Hispanic minority is growing very fast and is likely to out-number blacks by 2005. The average household income of blacks is 63 per cent of that for whites. In some areas such as education the racial gap has decreased and there is a growing black middle class. However, black rates are at least double those of whites on a range of measures of deprivation including:

• unemployment
• single parenthood
• welfare dependence
• incarceration.

The modern civil rights movement began as a struggle for integration in the south. The Civil Rights Act of 1957 was passed to enforce racial desegregation in the south following a 1954 Supreme Court decision outlawing 'separate' but 'equal' facilities in which racial segregation was allowed so long as facilities provided for each race were of equal quality. Racial problems involving discrimination, poverty, unemployment and poor housing, led to major riots in the ghettos of many North American cities in the early 1960s.

In the late 1960s 'affirmative action', or *positive discrimination*, in the form of setting quotas for black entrants into some education programmes was instituted. This policy has now been undermined by a 1997 Supreme Court decision that state laws which prohibit this are legal. A referendum in California supporting the abolition of affirmative action in the state has been passed.

The issue of race continues to occupy a central place in social policy debates in the US in relation to crime, housing, social benefits and equal opportunities laws. There is a racial divide in politics with about 90 per cent of black votes going to the Democrats in the 1993 Presidential Election. Racism is still a major feature of American society as recent debates on the existence of a black and Hispanic 'underclass' (see 2.17) show.

> The welfare benefits system, alongside the law enforcement, health care and social services agencies, functions to maintain and control the underclass. Ironically the enfranchisement of black people in the welfare state created a system which entraps and polices many of them, while preventing absolute destitution.
> (Ginsburg, 1992: 117)

RELATED TOPICS

2.17 Poverty: right-wing view
2.20 Race: right-wing view
2.21 Race: reformist view
4.12 Positive discrimination
4.13 Empowerment
9.15 Race

FURTHER READING

Ginsburg (1992) pp 114–17

8.27 CANADA: BACKGROUND

Canada is a mainly English-speaking country with a minority of 25 per cent French speakers mainly in Quebec. Canada has a mixed political culture with a significant *reformist* tradition as well as strong support for the values of the *conservative* and *liberal* right.

> Although liberalism is the predominant political paradigm ... Canada, unlike the United States (US), contains an important non-liberal element ... the presence in Canada of universal family allowances and national state health insurance reflects a more collectivist political culture than that of the United States ... Canada's French settlers brought with them the Tory conception of society as organic and hierarchic. The state took precedence over the individual and was seen as having responsibility for guiding the new society, particularly its economic development.
> (Bellamy and Irving, 1989: 48)

The principal parties, the Liberals and Conservatives, do not have widely divergent principles and policies and both support a relatively restricted welfare state. Social reform has been championed by the New Democratic Party formerly known as the Co-operative Commonwealth Federation (CCF) which has a *reformist* democratic socialist ideology.

Federal–provincial relations and bargaining are an important factor in Canadian politics. Quebec has special provisions to safeguard its French language and culture. Separatist sentiment is strong and has been tested in referendums in 1980, 1985 and 1995. The administrative arrangements for social policies are highly variable and complex across the ten provinces and two territories. Central government has often claimed that welfare policies are a local responsibility in line with the poor-law tradition. Social policies were developed by the individual states up until the 1920s.

The first major federal government initiative in social policy was the introduction of *means-tested* pensions in 1927. The 1940 Unemployment Insurance Act set up a scheme which was paid for by contributions from employers and employees with benefits set at 60 per cent of earnings.

The ideas of Beveridge (see 4.6) inspired Marsh's 'Report on Social Security in Canada' of 1943 which was a blueprint for the Canadian system of welfare. Marsh had close personal links with Beveridge and was also associated with the International Labour Organization (ILO). Like Beveridge, the Marsh Report also recommended free medical care, child allowances and a back-up scheme of means-tested public assistance. The Marsh Report proposed a workers' insurance scheme for employment risks such as injury or joblessness and a general insurance programme for risks such as sickness and old age. The Marsh Report was not implemented in full but it remained an important point of reference for reformists in the post-war period.

A wide-ranging system of means-tested benefits under the control of the provinces was established by Canada Assistance in 1966. This provides the provinces with federal funds for equal cost sharing for spending on means-tested social assistance. National health insurance legislation was passed in 1966 although it took five years for the provinces to implement it fully. The federal government is responsible for universal programmes covering children, the unemployed and the elderly.

While the Canadian economy grew throughout the 1960s and 1970s unemployment remained relatively high. From the mid-1970s *new-right* ideology has been associated with cuts in welfare spending. In 1984 the Progressive Conservatives were elected on a programme committing them to maintaining social expenditure though after the election reduction of the budget deficit was given priority. Reviews of social policy were undertaken though the recommendations to cut Canada Assistance and to subject pensions to means tests created a great deal of public opposition and they were withdrawn. Changes were made to the benefit system which caused many of the unemployed to lose benefit entitlement, leaving them reliant on social assistance or charity. The principle of 'social responsibility', meaning the use of *means testing*, was applied to all areas except health care. Partly as result of these social policy changes the government became deeply unpopular.

In the general election of 1993 the Conservative Party was virtually eliminated, winning only 2 of the seats, having previously held 154, leaving the Liberal Party with a large majority. The Liberal Party was re-elected in 1997 but with only a small overall majority. The right-wing populist Reform Party is now the official opposition with 60 seats, since it now has more seats than the Conservatives. The separatist party in Quebec lost some of its support but still dominated the French-speaking area of Canada. The leftish New Democratic Party increased its representation from 9 to 21 seats.

RELATED TOPICS

1.11 Right-wing approaches: general features
1.15 Conservative paternalism
1.18 Reformist approaches: general features
4.4 Means-testing and selectivity
4.6 National Insurance

FURTHER READING

Bellamy and Irving (1989)
Mishra (1990) Chap 4

8.28 CANADA: POVERTY

Canada did not pursue a full-employment policy in the years of the long boom and unemployment often reached high levels during downturns of the business cycle. In 1956, a federal scheme of means-tested benefits for the unemployed was set up under the Unemployed Assistance Act. However, the main safety net for the poor is Canada Assistance, which was established in 1966. The Canada Assistance Plan has failed to act as an effective back-up for all those not otherwise eligible for benefits. Means-tested social assistance goes mainly to the aged, disabled, unemployed or to single parents.

... the Canada Assistance Plan ... established for the first time a major federal role in sharing the cost of conditional aid to mother-headed families as well as in sharing the cost of social services and health care not covered by national health insurance. (Leman, 1980: 37)

From 1973, schemes to supplement the wages of low-paid workers began to be developed by the provinces. There is a selective child-tax credit, which is index-linked and taxable though with some variation around the country.

By the early 1980s, unemployment was over 10 per cent. Policy has concentrated on job creation through *neo-liberal* policies of private sector growth, deregulation and tax cuts to high earners. Voluntary 'food banks' designed to distribute surplus food to the poor have been set up in many parts of Canada indicating continuing high levels of deprivation.

Cuts in benefit levels and entitlements have taken place. In 1985, pensions and family allowances were raised by inflation minus 3 per cent rather than in line with inflation. Severe deprivation occurs since benefit levels are one half or less of the poverty level. Figures from the UN Human Development Index show that in 1992 Canada had the fourth-highest score for inequality amongst 53 industrialised states.

RELATED TOPICS

2.17 Poverty: right-wing view
2.18 Poverty: reformist view
2.19 Poverty: Radical view
4.4 Means-testing and selectivity

FURTHER READING

Leman (1980) pp 33–41

8.29 CANADA: HEALTH CARE

There is a long history of state support for health going back to grants to voluntary bodies in the 1840s. The health-care system is a combination of publicly and privately financed services largely delivered by the private sector.

In 1957, the Hospital Insurance and Diagnostic Services Act provided federal cost sharing for provincial plans for health insurance for acute hospital care. This produced a 'socialised' system of payment for medical care but not for the delivery system.

The Medical Care Act of 1966 was partly based on developments under way in Saskatchewan since 1961 introduced by the Co-operative Commonwealth Federation. The act provides 'medicare', consisting of all doctor services, on an insurance basis. By 1971, all provinces were participating with 50 per cent of the cost paid by federal government.

The costs of health provision have risen rapidly from 3.4 per cent of GNP in 1956 to 8 per cent in the 1980s. As the costs rose and the state attempted to reduce payments to doctors, top-up bills began to be presented to patients. These direct charges undermined the principle of a free health service and deterred some people from seeking medical care. In 1984, the Canada Health Act replaced this system with one allowing greater control of bills and costs by the federal government. Provincial variations in health expenditure and the range of available specialist services continue to exist.

The Canadian health care system continues to be organized around the individual physician and fee-for-service payments, all within the framework of universal state health insurance. It is considered to be in a state of almost continual crisis. Escalating costs, particularly payments to physicians, has been the major contributing factor to this crisis. (Bellamy and Irving, 1989: 67)

RELATED TOPICS

4.6 National Insurance

FURTHER READING

Bellamy and Irving (1989)

8.30 CANADA: THE OLD

Pensions were first introduced in the Old Age Pensions Act of 1927, which allowed the federal government to reimburse provinces for means-tested payments made to the over-70s. Old Age Security (OAS) was set up in 1952 to give a nearly *universal* index-linked flat-rate pension for 20-year residents at age 70. The age limit was lowered to 65 from 1970. The spouse of a recipient of OAS is also entitled to a means-tested spouse allowance.

The Canada/Quebec Pension Plan (C/QPP) was established in 1966 to cover retirement, survivors' benefits and disability. It is a wage-linked scheme giving a pension of 25 per cent of earnings up to a specified maximum payment. Since 1967 there has been a means-tested Guaranteed Income Supplement (GIS) to OAS pensioners in need. Around half the population also accrue pension rights through tax-relieved pension contributions, though these are most common for public-sector workers.

The older people in Canada experience three major problems: economic insecurity, social neglect and psychological alienation. Economic insecurity is due to the lack of adequate income after retirement ... Because older people have no significant social role to perform they feel isolated and alienated from the mainstream of society ... (Yelaja, 1978b: 163–4)

Other services for the care of the old are the responsibility of the provinces. Since 1972, the Ontario Health Insurance Plan (OHIP) has provided insurance cover for homes for the aged and for nursing homes and similar schemes are found in other provinces, though there is no national policy.

RELATED TOPICS

4.4 Means-testing and selectivity
6.5 The old: social status

FURTHER READING

Yelaja (1978b)

8.31 CANADA: RACE

Canada is an ethnically diverse society with two major language groups, the French and English speakers, various indigenous peoples and immigrants from many countries. From 1845, Canada had a relatively open-door policy on immigration but from 1896 a racist policy excluding blacks was operated. Restricting immigration by race and ethnic characteristics was also required by an Immigration Act in 1953 which gave preference to those from the white Commonwealth. During the long period of post-war labour shortage immigration rules were relatively unrestrictive, though from 1967 educational criteria were employed. In the 1970s there was substantial immigration of Afro-Americans, Caribbean people and Asians.

From the eighteenth century indigenous Canadian Indians were subjected to the usual colonial processes including:

- subjugation
- suppression of traditional culture
- deprivation of lands
- denial of citizenship rights
- economic exploitation.

While it was expected that they might slowly assimilate by becoming 'civilised' and 'Christianised', federal voting rights were not given to Canadian Indians until 1960. The White Paper 'Statement of the Government of Canada on Indian Policy' in 1969 introduced a *reformist* approach. This proposed the removal of discrimination, equal rights, provision of extra assistance for the most oppressed and the return of control of Indian lands. The 'Statement' was viewed by many Indians as an attempt to enforce cultural assimilation rather than to recognise the distinctive features of Indian life and identity. Commitment to the maintenance of Indian social and cultural identity has been developing over the past few decades and assimilation now appears unlikely.

> The Indians, Inuit and Metis are not satisfied with the Canadian social welfare state at all. They reject it not only because of the inadequacy of the benefits it provides to them, nor because they have been the subject of deliberate measures intended to exert control and to force assimilation ... Their rejection stems from their demand that they be recognised as separate national peoples within the larger Canadian society. (Armitage, 1991: 256)

The existence of the English and French communities has also been a source of tension. Policy has generally been based on 'bilingualism and biculturalism'. In 1971, the official policy became one of multi-culturalism within a bilingual framework. In a referendum in 1980 in Quebec there was a 40 per cent vote for secession while the referendum in 1995 produced only a tiny majority in favour of Quebec's remaining a part of Canada. Regional, national and race issues played a key role in the 1997 general election. There was continued support in Quebec for the separatist party and the emergence of the right-wing populist Reform Party in the west of Canada.

RELATED TOPICS

2.20 Race: right-wing view
2.21 Race: reformist view
4.13 Empowerment
9.15 Race

FURTHER READING

Patterson (1978)

CHAPTER 9

Globalisation and social policy

Part 1 Global perspectives

9.1 GLOBALISATION

Globalisation in the study of social policy focuses on:

- social policy as a worldwide phenomenon
- policy making by supra-national bodies
- social policy implementation on an global scale.

The stress on globalisation corresponds to developments in the other social sciences in which this theme is emphasised. Global changes are not only important in themselves, they are also vital in understanding many apparently local issues. Local unemployment, ill-health, community breakdown and poverty can often be associated with global causes such as shifts in global employment patterns.

Globalisation is most evident in the economic sphere with the opening up of world markets. Global movements of labour and capital have been a feature of capitalism for centuries. The world economy is now dominated by transnational corporations (TNCs).

> ... globalisation ... is creating a world of increasingly porous borders, in which governments are being superseded by formidably powerful transnational companies (TNCs). The deregulation of markets and the growing power of international financial institutions have contributed to this trend. (Watkins, 1995: 3)

The growth of a global culture has taken place through the organisation of mass communications by giant media TNCs. These make widespread use of common programming patterns exposing many national populations to the same ideas, images and symbols. Developments in electronic communications such as satellites and fibre-optic cables have accelerated this aspect of globalisation.

In the area of social policy, world population has been a concern for some decades. Other central concerns in social policy can also be examined from a global perspective. *Poverty*, inequality and health are issues to which a global perspective can be applied.

Global organisations have been playing an increasingly important part in social policy over the past few decades. The World Health

Organization (WHO) and bodies like the *World Bank* and the *International Monetary Fund* (IMF) have a role in social policy-making:

1. Their influence may come from control of resources which they can dispense to states for specified purposes.
2. They may also be able to intervene in domestic debates on social policy through publication of reports, conferences and other public events.
3. They may be able to influence policy at 'insider' level through direct contact with policy makers such as politicians and civil servants.

Social policy making in global organisations shares some of the characteristics of policy-making at national level with the emergence of what can be described as a global 'civil society'. There are pressure groups or non-governmental organisations (NGOs) which attempt to influence global social policy making in a *pluralist* fashion. Many charities which in the past were mainly involved with fund raising are now attempting to influence policy at national and international level. These groups are becoming more effective through the creation of global networks and organisations. Recent international conferences have given an institutional role to NGOs, representing a range of charities and pressure groups concerned with the issue raised by the conference. They are now being drawn into the implementation of the policies of official agencies where these are eager to deflect criticism and develop new policies.

Political conflict can also be examined on a global scale.

1. This conflict may be affected by social divisions such as those based on *class*, *gender* and age, which can be viewed globally.
2. The major political ideologies have their own distinctive views on international issues and the proper organisation of the international system.
3. We can see the part played by 'world opinion' and the 'international community' in debates on global social policy issues.

Social policy debates in the international arena also have an impact on domestic policies through the influence they have on governments and public opinion:

- providing participants with information
- legitimating particular concerns
- adding authority to critics when domestic policies are author-itatively judged to fall short of international standards
- 'auditing' compliance with international standards.

RELATED TOPICS

1.18 Reformist approaches: general features
1.23 Welfare pluralism
3.4 Democratic elitism and technocracy
3.5 Social betterment
3.6 Pluralism
3.9 Marxism
3.10 New social movements
3.11 Feminism

FURTHER READING

New Internationalist, a monthly journal, is an indispensable source
   for most of the issues in this chapter
Deacon et al. (1997) Chap 1
Jones (1990) Chap 14
Townsend (1995)
United Nations (1994) Chap 1
Watkins (1995) Introduction

9.2 LIBERALISM

The principles of *liberalism* include:

* free speech
* legal equality
* freedom of movement
* freedom from arbitrary acts of government
* economic freedom
* political freedom.

Liberalism began as a revolutionary creed based on individual
freedom, and developed in opposition to aristocratic and autocratic
forms of government which denied personal freedom and
democracy. It was the ideology which was central to both the
American and French revolutions of the late eighteenth century.

   According to the liberal viewpoint, where freedom exists everyone
is able to develop their own capabilities to the full and conditions
are present for the greatest possible economic, social and cultural
development. Liberals claim that with free trade and national self-
determination the separate states will be able to develop fully to
the benefit of their own people and of world society as a whole.

   Free international trade would have even greater benefits: to trade
   itself, to world peace and to government expenditure through a
   limitation in armaments. The reduction of taxes consequent to
   this policy of non-intervention would in turn benefit the domestic
   economy. Colonies should be liberated and commercial ties

between nations should replace relationships of military and diplomatic superiority and inferiority ... Free Trade was the key to international peace and prosperity. Just as Cobden believed that freedom would see no essential hostility between the middle and working classes but rather the reverse, so with relations between nations in a climate of free competition. (Pearson and Williams, 1984: 47–8)

In the twentieth century liberalism has been associated with the idea of *citizenship* in which individuals actively shape the policies of government. The civil and political rights of individuals within a nation state have a parallel in the rights of states in international society. When these ideas are applied to the international system the relations between nation states should mirror those between individuals. Each state should be free, with full rights to self-determination. Liberal theory is thus opposed to all forms of colonialism and imperialism.

The implications of the liberal view for global social policies is that they are not needed. The best possible conditions of life for all will generally be ensured by free trade and completely free relations between the peoples of different countries.

RELATED TOPICS

1.17 Neo-liberalism (the new right)
2.15 Citizenship: reformist view
4.2 Privatisation
4.3 Provider markets

FURTHER READING

Pearson and Williams (1984) Chap 2

9.3 REFORMISM

Reformism always rests on the belief that organised intervention is necessary to achieve socially desirable goals. Attempts to create global institutions to regulate relations between states go back to the founding of the League of Nations in 1919. When the *United Nations* (UN) was founded in 1945 its aims were defined more broadly to create something like a system of global regulation affecting political, military, economic, social and cultural relations between states.

Global *reformism* seeks a world regulated by international law, economic agreements on trade, management of the international economy and aid for developing states. Global reformism has for long been evident in the field of economic management, where a broadly Keynesian system of international economic regulation was established in 1945 which operated until the early 1970s. In the post-war period global reformism has extended to cover many traditional areas of social policy such as *poverty* and health.

> ... social welfare provision is central to poverty reduction and economic growth. Healthy and educated people can, through productive employment, contribute effectively to economic growth. They can also benefit more from that growth. It is often argued that developing countries lack the resources substantially to improve the health care education, and nutrition of poor people. But what is actually lacking in most cases is the political will to make these resources available and to invest them in an equitable manner. (Watkins, 1995: 37)

According to the reformist view the *liberal* belief that free trade will lead to growing prosperity for all is incorrect. The process of market-led growth will generally lead to widening inequalities. Regions which are already developing benefit from a process of 'cumulative advantage'. They then attract further investment and continue to grow while other areas stagnate or even regress. Planned intervention is required to even out the process of development so that everyone can benefit from it. The international market is unstable and needs to be regulated by a system of global economic management.

The aim of international economic regulation is to stabilise international economic relations in order to increase prosperity, reduce economic fluctuations and cut domestic unemployment. The *International Monetary Fund* was originally designed to allow a system of fixed exchange rates to operate. With stable currency values, companies involved in importing raw materials and exporting their products would have a clear idea of future costs and revenues and be able to plan ahead with less uncertainty.

In the area of social policy similar considerations apply in that some problems may be global in scale and will not be solved without intervention. Poverty, ill-health, denial of rights, inadequate educational provision and social exclusion are all problems which need to be tackled on a global as well as a national scale. A global social policy in the form of organised international intervention is therefore required.

RELATED TOPICS

FURTHER READING
Deacon et al. (1997) Chap 6
Watkins (1995) Chap 7

9.4 RADICALISM

Radicals see the world economy as dominated by powerful capitalist states and by giant capitalist enterprises. *Marxism* uses the term 'uneven development' to describe the process by which the centre of gravity of capitalist economic development shifts over time from one country or region to another. There are two broad radical interpretations of the way in which the international economic system develops.

> In the classical Marxist account ... capitalism emerges first in a few centres ... Capitalism spreads, starting the same process in other areas. Different parts of the world [are] runners in the same race, in which some started before others. Any advantage gained by one at the expense of others is incidental.
>
> The alternative view [is of] Capitalism [as] production for profit within a world system of exchange and [of] the exploitation of some areas by others. The 'metropolis' or 'core' exploits the 'satellites' or 'periphery' by direct extraction of profit or tribute, by 'unequal exchange' or through monopolistic control over trade. Underdevelopment is not a state of original backwardness, but is the result of the imposition of a particular pattern of specialisation and exploitation in the periphery. (Brewer, 1980: 17)

The operation of capitalist firms is seen as playing an important part in the 'polarisation' of the international economy with the rich getting richer and the poor getting poorer. In the decade 1985–95 living standards in Africa fell by 2 per cent annually while the *Asian Tigers* grew by 5–10 per cent annually.

Foreign direct investment (FDI) is unevenly spread and contributes to the economic strengthening of a few regions. In 1993, 40 per cent of FDI was in developing countries with most of this concentrated in a handful of states in Asia and Latin America.

Transnational companies (TNCs) now account for a third of global output with the top 100 companies responsible for about 30 per cent of all direct foreign investment. The economic dominance of the TNCs allows them to play a major part in shaping global policies. They do this in part by dominating the institutions which undertake global regulation. TNCs also dominate the emerging global culture. TNCs are very difficult to regulate because their multinational operations put them outside the control of national governments. They encourage budgetary policies which reduce public expenditure and the use national social policies to support the capitalist system. They are often able to impose their own patterns of wages, training and industrial relations in the states where they operate.

Many radicals employ the concept of imperialism to describe the relations between the economically powerful states such as the US and the poorer states they deal with. The concept of neo-colonialism is used to describe the extensive patterns of influence which developed states sometimes exercise over the government of other states even in the absence of the direct political controls typical of classical colonialism.

According to the radical view, major international regulatory bodies such as the *World Bank* and the *International Monetary Fund* are dominated by capitalist interests. These bodies will normally attempt to solve crises by encouraging wage cuts and weakening worker organisations so as to increase the share of income going to profits. Radicals view economic crisis as a normal feature of the international capitalist economy. International control on the basis of radical principles is needed if the interests of people are to prevail over those of profits.

RELATED TOPICS

1.25 Radical approaches: general features
1.26 Marxism: 1 Capital logic
1.27 Marxism: 2 Balance of social forces
3.9 Marxism
3.10 New social movements
9.7 World Bank
9.8 International Monetary Fund

FURTHER READING

Brewer (1980) Part IV
Navarro (1982b) Chap 2

Part 2 Global agencies

9.5 THE UNITED NATIONS

The United Nations (UN) was formed in 1945 in an attempt to guarantee a world order for the post-war period. In 1945, the UN had 51 members and this had risen to 184 by 1994. The major victorious powers – Britain, the US and the USSR – were given permanent seats on the Security Council. The decisions of the Security Council are binding on members states though those of the General Assembly are not. A handful of the most powerful states provide most of the funds for the UN. The US pays 25 per cent of the budget and Germany, Japan, Russia, UK, France and Italy in total pay 44 per cent. The UN has an important peace-keeping function but about 70 per cent of its budget goes on development and on what can broadly be termed social policy.

The United Nations Economic and Social Council (ECOSOC) is the organisation in charge of social-welfare and health questions. It is composed of 27 members elected by the General Assembly, with a president elected for a one-year term.

The functions of the Council are the following:

1. to make or initiate studies, reports, and recommendations on international economic, social, cultural, educational, health and related matters
2. to promote respect for and observance of human rights and fundamental freedoms
3. to call international conferences
4. to prepare draft conventions for submission to the General Assembly on matters within the purview of the Economic and Social Council
5. to negotiate agreements with specialised agencies defining their relationship with the United Nations
6. to coordinate their activities by consultation with them and by further recommendations to the General Assembly and the members of the United Nations.

Among the commissions of the Council, several have important influence in the field of social welfare: the Population Commission, the Social Commission, the Commission on Human Rights, the Commission on the Status of Women. and the Commission on Narcotic Drugs. (Friedlander, 1975: 34)

The UN runs a series of specialised agencies such as:

- UN Children's Fund (UNICEF)
- UN High Commission for Refugees (UNHCR)
- UN Food and Agriculture Organization (FAO)
- World Health Organization (WHO)
- UN Educational, Social and Cultural Organization (UNESCO)
- UN Development Programme (UNDP)
- UN Conference on Trade and Development (UNCTAD).

The UN has sponsored several important conferences which have attempted to formulate policies on a range of economic and social issues. These include:

- the 1992 Earth Summit
- the 1994 Population Conference
- the World Summit on Social Development
- the 1995 Women's Conference.

The conferences usually end with a declaration signed by the participants setting standards or specifying policy goals.

Proposals have been made to restructure the UN in line with the changed global economic and political system. The Commission on Global Governance proposed various reforms:

- expand the Security Council by adding non-veto members from Europe (e.g. Germany), Asia (e.g. Japan) and from large states in the South (e.g. India, Brazil or Nigeria)
- establish an Economic Security Council to coordinate the response to global economic crises
- abolish the Economic and Social Council
- abolish the United Nations Conference on Trade and Development
- abolish the United Nations Industrial Development Organization.

In early 1997 Kofi Annan was elected UN Secretary-General with a brief to reform the UN bureaucracy. A deputy secretary-general will be put in charge of collaboration amongst UN organs. Human-rights issues will be given increased prominence. The UN will consolidate its programmes for international law enforcement by creating an office of drug control and crime prevention in Vienna. The work of aid agencies will be reorganised by placing them in one of two groups dealing either with humanitarian affairs or with development.

RELATED TOPICS

1.18 Reformist approaches: general features
3.3 Bureaucratic self-interest
3.4 Democratic elitism and technocracy
3.5 Social betterment
4.8 Administrative reorganisation

FURTHER READING

Commission on Global Governance (1995)
Deacon et al. (1997) Sections 3.9–10
Friedlander (1975) Chap 2

9.6 THE EUROPEAN UNION

What is now called the European Union (EU) began as the European Economic Community (EEC) which was founded as a customs union in 1957 by the Treaty of Rome. This involved internal free trade between the members with a common external tariff along with common policies towards agriculture, industry and energy. Effective power resides in the European Commission in partnership with the Council of Ministers. Moves have been made in the direction of greater democracy through direct elections for the European Parliament.

The founders of the EEC were partly inspired by a form of Catholic *corporatism* linked to the principles of Christian Democracy blending market efficiency with social solidarity. They sought to unify Europe around common institutions with a free-market economy managed through the participation of the 'social partners' (see 3.8).

The main EEC policy in terms of spending has been the Common Agricultural Policy (CAP), which began in 1964. This supports farm incomes by restricting sales of agricultural products in order to keep the prices at designated levels. Surplus production is bought and stored by the EEC. This policy involves a substantial redistribution from consumers to farmers. Since its formation in 1957 the EEC has gradually developed new initiatives with an explicit social policy dimension.

1. The Regional Fund was set up in 1972 to reduce regional inequalities and the *poverty* and unemployment they involve. The EU now dispenses regional funds to a range of groups and local authorities rather than to the national governments of member states.
2. Attempts have been made to develop common social policies amongst the member states. These have involved Directives from the European Commission requiring member states to adjust their social-policy legislation in order to ensure *gender* equality with equal social and employment rights for men and women.
3. The European Union (EU) Maastricht Treaty of 1991 contains *neo-liberal* provisions for 'fiscal convergence' and price stability which may necessitate public expenditure cuts. There is extensive social provision in its 'Social Chapter', which is based on the EU Social Charter. The Social Chapter contains a series of provisions relating to minimum standards in employee relations, social benefits and equal opportunities though the UK negotiated an 'opt out' from its terms. The Labour government elected in Britain in 1997 proposed to adopt the Social Chapter.
4. There is a Social Fund, which was originally intended to improve the geographical and occupational mobility of labour by assisting with training and retraining. It now also deals with health and safety, the living standards of workers and with 'social exclusion'.

The priority which has constantly, and understandably, been given to economic objectives has gone hand in hand with an emphasis on workers' rather than citizenship rights. If social policy is by definition applicable and redistributive, then the focus on workers could be seen as creating a serious deficit in coverage. (Hantrais, 1995: 197)

The EU also has a global social policy role through foreign aid regulated by the Lome Convention which manages its relations with 70 developing world countries. *Radical* critics argue that the EEC is based predominantly on support for private capital. Supporters of the *new right* are opposed to *reformist* social policies such as the Social Chapter, since they see employee rights as undermining the competitiveness of firms.

The *reformist* viewpoint seems to be gaining support. In early 1997 the issue of unemployment began to be given more prominence in the EU with concern about the 18 million jobless in the EU. The election of moderate socialist governments in France and the UK contributed to this process. There have been proposals to add a chapter on jobs to the criteria specified for monetary union in the Maastricht Treaty. It has also been argued by the French government that European Union governments must coordinate their economic policies and promote growth by stimulating demand, not by trying to compete with each other through 'social dumping' – lowering wages and reducing welfare provision.

The further development of 'social Europe' is seen as a priority. This is partly reflected in the terms of the Treaty of Amsterdam of 1997. The treaty outlaws all discrimination based on *gender, race,* religion, sexual orientation, age or disability. There will be more emphasis on combating social exclusion affecting the unemployed, the poor, the elderly and the disabled. The 'democratic deficit' in the EU will be reduced by giving the European Parliament law-making powers equal to the Council of Ministers in more policy areas.

RELATED TOPICS

1.14 Social imperialism
1.17 Neo-liberalism (the new right)
2.6 Gender: reformist view
8.7 Ireland: background

FURTHER READING

Burkitt and Baimbridge (1995)
Cochrane (1993b)
Deacon et al. (1997) Section 3.8
Moore (1993) Chap 10

9.7 WORLD BANK

The World Bank was founded in 1944 at the Bretton Woods conference. It lends to developing countries, which use the money to pay for development projects. It runs the International Development Association (IDA) with 155 members. This channels foreign aid from donor countries to the poorest nations. More than half of the money lent by the IDA goes back to companies in wealthy countries as payment for goods and services.

> The World Bank's statutes specifically enjoin it to promote the flow of private investment to underdeveloped countries, and an internal memorandum states that it must not lend to countries that nationalise without adequate compensation, default on their debts or act in other ways unsatisfactory to private investors. (Hayter, 1983: 88)

From the 1970s the bank worked in cooperation with the IMF to reform the economies of aid recipients through Structural Adjustment Programmes (SAPs). SAPs are based on *new right* principles of reduced state spending, monetary restriction and privatisation. These policies were supposed to create the conditions for growth by eliminating inflation. In reality they often led to increased *poverty* and inequality as large numbers of people lost their jobs with the destruction of labour-intensive industries.

In recent years the bank has not made much of a net contribution to development funds and in 1993–4 in net terms it lent minus $700 million due to repayments of loans. The bank has until recently refused to consider writing off these loans, which account for 36 per cent of all foreign debt in Africa.

For many years the bank concentrated on financing very large projects. In recent years this has been strongly criticised on economic, social environmental grounds. Major projects were said by critics to have:

- increased inequalities
- led to the displacement of populations
- failed to bring economic benefits.

There is some evidence that the World Bank is moving away from its past approach and endeavouring to become more responsive to *reformist* criticism. In 1987, the president of the bank admitted to major shortcomings and it has developed a range of social policies to supplement its economic objectives. Following the Earth Summit in 1992 the bank now has the job of giving out environmental loans under the Global Environmental Facility. The bank is now involved with environmental assessments, assisting with pollution control, 'sustainable' agriculture and conservation of natural resources.

Support for the Arun dam project in Nepal was abandoned in 1995 after strong criticism, some of it from within the bank. A micro-loan scheme was proposed in 1995 in the report 'The World Bank's Strategy for Reducing Poverty and Hunger' and $200 million was earmarked project to provide funds to develop small businesses.

The bank plays a role in developing higher education and has lent over $5 billion for this since 1980. It produced a report in 1994 which argued that students should pay tuition fees to help to pay for their own education, since many are from better-off families while poorer students could be given loans or grants. It also favours greater use of private finance, including private universities.

In 1993, in its yearly 'World Development Report' the World Bank entered the field of health. It cooperated with the WHO to assess the impact of diseases using a new measure, DALYs (Disability Adjusted Life Years). The World Bank has also intervened in the debate on old age on the grounds that the increasing numbers of old people are creating a crisis for social expenditure.

In a policy statement in 1994, entitled 'Embracing the Future', the bank claims that its central aim is to improve human and social welfare. This involves:

- support for (moderate) trade unionism
- encouragement for labour protection
- a strategy designed to create jobs.

The bank now states that the reduction of *poverty* is a central objective and the criterion by which it should be judged. However, criticism from radicals has been continuous since the late 1980s. In 1988, protesters in Berlin set up a tribunal to 'try' the bank and the IMF for 'destroying global ecological stability and organising the poverty of the world people'. The policies of the bank have been opposed by radical NGOs on the occasion of its 50th anniversary under the slogan 'Fifty years is enough'. In a partial response the bank plans that about half its lending from 1994 will be done in partnership with NGOs. The bank's World Development Report for 1997, entitled 'The State in a Changing World', comes down against the *liberal* conception of the minimalist state in favour of an 'effective state' whose key tasks include investing in basic social services and infrastructure.

RELATED TOPICS

FURTHER READING
Brand (1994)
Deacon et al. (1997) Section 3.4
Watkins (1995) Chap 3

9.8 INTERNATIONAL MONETARY FUND

In 1945, the International Monetary Fund (IMF) was established to regulate exchange rates and to prevent balance-of-payments crises in member countries from destabilising the international monetary system. The IMF was intended to pursue what was seen as the common interest of all states in stable trading conditions. The international payments system was to be based on fixed but adjustable exchange rates. It was designed on modified Keynesian lines to assist states in temporary difficulties.

For much of the post-war period the role of the IMF was to support the trading system dominated by the industrialised states. Most of its larger loans were given to advanced states which were experiencing balance-of-payments problems. When the era of fixed exchange rates ended in the early 1970s the original rationale for the IMF disappeared and it was, in effect, given the new role of propagating the economic doctrines of the *new right*.

In the 1980s loans were more commonly made to countries outside the small circle of advanced capitalist economies only on condition that Structural Adjustment Policies (SAPs) (see 9.7) were adopted and *neo-liberal* monetarist policies were pursued. This was based on the assumption that these policies would improve social welfare, since its benefits would 'trickle down' to the poorer members of society. The recommended policies involved cuts in state spending and reductions in social welfare budgets. This policy was based on the liberal belief that minimal state intervention and freedom from restrictions on trade and investment was the only way in which governments could achieve economic advance.

> ... structural adjustment ... refers to the process by which many developing nations are reshaping their economies to be more free market oriented ... structural adjustment assumes that an economy will be most efficient, healthy and productive in the long run if market forces operate, and products and services are not protected, subsidised, heavily regulated or produced by the government. (Sparr, 1994: 1)

The success of the *Asian Tigers* such as South Korea and Hong Kong has caused a partial re-think of the rigid free market doctrine. In these countries rapid economic growth has been linked to various forms of state intervention. In several cases these have involved:

1. incentives for manufacturing exports
2. protection of domestic industries
3. massive state spending on economic infrastructure
4. controls on interest rates in order to provide business with cheap loans.

The issue of how to deal with the former communist states after the collapse of the pro-Soviet regimes in 1989 highlighted divisions about the role of the IMF. The IMF wished to use substantial resources to 'stabilise' Eastern Europe at the expense of developing world countries and massive stand-by credits were given to Poland and Hungary in 1993. This was opposed by states in the developing world, which saw this as involving a reduction in the funds available to them.

In recent years the issue of debt relief has created considerable difficulty for the IMF. There have been proposals to reduce or even write off some developing-world debts but agreement on how to do this has proved hard to obtain. Disagreement has centred:

• on eligibility criteria
• on which countries to include
• on whether to sell off some of the IMF gold reserves to pay for debt relief.

A limited plan was finally agreed in 1996 to deal with some of the HIPCs (Heavily Indebted Poor Countries).

There also some indications that the IMF is beginning to reassess the value of free-market policies and showing interest again in managed exchange rates. This is a move to more *reformist* policies, which partly mirror the changes currently taking place in the World Bank.

RELATED TOPICS

1.17 Neo-liberalism (the new right)
1.18 Reformist approaches: general features
7.3 The Asian Tigers
7.10 The former USSR and the new Eastern Europe
9.7 World Bank

FURTHER READING

Brand (1994)
Deacon et al. (1997) Section 3.3
Watkins (1995) Chap 3

9.9 GATT AND THE WORLD TRADE ORGANIZATION

The General Agreement on Tariffs and Trade (GATT) was founded in 1947 by 23 of the world's richest countries in order to liberalise trade. GATT has now been succeeded by the World Trade Organization (WTO). GATT was designed to reduce protectionism and members agreed to negotiate tariff reductions in order to increase trade. One effect was to make it very hard for poorer countries to develop their own manufacturing industries. Critics argue that this involved a covert policy to keep poor countries reliant on the export of 'primary' agricultural or mineral products. GATT has operated as a forum for negotiating reductions in tariffs at a series of 'rounds' since the end of the Second World War. The last of these was the Uruguay round, which was completed in 1994.

> In contrast to the GATT, its successor has wide-ranging powers to enforce compliance with the principles of trade liberalisation ... the Uruguay Round agreement, which the WTO will oversee, does not address many of the interlocking problems facing developing country exporters, such as commodity price stabilisation ... the GATT agreement on agriculture, which the WTO will implement, does little to address long-standing problems of subsidised over-production in the industrialised countries. There is also a growing concern that the WTO does not create a viable framework for the social and environmental regulation of international trade. While the treaty includes a commitment to promoting sustainable development, its rules are focused almost entirely upon the narrower objective of trade expansion. (Watkins, 1995: 117)

A new development is the plan for a 'social clause' dealing with the issue of labour standards which is to be included in the next set of GATT negotiations. The subjects to be covered are safety at work, union rights, discrimination at work and child labour. Critics in some poor countries believe that these clauses may be used to justify discriminating against their exports by making it more difficult for their manufacturing industries to trade profitably. The International Confederation of Free Trade Unions' proposal for the social clause suggests incorporating the internationally recognised core International Labour Organization conventions, covering the rights to freedom of association, collective bargaining, freedom from discrimination, equal remuneration, forced labour and child labour.

RELATED TOPICS

1.17 Neo-liberalism (the new right)

1.18 Reformist approaches: general features
9.2 Liberalism

FURTHER READING

Watkins (1995) Chap 4

9.10 THE OECD

The Organization for Economic Co-operation and Development (OECD) is made up of representatives from 29 advanced capitalist states along with some of the states of the *new Eastern Europe* including Hungary and the Czech Republic. The OECD works through its contacts with ministers and top officials involved with economic policies in member states. The OECD exercises an important influence over its member states through regular and special reports on a range of policy issues, many of which are central to social policy. It also intervenes by influencing public opinion and domestic policy debates through well-publicised reports on a range of topics including social policies.

Within the OECD an important role has been played by the 'Group of Seven', the UK, US, Canada, Japan, France, Germany and Italy. However, the balance of world economic power is now shifting away from the Group of Seven with the sustained high growth rates of the *Asian Tigers* and of *China*.

In the 1980s the OECD strongly supported *neo-liberal* policies recommending restrictions on welfare spending. However, in the mid-1990s, after a sustained period of high unemployment the OECD has starting to argue for 'active labour-market measures' to increase the number of jobs. The OECD now favours state action to improve the employment prospects of minorities and other disadvantaged groups in part because this increases economic efficiency by widening the pool of talent available to employers. This might appear as a shift in the direction of *reformism* from the traditionally free-market policies of the OECD. However, given that this new concern about unemployment is due to its view that 'social cohesion' will otherwise be undermined, it can also be interpreted as a *Bismarckian* approach.

There does appear to have been a shift in policy from *neo-liberalism* towards social *reformism*. The OECD Employment Outlook for 1996 criticised the widening gulf between workers, especially in the US and the UK. It argues in favour of minimum wages saying that they do not appear to cause job losses among the most affected groups – women, young people and the unskilled. In 1997, the OECD announced that it no longer supported the view that the existence of trade unions increased unemployment.

9.11 OFFICIAL AID PROGRAMMES

Much of the foreign capital received by emergent nations consists of aid. Aid can be 'bilateral', where one country provides aid to another, or 'multilateral', where some agency such as the *IMF* or the *World Bank* dispenses aid on behalf of a number of donors. Aid may involve grants, loans, technical assistance or military aid.

Most aid consists of loans tied to particular projects with economic or political conditions attached to its receipt. Aid in the form of loans has given rise to a huge burden of debt which continued to increase during the 1980s. It has also given the creditors the power to intervene in the domestic affairs, including the social policies, of the debtor countries through bodies such as the IMF and World Bank. The 'Structural Adjustment Programmes' (SAPs) (see 9.7) that have been imposed have not solved the debt crisis.

Aid is used for political and strategic purposes as well as having a humanitarian role.

- The US used to concentrate aid on Latin America and on nations bordering the Soviet Union.
- There is now greater concern with the *new Eastern European* states which were formerly in the Soviet bloc and aid is designed to integrate them into the Western capitalist order.
- British aid policies are mainly directed towards the Commonwealth, which receives 80 per cent of the funds distributed.

The institutions providing funds – especially the two most powerful, the World Bank and the International Monetary Fund – insist that their advice is purely technical, value-free and objective ... But in fact the recommendations follow a predictable pattern, which accords with an easily recognisable right-wing ideology and which has at times caused considerable hardship to the peoples of the countries receiving 'aid'. (Hayter, 1983: 97–8)

In 1993 the British aid programme, at 0.28 per cent of GNP, fell well short of the UN aid target of 0.7 per cent. British aid favours countries that purchase substantial British exports or that provide important raw materials. Aid is also made available to countries that purchase British arms, as the Pergau dam affair showed. Arms worth £1.3 billion were sold to Malaysia as part of a deal involving aid of £234 million for the Pergau dam. The Labour government elected in 1997 has announced that the 'aid and trade' policy will be abandoned.

There is considerable debate about whether aid is of great benefit to recipient states. The *liberal* view is that poor countries benefit from the 'trickle down' of wealth from the advanced states and that aid is unnecessary. Many liberals believe that aid also encourages government inefficiency and corruption in recipient states. The *neo-liberal* Institute of Economic Affairs has recently proposed that multinational companies should be given the right to run whole countries. Companies would have to tender for leases of up to 21 years, promising to provide specific services in return for pre-set tax revenue.

Radicals argue that:

• Aid may lead to an unbalanced pattern of development, technological dependence, massive outflows of capital and crippling debt repayments.
• Food aid for countries with an agricultural deficit may lead to the destruction of indigenous agriculture.
• Aid for agricultural development in the form of the 'green revolution' which uses high-productivity crop strains can also be counter-productive. These new plants require high inputs of fertiliser and machinery and the richer farmers who can afford them buy up neighbouring smaller plots and invest in more machines leaving the previous occupants unemployed and increasing social and economic inequalities.

The *reformist* approach to aid is most clearly articulated in the Brandt Report of 1980. The Brandt Report proposed a transfer of purchasing power to poorer countries through aid and the reform of international economic institutions to give more weight to the interests of the developing world. Reformists also argue that aid budgets should be restructured with less spent on technical assistance by Western experts and professionals at the same time as the pool of highly educated indigenous people is being depleted by migration to the West. The Human Development Report produced by the UN Development Programme suggests the aim of aid should be 'human security' rather than 'national security'.

There have been pressures from radicals and reformists to adopt a more *pluralist* approach to administering aid. In response the US has announced that 40 per cent of its future aid will be dispensed through the relevant NGOs (non-governmental organisations) rather than governments. In the mid-1980s the idea of focusing aid on basic needs such as education, sanitation, nutrition, health care and family planning became more influential.

RELATED TOPICS

1.23 Welfare pluralism
3.5 Social betterment
3.6 Pluralism
4.2 Privatisation
9.7 World Bank
9.8 International Monetary Fund
9.18 Poverty

FURTHER READING

Brandt (1983)
Elson (1982)
Hardiman and Midgley (1982) Chap 10
Hayter (1976)
Hayter (1983) pp 82–96
Hayter (1985)
Watkins (1995) Chap 6

9.12 THE VOLUNTARY SECTOR

The voluntary sector plays a significant and growing part in the international arena both in exerting pressure for particular services and by providing services directly or as the agents of governments or international bodies. What are now termed NGOs (non-governmental organisations) not only influence policy but are increasingly being taken on by official agencies in a partnership role in the making and implementation of policy. The development of *new social movements* operating on an international scale has had an important impact on policy. The green movement and feminism have both played a major role in recent debates about global social policies.

... thousands of NGOs ... lobbied the Earth Summit in 1992 and the World Summit for Social Development in 1995. The communiqués agreed at those Summits bear the imprint of their influence. Some NGOs are now working to encourage the public pressure for change which will be needed to translate the agreed principles into practice. Others are working together in regional and international networks to address human development problems associated with conflict, trade, and finance, in an attempt to force the interests of the poor on to the agendas of the world's governments. (Watkins, 1995: 2–3)

Charities are a significant element in the international voluntary sector. The three main relevant types are:

1. agencies such as Christian Aid and Oxfam which undertake general aid work
2. missionary evangelical societies which seek converts
3. sponsorship bodies which send aid to individual people or localities.

Charities obtain most of their funds from voluntary donations but they may also receive some government funds. In Britain state funding accounts for 16 per cent of the income of Oxfam and over 33 per cent of that of Christian Aid (UK). The incomes of many of these charities have grown substantially in recent years. The income of Christian Aid (UK) rose by 204 per cent and Save the Children (UK) by 274 per cent from 1983 to 1993.

Some of the major charities have changed the scope of their activities and developed new modes of intervention. Oxfam began in 1942 with a focus on famine relief and for many years it worked principally as a fund-raising body. In the 1960s, when awareness of developing world *poverty* and under-development increased, it began to take an interest in development issues and in the provision of development aid rather than emergency relief. Within charities like Oxfam there was also a move towards a more *radical* approach with an emphasis on political liberation and global political change.

In the 1970s, there was a general shift from paternalism towards working with, rather than for, the peoples of developing countries. In the 1980s both emergency aid and development became important political issues in some Western states.

RELATED TOPICS

1.23 Welfare pluralism
3.6 Pluralism
3.11 Feminism
3.10 New social movements
4.9 Participation
4.13 Empowerment

FURTHER READING

Deacon et al. (1997) Sections 5.1–3

Part 3 Global social divisions

9.13 CLASS

Radicals view the operation of the international economic system as involving the exploitation of developing world countries in a way that parallels the exploitation of the working class by the capitalist class. Direct foreign investment can lead to:

- economic and technological dependence
- the destruction of local industries
- capital export in the form of the repatriated profits of TNCs.

Many new states suffer from the legacy of colonial trade patterns based on exports of primary products. Many developed states have erected barriers to the import of manufactured goods from the emergent states by the use of tariffs, quotas, foreign-exchange restrictions, licences and anti-dumping regulations.

> Northern governments, which control the governance of the world economy, are content to tolerate and maintain trade and financial structures which concentrate wealth in the industrialised world, while excluding the poorest countries and people from a share in global prosperity. For their part, most Third World governments ... maintain systems of income and land distribution which exclude poor people; they concentrate public investment in areas where it maximises returns to the wealthy and minimises returns to the poor; and all too often they waste vast sums on armaments ... (Watkins, 1995: 6)

The gap between the richest and the poorest countries is increasing. Between 1960 and 1979 the share of world income going to the richest 20 per cent of the world's people increased from 70 per cent to over 82 per cent. The poorest 40 or 50 countries with a fifth of the world's population get less than 1.5 per cent of world income. The UN Human Development Report for 1996 called for a three-way strategy to reverse increasing income inequalities:

- a target of 3 per cent per capita growth in the poorest countries
- an emphasis on making expansion sustainable and more equitable
- action to avoid the five forms of undesirable growth:
  1. jobless growth
  2. ruthless growth where only the rich benefit
  3. anti-democratic voiceless growth
  4. unsustainable futureless growth
  5. rootless growth which tramples on cultural identities.

The employment picture in developing countries varies. A few countries such as Taiwan and South Korea have a labour shortage. Much of sub-Saharan Africa has urban unemployment rates of around 20 per cent and in Latin America they are about 10 per cent. Employment in many countries is becoming increasingly precarious with large firms reluctant to take on permanent staff.

'Under-employment' is becoming common with the under-employed often working in the informal sector as small-scale own-account workers in unofficial and casual employment. Globally around 700 million people are unemployed or under-employed, making up massive global reserve army of labour (see 2.7).

Migration in search of work and better wages has resulted in around 100 million people living in 'foreign' countries often as illegal immigrants. These workers may lack rights and be subject to the discrimination commonly experienced by ethnic minorities.

There is little sign that global class divisions are decreasing. In the 1980s policies pursued at an international level appear to have increased them. The debt crisis and the consequent imposition of Structural Adjustment Programmes (SAPs) has increased inequalities in the countries affected.

RELATED TOPICS

1.25 Radical approaches: general features
1.26 Marxism: 1 Capital logic
1.27 Marxism: 2 Balance of social forces
2.22 Race: radical view
3.9 Marxism
9.18 Poverty

FURTHER READING

Deacon et al. (1997) Section 2.4
George (1992)

9.14 GENDER

In the past two decades issues concerning women have become central to the global debate on development:

- *Radicals* and *reformists* have sought to advance women's rights and the achievement of equality.
- *Conservatives* have advanced their traditionalist views on family planning, abortion, sexuality and women's role as mothers, through fundamentalist *Islamic* and Christian movements, and the Vatican.
- *Feminists* have argued that investment in women is the key to development and that women's education is essential for their health and for that of their children.

The first UN Conference on Women was in 1975 and in 1979 the UN General Assembly supported a convention on the elimination of discrimination against women. Some 41 countries did not sign, and 43, including Britain, only ratified it with reservations. The third UN Women's Conference in 1985 produced a plan for women's equality in UN member states by the year 2000 with progress to be monitored every five years.

Women's political participation varies greatly, measured by the proportion of female parliamentary representatives. Sweden is at the top with 42 per cent while Australia, France, Greece and Japan have below 10 per cent. In some countries such as Bahrain, Kuwait and the United Arab Emirates women cannot stand for election or vote.

> Women are subject to multiple forms of deprivation from the cradle to the grave. Throughout the world, women play a key role in household livelihood systems in a productive and reproductive capacity. As producers, they provide most of the food consumed by poor households, performing more than threequarters of agricultural labour in many countries. In addition, they manage common resources, and are responsible for collecting water and firewood. Female labour also accounts for a growing proportion of employment in commercial agriculture and industry. Despite this contribution, women face a bewildering array of social, economic, cultural, and religious barriers to their equal participation in society. (Watkins, 1995: 26)

According to research undertaken using a Gender-related Development Index (GDI) comparing literacy, life expectancy and economic data, there is no society in which women fare as well as men. Sweden scores best with 92 per cent but 45 of 130 countries score below 50 per cent.

Gender issues cover various aspects of global social policy:

- Equality of property rights is an issue in those countries in Asia, Africa and the Middle East which employ customary law.
- Inequalities in access to education are common in Africa, South Asia and the Middle East.
- According to the WHO report 'Bridging the Gaps', inequality in health between the sexes is increasing.
- Poverty generally is 'feminised' and this is accentuated in old age.

The promotion of *neo-liberal* policies has had an adverse impact on women.

> ... research suggests that when the various policies associated with moving towards a more free-market economy are taken together, they potentially have profound and wide-ranging effects on the lives of women and girls. They influence: women and girls'

health and safety; educational attainment; income; employment; working conditions; access to land; marital status; family relationships; mental health; self concept; birth rates; marriage decisions ... and their understanding of their role and possibilities in life. (Sparr, 1994: 20–1)

According to the International Labour Organization (ILO) the gap between the wages of men and women only closed slightly in the decade 1985–95. The proportion of working women is rising globally and by 2000 women will make up half the labour force as against a third in 1990. The fifth annual Human Development Report for the UN Development Programme on women's economic position shows that globally women make a major contribution to economic output through unpaid work. Two-thirds of women's work (and a quarter of men's) is unpaid and amounts to 70 per cent of annual global output of $23,000 billion. On average, women work 13 per cent more than men though there are marked national differences.

Women also suffer globally from violence directed towards them:

- The ILO has taken up the issue of sexual harassment of working women and found that 15–30 per cent had experienced this.
- Owing to nutritional neglect and sometimes infanticide about 100 million women are 'missing' from the population of the developing world. More than half a million mothers die in childbirth every year.
- In many countries women are subject to a high risk of domestic violence. In India up to 4,000 women a year are murdered in conflicts over dowries.
- Women suffer disproportionately from the impact of political violence. About 80 per cent of all refugees are women and their dependent children.

In 1997 for the first time UNICEF included a section in its annual Progress of Nations report on violence against women. It also employed the notion of 'gender crime' to refer to such actions as bride-burning, domestic violence and genital mutilation.

RELATED TOPICS

2.5 Gender: right-wing view
2.6 Gender: reformist view
2.7 Gender: radical view
2.16 Citizenship: radical view
3.10 New social movements
7.11 Islamic social policy

FURTHER READING
Jones (1990) Chap 11
Mosse (1993)

9.15 RACE

In the past the concept of *race* was used to classify people genetically into four distinct races: Caucasian, Negroid, Asian and Mongoloid. While this classification is not so widely used today as it once was, the concept of race is still important. It is useful to distinguish between race and ethnicity. A race or racial group is socially defined by physical characteristics such as colour or facial appearance. An ethnic group is defined by cultural criteria such as language, diet, dress or accent. Racism involves a negative view of a group based on its perceived physical characteristics.

Racism has strong roots in the slave trade where black people were treated as commodities to be bought and sold and worked for profit. Racism lives on in ex-colonies and in the states formerly involved in the slave trade. Immigrants from ex-colonies are often brought into the former colonial country as a source of cheap labour. They commonly become the victims of racism. Racial minorities are often subject to high levels of discrimination, unemployment, criminal victimisation and incarceration. In the industrialised states 'institutional racism' may be built into state policy.

In the past 50 years around 40 ethnic groups have been subject to state-organised genocidal attacks. Nation states have often persecuted indigenous peoples. Many are still being subjected to genocidal repression or forced into subjection to dominant groups.

> The degree of violence so frequently generated by racial and ethnic relations raises a further set of fundamental issues ... Two of the most extreme manifestations of violence, warfare and genocide, are rarely even mentioned in textbooks on race relations ... One extreme argument maintains that it will be a 'race war', not class conflict or war between states, that will fuel the next major outburst of global violence. (Stone, 1985: 152–3)

There is evidence of the growth of racism in Europe affecting the 17 million ethnic-minority members. In response it has been proposed that the *European Union* should take action. According to the Kahn Report, commissioned after the 1994 EU Corfu summit, the Maastricht Treaty should be amended to criminalise discrimination. The report recommends an approach mainly based on *reformist* principles of enforcing rights and employing education. This would give the EU the right to oppose discrimination on racial, ethnic or religious grounds and serve directives to enforce this on member states. It proposes:

- a code of ethics against racism
- a European ombudsman
- teaching human rights and non-discrimination in schools
- producing an anti-racist handbook setting out rights.

RELATED TOPICS

1.9 Clarke, Cochrane and Smart: ideologies of welfare
2.19 Poverty: radical view
2.20 Race: right-wing view
2.21 Race: reformist view
2.22 Race: radical view
3.10 New social movements
9.6 The European Union

FURTHER READING

Banton (1988) Chap 1
Eriksen (1993)
Stone (1985) Chap 1
United Nations (1994) Chap 13

Part 4 Global social policy

9.16 POPULATION

The issue of *population* provokes sharp ideological divisions.

> The neo-Malthusian arguments ... include the [view that] the developing countries are overpopulated [and that] rapid population growth makes it impossible to achieve satisfactory social and economic progress ... The conclusion from these arguments is that all efforts must be concentrated on family planning programs. The anti-imperialist ideology ... purports that the concept of 'overpopulation' is unscientific ... It has become so popular because [it] creates the impression that the chief reason why there is so much poverty, unemployment, large slum areas in too rapidly expanding cities, and slow economic development is because there are 'too many people.' (Hofsten, 1982: 173–4)

The orthodox view on population in the 1950s and 1960s was that economic growth was the key to reducing the rate of population expansion. As people became better off it was believed that the incentive for having larger numbers of children would be reduced, since parents would no longer need large families to ensure that some children survived and that there would be children to care for them in old age. This view has always been challenged by proponents of limiting population through family planning.

The UN Population Fund which is responsible for family planning wishes to stabilise world population at 7.8 billion by 2050. Population growth rates have been falling in many countries without increases in per capita income, owing to the increased use of contraception. In the 1970s attempts at compulsory family-size limitation were tried in India. Similar methods are being employed in China's 'one-child family' policy which includes compulsory sterilisation and abortion.

Another population issue concerns the global capacity to expand food output. The Worldwatch Institute report 'Full House' argues that food scarcity is a major emerging global problem. It predicts world population will rise to 8.9 billion by 2030 with the biggest increases in the poorest areas. It points to declining fishing catches and a falling growth in crop yields.

Worldwatch also suggests the problem is exacerbated by rising income inequalities, since the richest and the poorest do most ecological damage. The rich consume huge quantities of energy, raw materials and manufactured goods. The poor often grow crops, graze cattle or fell trees in ways that harm the earth. In contrast to the Worldwatch view, the UN Food and Agriculture Organization (FAO) believes output growth will continue at high rates.

RELATED TOPICS

1.16 Eugenics
1.29 Illich and anti-industrialism
7.9 China

FURTHER READING

Hardiman and Midgley (1982) Chap 3
Hofsten (1982)
Jones (1990) Chap 12
United Nations (1994) Chap 5

9.17 CITIZENSHIP AND RIGHTS

The notion of rights originates in *liberalism* though it has been extended to new areas such as sexual orientation and to groups not previously designated for this purpose such as the disabled and children.

Rights' theorists claim that there are basic and universal features of human life which can be recognised as existing within any moral, ideological or religious framework. Whatever the belief system, certain universal human rights can be recognised. Two criteria are crucial: universalism and moral relevance. The universal feature of humanity in terms of which rights should be recognised is ... the capacity of human beings for agency, deliberation, and choice. (Hill, 1992: 2)

There is a European Convention on Human Rights. This covers the following rights, which are enforceable by the European Court of Human Rights:

- the right to life, liberty and security of the person
- the right to a fair trial and access to justice
- respect for private and family life, home and correspondence
- freedom of thought, conscience and religion
- the right to free expression, including freedom of the press
- freedom of assembly and association, including the right to join a trade union
- the right to marry and found a family
- the right to peaceful enjoyment of possessions
- the right to education
- the right to free elections by secret ballot
- the prohibition of torture, inhuman or degrading treatment
- the prohibition of slavery, servitude or forced labour
- the prohibition of criminal laws that are retrospective.

The *United Nations* has a Charter of Human Rights and a Commission to promote it and a charter for The Rights of the Child. In 1993 there was a UN World Conference on Human Rights in Vienna. This created the office of Commissioner for Human Rights with a budget of £30 million per year and 450 staff, many of whom are involved in monitoring human rights in selected states. Amnesty International has criticised the organisation for 'diplomatisation', i.e. dealing with human rights by behind-the-scenes negotiation rather than by public campaigning. In 1997, the former President of Ireland, Mary Robinson, was appointed Commissioner and a more vigorous approach is anticipated.

There are competing views of human rights. The West tends to focus on individual rights linked to the principles of *liberalism* such as free speech, freedom from torture and freedom of conscience. Representatives from the developing states tend to focus more on the right to social and economic progress and on community rights.

The distribution of different types of political regime is an important factor in human rights. In 1993 5 per cent of the global population lived under military rule, 30 per cent in one-party states and 65 per cent in multi-party regimes. Human rights are generally better protected in pluralist democracies. Human rights are often violated in conditions of civil war or intense political conflict where the state organises or condones the use of 'death squads' or the 'disappearance' of political opponents. In Latin America in the 1970s and 1980s these methods of suppression of opposition were widely used under the tutelage of the US. Human-rights violations include:

- transgression of the rules of war
- imprisonment of opponents
- attacks on civilians, including the organised rape of women.

Many people lack enforceable human rights because they do not qualify as citizens of the state they live in or because the state does not assign *citizenship* rights to them. These groups include:

1. refugees
2. stateless people
3. slaves
4. indentured labourers.
5. indigenous peoples.

The UNHCR was set up in 1950 to take responsibility for the care of refugees though its budget has not kept pace with the increased numbers of refugees in the 1980s. Palestinian refugees are covered by the UN Relief and Works Agency for Palestinian Refugees (UNRWA). Officially, refugees are people who have been expelled from or fled from their country of origin because of persecution. Under the 1951 Convention Relating to the Status of Refugees, states may not send refugees back to a country where their freedom or life would be in jeopardy.

The process of decolonisation and the establishment of new national boundaries caused many people to become refugees. There are many other 'displaced persons' who have left because of famine, poverty, natural disaster or war. In 1991 there were about 15 million refugees and 30 million displaced persons across the globe, many living in camps with women, children and the old most affected. Most refugees and displaced persons are from developing-world countries. Many asylum speakers face restrictive legislation and punitive treatment in the countries where they seek refuge.

Trade-union rights are promoted by the ILO, which has published a series of 'Conventions' which signatory states agree to uphold. The Survey of Trade Union Rights (May 1993) undertaken by the International Confederation of Free Trade Unions (ICFTU) shows that these are denied in many countries especially in Africa, Latin America, the Middle East and East Asia.

The rights of indigenous peoples are currently the subject of controversy. Apart from normal human rights there have been moves to prevent the patenting of the, often distinctive, human genetic material of indigenous peoples. The 1995 Treaty for Lifeforms and a Patent-Free Pacific is a case in point. It is designed to prevent drug companies from profiting from obtaining a legal monopoly of the commercial use of genetic material obtained from human beings.

There is a global debate on human rights with active national and international pressure groups. Consumers may boycott products from states where rights are being violated. The Fairtrade Foundation run by Christian Aid has launched a campaign to get foreign suppliers of goods to British supermarkets to improve wages and conditions for their workers. Amnesty International is a leading international NGO which campaigns for 'prisoners of conscience' and against torture.

RELATED TOPICS

2.15 Citizenship: reformist view
2.16 Citizenship: radical view
3.6 Pluralism
9.15 Race
9.21 Children

FURTHER READING

Beddard (1993) Chap 1
Hill (1992)

9.18 POVERTY

Explanations of world *poverty* mirror the explanations given for poverty in individual states. They differ according to the ideological perspective within which they are formulated. Right-wing explanations often focus on the characteristics of the poor themselves and ignore the structural conditions in which they have to live.

> ... the question addressed is not usually the question of why the international distribution of income is so unequal. Explanations are attempted to show why the peoples of underdeveloped countries are 'poor', but the existence of their poverty is not related to the wealth accumulated elsewhere. Moreover, the picture given is usually a static one ... Attempts to provide historical explanations are dismissed as irrelevant ... The explanations, such as they are, tend to be based on what might tactfully be called a Eurocentric view of the world, which is itself a product of historical circumstances, and of colonial mythology in particular. Europeans ... gradually built up theories of racial superiority. (Hayter, 1983: 18–19)

Over the past 25 years there has been some reduction in world poverty. There is evidence of improvement in the *World Bank* report on Social Indicators of Development 1994. Over the past 30 years under-nourishment has been falling globally except in Africa. From 1969–94 global life expectancy rose from 53 to 62 years and infant mortality fell from 110 to 73 per 1,000 births. The countries of the Pacific have shown most improvement, while conditions in sub-Saharan Africa have worsened. However, poverty still affects over 1 billion people, making up 30 per cent of the population of the developing world.

International agencies are now at least giving the appearance of addressing this issue. The *OECD*, for example, has set as a target the reduction of poverty by half by the year 2015. The UN World Summit on Social Development in 1995 had the aim of planning the total eradication of poverty. Its Programme of Action states that aid should aim to improve the basic rights of the poor rather than economic growth rates. The year 1996 was designated as the International Year for the Eradication of Poverty. A new proposal has been for what has been termed a 20:20 strategy in which 20 per cent of aid budgets and 20 per cent of state spending in the recipient countries is spent on basic needs. The *World Bank* has also become involved in the issue of poverty through the micro-loan scheme. This is designed to finance small-scale projects in conjunction with NGOs including development charities.

Poverty globally is feminised. Policies pursed by major international agencies may disadvantage women. The *neo-liberal* economic theories on which SAPs (Structural Adjustment Programmes) (see 9.7) have been based can be viewed as biased against women:

- Women suffer most from cutbacks which rely on 'community care', which, in reality, is often the unpaid labour of women.
- They are most likely to become unemployed.
- They suffer most from the domestic stress caused by poverty.
- As the most vulnerable section of the labour force they suffer most from reductions in labour rights.

Poverty in the industrialised states has also re-emerged as a major problem largely because of persisting high levels of unemployment. The OECD 'Employment Outlook' report for 1995 predicts unemployment of 7 per cent or more for the rest of the century. In the *new Eastern Europe* poverty has increased, unemployment levels are now much higher than before 1989 and the welfare safety net has often been reduced as part of the move to free-market policies.

RELATED TOPICS

2.6 Gender: reformist view
2.17 Poverty: right-wing view

FURTHER READING

Galbraith (1980) Chap 1
Hayter (1983) pp 16–27
Jones (1990) Chap 2
Townsend (1993) Chap 1
United Nations (1994) Chap 4
Watkins (1995) Chap 1

9.19 HEALTH

Health issues have been part of international debate for some years. Radicals have argued that imperialism has been a factor in the health problems of many developing-world states.

> The diseases of underdevelopment, and the high mortality rates which accompany them, are not somehow a natural, and therefore inevitable aspect of life in the third world. Rather, they are a direct consequence of the wretched material conditions imposed on most inhabitants of third world countries. While certain elements of medical technology are of undoubted value in dealing with some of these diseases, modern medicine cannot provide any real solution to the health problems of the third world while social and economic conditions remain unchanged. (Doyal, 1979: 137)

In the poorest countries life expectancy is 43 years while in the richest it is 78 and the gap is currently widening. Communicable diseases such as tuberculosis along with maternal and infant deaths cause 20 million deaths annually, with 99 per cent occurring in the developing world. Infectious diseases are still the leading global cause of death, killing at least 17 million people, mostly young children, each year. The control of infectious diseases has become increasingly difficult with diseases that seemed to be under control such as tuberculosis and malaria re-emerging as a major threat. Some, such as cholera and yellow fever are reappearing in regions from which they had apparently been eliminated.

The World Health Organization (WHO) acts as a global public health agency setting goals and monitoring standards. WHO has campaigned against particular diseases such as smallpox which has now been eradicated. A major area of conflict concerns whether the priorities of the WHO should be the health problems of the developing world or high-profile diseases such as AIDS which also affect the industrialised states. Policy changes linked to the activities of other international agencies may also have an impact on health problems. Agencies such as the *World Bank* have now developed policies on global health issues.

The World Health Organization Annual Report for 1997 predicts changes in the future pattern of disease. There will be a growing toll from cancer, heart disease and strokes, mental disorders including dementia, chronic lung conditions and musculoskeletal problems such as arthritis. Developing countries will continue to face infectious diseases while also being increasingly afflicted with the lifestyle illnesses seen in more affluent countries.

Misguided but well-intentioned technical aid policies which lead to the importation of high-technology medical services may also adversely affect health services in poorer countries. They have the effect of using disproportionate amounts of resources for curative services when public-health improvements and preventative measures would be more appropriate.

The activities of TNCs have been criticised by radicals for damaging health. There has been a campaign against Nestlé for marketing inappropriate baby foods in developing-world countries.

With the collapse of communism and the emergence of the *new Eastern Europe*, the imposition of *neo-liberal* policies, with the support of the *International Monetary Fund* and the *World Bank*, has brought new health problems. In these states there has been a substantial rise in TB associated with the abandonment of free health services.

NGOs such as Oxfam also argue that social deprivation and poor health are linked in both less developed and advanced countries. In a shift towards a *radical* approach the WHO 1995 Annual Report 'Bridging the Gaps' identified *poverty* as the major cause of ill health.

RELATED TOPICS

1.29 Illich and anti-industrialism
5.20 Death and disease: reformist view
5.21 Death and disease: radical view
7.10 The former USSR and the new Eastern Europe
9.7 World Bank
9.11 Official aid programmes
9.18 Poverty

FURTHER READING

Doyal (1979) Chaps 3 and 7
George (1986)

Hardiman and Midgley (1982) Chap 6
Jones (1990) Chap 6
Navarro (1982a) Chap 2
United Nations (1994) Chap 7

9.20 DISABILITY

The UN Human Rights Declaration on Disability of 1975 sought
to give the disabled defined rights. Some national states now
promote the rights of disabled people. Since 1990 the US has had
anti-discrimination legislation and charters for the disabled exist
in Canada, Sweden and some Australian states. The *European
Union* in 1997 agreed to ban discrimination based on disability.
About 500 million people in the world are disabled with about 60
per cent living in developing countries. Industrialisation often
worsens the status of the disabled because they are usually excluded
from factory production. In many industrialising societies disabled
people have been placed in institutions and today many are still
segregated.

The Independence 92 and Disabled People's International
conferences took place at the end of the UN Decade of Disabled
Persons. The Disabled People's International is an umbrella
organisation for disability groups around the world. The disability
movement in the industrialised states has pursued the goal of
independent living and *empowerment* in which disabled people can
speak for themselves and campaign collectively. In the developing
world disabled activists focus more on nutrition, preventative
health measures and training. Many disabled people are deprived
of an adequate education. In poor countries very few disabled
children go to school and in rich countries most still receive a
segregated education.

Eugenic policies are still being employed. Biotechnology and
pre-natal genetic screening are being used to try to eliminate
disability by preventing the birth of disabled babies. In Gansu
Province in China more than 5,000 people were sterilised from
1988–92 and many pregnant disabled women were subjected to
compulsory abortions. Many disabled people see this as a means
of portraying them as unfit to live. Many disabled people reject the
medical model of disability and argue that their problems are due
to social and environmental factors. Disability is usually the result
of social rather than genetic causes:

- Over 90 per cent of infant disability is due to factors such as
  disease and poverty.

- About 85 per cent of adult disability is caused after the age of 13 with physical abuse, industrial accidents and environmental pollution the major causes.
- Over 100 million people are disabled as a result of malnutrition.
- Iron deficiency, anaemia and early pregnancy are major causes of disability in women in poor countries.
- War and violence cause disability with landmines being a major problem.

Landmines have been causing over 25,000 casualties annually. In 1995, at a UN conference to review the 1980 Inhumane Weapons Convention NGOs and radicals supported an (unsuccessful) attempt to ban landmines. In 1997, the Labour government in the UK announced a ban on their production and use, though the government of the US is opposed to the ban.

RELATED TOPICS

1.16 Eugenics
2.15 Citizenship: reformist view
2.16 Citizenship: radical view
4.13 Empowerment
5.19 Death and disease: right-wing view
6.8 Mental disability
9.6 The European Union

FURTHER READING

Boylan (1991) Chap 1
Oliver (1990)
Shakespeare (1995)
UN Economic and Social Council (1991)

9.21 CHILDREN

The UN has a Declaration on the Rights of the Child produced by UNICEF in 1990. This sets down standards for the legal status and treatment of children covering areas such as the right to life, a name, nationality, freedom of speech and religion, and protection from abuse. The convention also prescribes standards for adoption, education and disability.

In some countries, including Brazil, children's right to life is violated by death squads which exterminate 'street children'. Sexual exploitation of children is also common and may involve incest, sexual abuse, forced marriage of young girls and the use of young people in prostitution and pornography. The first World Congress on the Commercial Sexual Exploitation of Children in 1996 revealed the extent of child sex abuse. Abuse affects development, self-esteem and confidence. Many sexually exploited children are denied the right to education and they may be rejected by their families and communities.

The 1990 World Conference on Education called for education for all by 2000. The right to an education is included in the Rights of the Child. Worldwide, around 400 million school-age children do not get an education at all. In developing countries 90 per cent of children now start school but nearly half fail to complete four years. Globally there are 900 million people who cannot read and write and two-thirds of these are women.

> ... 40 years after the Universal Declaration of Human Rights asserted that 'everyone has a right to basic education', there are 130 million children of primary-school age not enrolled in school. Unless policies change, the absolute number of children not attending school is likely to reach 162 million in the year 2015. In Africa, where 50 per cent of primary school age children are not attending school, enrolment rates are decreasing on average ... (Watkins, 1995: 25)

The UNICEF report on Progress of Nations compares states in terms of health standards, education, access to clean water and political participation compared with what would be expected from their GNP. According to the report, some poor countries, including Sri Lanka, Nepal, Cuba and Burma, have better infant-mortality rates and junior-school attendance than would be expected from their GNP.

The World Summit for Children in 1990 set targets to improve health, education and nutrition. Over a decade these seek to cut child deaths by a third and malnutrition by a half. Polio was to be eradicated, measles and diarrhoea brought under control, and 80 per cent of children were to complete primary school. Current improvements in child health involve a reduction in deaths from malnutrition, disease and through being disabled.

According to the International Labour Organization (ILO) child labour is common with between 70 million and 100 million children aged 10–14 working. The figures for child labour vary from 3 per cent in Europe to 22 per cent in Africa. Most child workers are not employees but work at home on the family farm or in village industries, where their work is a key element in their family's survival. In 1996 both UNICEF and the ILO estimated that the global total of child workers was 250 million. Some attempts have been made to organise economic sanctions against firms employing them including the unsuccessful Harkin Bill introduced into the US Congress in 1992. However, polices which suddenly eject children from an industry without ensuring that they then attend school may simply drive them into other hazardous forms of employment.

The condition of children in virtually all English-speaking industrialised countries worsened in the 1980s owing to the imposition of *neo-liberal* economic policies or deregulation and rising unemployment. The US has the worst record, with one-fifth of children living below the poverty level. In 1994 the UN undertook an audit of children's rights in Britain and reported substantial failings in policy. These included child poverty, and the use of physical punishments and imprisonment. It called for changes in policy, for independent monitoring, for a children's ombudsman and training in children's rights for those working with children. A recent report on Children in Europe examines legislation, policy and practice in the *European Union*. It shows that:

- children's interests are largely ignored in EU policy-making
- there is no mention of children in the Treaties of the EU
- the key social partners (see 3.8) are from business and from trade unions rather than from welfare service providers.

RELATED TOPICS

1.17 Neo-liberalism (the new right)
1.26 Marxism: 1 Capital logic
2.16 Citizenship: radical view
6.2 Children: social status and rights
6.3 Parentless and abused children
9.6 The European Union

FURTHER READING

Graham-Brown (1991)
Ruxton (1996)
United Nations (1994) Chap 8A

9.22 OLD AGE

Global economic development is increasing the proportion of old people owing to declining fertility and increased life expectancy. By 2025 the world population of over-60s is likely to treble to 1.2 billion people, around 14 per cent of the total. The elderly population of developing countries is increasing fastest. Around 70 per cent of old people have no pensions and no savings. In order to make a contribution to family incomes old people in many developing world countries may continue to work.

Poverty in old age is feminised. A higher proportion of old women than men live alone and in poverty, because women live longer than men and they are likely to marry men older than themselves. Social and economic changes are compounding the problems of the old because as more women work, family care of the old becomes more difficult.

A greater interaction between the WHO and the UN could ... considerably enhance the cohesion of a global strategy on ageing. Additionally, recent health and social sector reforms introduced by the IMF and the World Bank in developing countries have made it more difficult for them to address the needs of long marginalised groups such as the elderly. (Sen, 1994: 50)

In 1994 the World Bank produced a report entitled 'Averting the Old Age Crisis' which proposed a selective approach to policy. It argues that poor countries should employ *means-tested* minimum incomes for the old. Richer countries wishing to keep a *universal* flat-rate pension should raise the retirement age as people live longer. The World Bank argues that pensions do not redistribute income from rich to poor since the rich live longer. The bank recommends that:

1. Higher-income groups should make provision for themselves through personal savings, which could be made compulsory and be managed by the private sector.
2. Developing countries should try to preserve the informal systems for looking after the old, such as extended family arrangements and mutual aid societies.

RELATED TOPICS

4.2 Privatisation
4.4 Means-testing and selectivity
4.7 Universalism
6.5 The old: social status
9.7 World Bank
9.18 Poverty

FURTHER READING

Sen (1994) Chap 1
Tout (1989) Chap 3

References

Abercrombie, N., Hill, S. and Turner, B. S. (1988) *The Penguin Dictionary of Sociology*, Penguin, Harmondsworth.

Alcock, P. (1989) Why citizenship and welfare rights offer new hope for new welfare in Britain, *Critical Social Policy*, Issue 26, Vol 9, No 2, Autumn, pp 32–43.

Alcock, P. and Harris, H. (1982) *Welfare Law and Order*, Macmillan, London.

Allsop, J. (1984) *Health Policy and the National Health Service*, Longman, London.

Althusser, L. (1971) *Lenin and Philosophy*, Monthly Review, New York.

Anderson, D. C. (ed.) (1980) *The Ignorance of Social Intervention*, Croom Helm, London.

Andrews, G. (ed.) (1991) *Citizenship*, Laurence & Wishart, London.

Armitage, A. (1991) *Social Welfare in Canada*, 2nd edn, Mclelland and Stewart, Toronto.

Arnstein, S. R. (1971) Eight rungs on the ladder of citizen participation, in E. S. Cahn and B. A. Passett (eds), *Citizen Participation*, Praeger, London.

Baker, J. (1979) Social conscience and social policy, *Journal of Social Policy*, 8, pp 177–206.

Banfield, E. (1968) *The Unheavenly City*, Little, Brown and Co., Boston.

Banks, O. (1986) *Faces of Feminism*, 2nd edn, Blackwell, Oxford.

Banton, M. (1985) *Promoting Racial Harmony*, Cambridge University Press, Cambridge.

—— (1988) *Racial Consciousness*, Longman, London.

Barclay, P. (1982) *Social Workers: Their Role and Tasks*, Bedford Square Press, London.

Barker, M. (1980) *The New Racism*, Junction Books, London.

—— (1990) Biology and the new racism, in Chap 2 of D. T. Goldberg (ed.), *Anatomy of Racism*, University of Minnesota Press, Minneapolis.

Barrett, M. (1980) *Women's Oppression Today*, Verso, London.

Barry, B. M. (1970) *Sociologists, Economists and Democracy*, Collier-Macmillan, London.

Becker, H. S. (1963) *Outsiders*, Collier-Macmillan, London.

Beddard, R. (1993) *Human Rights and Europe*, 3rd edn, Cambridge University Press, Cambridge.

Bellamy, D. F and Irving, A. (1989) Canada, pp 47–88 of J. Dixon and R. P. Scheurell (eds), *Social Welfare in Developed Market Countries*, Routledge, London and New York.

Benyon, J. (ed.) (1984) *Scarman and After*, Pergamon, Oxford.

Benyon, J. and Solomos, J. (eds) (1988) *The Roots of Urban Unrest*, Pergamon, Oxford.

Beresford, P. and Croft, S. (1984) Welfare Pluralism: The New Face of Fabianism, *Critical Social Policy*, Issue 9, Vol 3, No 3, pp 19–39.

Berger, P. and Berger, B. (1983) *The War Over the Family*, Hutchinson, London.

Beveridge, W. (1942) *Social Insurance and Allied Services*, HMSO, London.

Beveridge, W. (1944) *Full Employment in a Free Society*, Allen & Unwin, London.

Biggs, S. (1996) A family concern: elder abuse in British social policy, *Critical Social Policy*, Vol 16, pp 63–88.

Blackledge, D. and Hunt, B. (1985) *Sociological Interpretations of Education*, Croom Helm, London.

Bland, L. , McCabe, T. and Mort, F. (1979) Sexuality and reproduction: three 'official' instances, in M. Barrett, P. Corrigan, A. Kuhn and J. Wolff (eds), *Ideology and Cultural Production*, Chap 4, Croom Helm, London.

Blaxter, M. (1990) *Health and Lifestyle*, Tavistock, London.

Bolger, S., Corrigan, P., Docking, J. and Frost, N. (1981) *Towards Socialist Welfare Work*, Macmillan, London.

Bonger, W. (1969) *Criminality and Economic Conditions*, Indiana University Press, Bloomington.

Bottomore, T. and Outhwaite, W. (eds) (1993) *The Blackwell Dictionary of Twentieth Century Social Thought*, Blackwell, Oxford.

Bottomore, T. B. (ed.). (1991) *A Dictionary of Marxist Thought*, 2nd edn, Blackwell, Oxford.

Bowlby, J. (1952) *Maternal Care and Mental Health*, 2nd edn, WHO, Geneva.

Bowles, S. and Gintis, H. (1976) *Schooling in Capitalist America*, Routledge & Kegan Paul, London.

Box, S. (1983) *Power, Crime and Mystification*, Tavistock, London.

Boylan, E. (1991) *Women and Disability*, Zed Press, London.

Boyson, R. (1970) The Essential Conditions for the Success of a Comprehensive School, pp 57–62 of C. B. Cox and A. E. Dyson (eds), *Black Paper Two*, Critical Quarterly Society, London.

—— (ed.) (1971) *Down with the Poor*, Churchill Press, London.

Brand, H. (1994) The World Bank, the International Monetary Fund and Poverty, *International Journal of Health Services*, 24, 3, pp 567–78.

Brandt, W. (1983) *North–South: A Programme for Revival*, Pan Books, London.

Breitenbach, H., Burden, T. and Coates, D. (1990) *Features of a Viable Socialism*, Harvester Wheatsheaf, Hemel Hempstead.

Bremner, M. (1968) *Dependency and the Family*, Institute of Economic Affairs, London.

Brewer, A. (1980) *Marxist Theories of Imperialism*, Routledge & Kegan Paul, London.

Brewer, C. and Lait, J. (1980) *Can Social Work Survive?*, Temple Smith, London.

Brown, M. (1983) The Development of Social Administration, pp 88–103 of M. Loney, D. Boswell and J. Clarke (eds), *Social Policy and Social Welfare*, Open University Press, Milton Keynes.

Brown, R. G. S. (1975) *The Management of Welfare*, Fontana, Glasgow.

Bryson, L. (1992) *Welfare and the State*, Macmillan, London.

Bullock, A. and Stallybrass, O. (eds) (1988) *Fontana Dictionary of Modern Thought*, Fontana, London.

Burden, T. and Campbell, M. (1985) *Capitalism and Public Policy in the UK*, Croom Helm, London.

Burkitt, B. and Baimbridge, M. (1995) The Maastricht treaty's impact on the welfare state, *Critical Social Policy*, Issue 42, Vol 14, No. 3, pp 100–11.

Burrows, L. (1988) Missing mothers: the effects of women working, Chap 9 of D. Anderson (ed.), *Full Circle*, Social Affairs Unit, London.

Busch, G., Rainer, M., Helga, N., Reithofer, H., Schmidt, H. and Wintersberger, H. (1986) Development and prospects of the Austrian welfare state, Chap 12 of E. Oyen (ed.), *Comparing Welfare States and Their Futures*, Gower, Aldershot.

Caherty, T., Story, A., Molly, M. and Ruane, C. (eds) (1992) *Is Ireland a Third World Country?*, Centre for Research and Documentation, Belfast.

Campbell, B. (1993) *Goliath: Britain's Dangerous Places*, Methuen, London.

Carr-Saunders, A. M. and Wilson, P. A. (1934) *The Professions*, Oxford University Press, Oxford.

Carrier, J. and Kendall, I. (1977) The development of welfare states: the production of plausible accounts, *Journal of Social Policy*, 6, 3, pp 271–90.

Carson, E. and Kerr, H. (1988) Social welfare down under, *Critical Social Policy*, Issue 23, Vol 8, No. 2, pp 70–82.

—— (1995) Revisiting social welfare down under, *Critical Social Policy*, Vol 15, No 2/3, pp 206–19.

Castles, F. G. (1985) *The Working Class and Welfare*, Allen & Unwin, Hemel Hempstead.

Castles, S. and Kosack, G. (1973) *Immigrant Workers and the Class Structure in Western Europe*, Oxford University Press, Oxford.

Caves, R. E. and Krause, L. B. (eds) (1984) *The Australian Economy*, George, Allen & Unwin, Sydney.

Cawson, A. (1982) *Corporatism and Welfare*, Heinemann, London.

Centre for Contemporary Cultural Studies (1984) *The Empire Strikes Back*, Hutchinson, London.

Clarke, J., Cochrane, A. and McLaughlin, E. (1994) *Managing Social Policy*, Sage, London.

Clarke, J., Cochrane, A. and Smart, C. (1987) *Ideologies of Welfare*, Hutchinson, London.

Clasen, J. and Freeman, R. (1994) *Social Policy in Germany*, Harvester Wheatsheaf, Hemel Hempstead.

Clutterbuck, R. (1978) *Britain in Agony*, Faber & Faber, London.

Coates, D. (1984) *The Context of British Politics*, Hutchinson, London.

Coates, D. (1990) Traditions of Thought and the Rise of Social Science in the United Kingdom, Chap 22 of J. Anderson and M. Ricci (eds), *Society and Social Science*, Open University Press, Milton Keynes.

Coates, D. (1991) *Running the Country*, Hodder & Stoughton, Sevenoaks.

Cochrane, A. (1993a) Comparative Approaches and Social Policy, Chap 1 of A. Cochrane and J. Clarke, *Comparing Welfare States*, Sage, London.

Cochrane, A. (1993b) Looking for a European Welfare State, Chap 9 of A. Cochrane and J. Clarke, *Comparing Welfare States*, Sage, London.

Cochrane, A. and Clarke, J. (1993) *Comparing Welfare States*, Sage, London.

Cockburn, C. (1977) *The Local State*, Pluto Press, London.

Commission on Global Governance (1995) *Our Global Neighbourhood: The Report of the Commission on Global Governance*, Oxford University Press, Oxford.

Corrigan, P. and Leonard, P. (1978) *Social Work Practice Under Capitalism*, Macmillan, London.

Cox, A. W. and McKay, D. H. (1979) *The Politics of Urban Change*, Croom Helm, London.

Craven, E., Rimmer, L. and Wicks, M. (1982) *Family Issues and Public Policy*, Study Commission on the Family, London.

Creighton, C. (1985) The family and capitalism in Marxist theory, in M. Shaw (ed.), *Marxist Sociology Revisited*, Macmillan, London.

Cronin, H. and Curry, D. (1996) Matters of Life and Death: The World View from Evolutionary Psychology, *Demos Quarterly*, 10.

Crosland, C. A. R. (1964) *The Future of Socialism*, rev. edn, Cape, London.

Crowther, M. A. (1978) The later years of the workhouse, pp 36–55 of P. Thane (ed.), *The Origins of British Social Policy*, Croom Helm, London.

Curry, J. (1980) *The Irish Social Services*, Institute of Public Administration, Dublin.

Cutler, T., Williams, K. and Williams, J. (1986) *Keynes, Beveridge and Beyond*, Routledge & Kegan Paul, London.

Dale, J. and Foster, P. (1986) *Feminists and State Welfare*, Routledge & Kegan Paul, London.

David, M. (1985) Motherhood and Social Policy, *Critical Social Policy*, Issue 12, (Spring), pp 28–43.

—— (1986) Moral and Maternal, in R. Levitas (ed.) (1986), *The Ideology of the New Right*, Polity, Cambridge.

Deacon, B. (1983) *Social Policy and Socialism*, Pluto Press, London.

Deacon, B. and Szalai, J. (eds) (1990) *Social Policy in the New Eastern Europe*, Avebury, Aldershot.

Deacon, B. with Hulse, M. and Stubbs, P. (1997) *Global Social Policy*, Sage, London.

Dearlove, J. and Saunders, P. (1984) *Introduction to British Politics*, Polity, Cambridge.

DHSS (1976) *Prevention and Health: Everybody's Business*, HMSO, London.

Dickson, D. (1974) *Alternative Technology*, Fontana, Glasgow.

Digby, A. (1989) *British Welfare Policy*, Faber & Faber, London.

Dixon, J. (1985) China, pp 21–62 of J. Dixon and H. S. Kim, *Social Welfare in Asia*, Croom Helm, London.

—— (ed.) (1987) *Social Welfare in the Middle East*, Croom Helm, London.

Dixon, J. and Kim, H. S. (1985) *Social Welfare in Asia*, Croom Helm, London.

Dixon J. and Macarov, D. (eds) (1992) *Social Welfare in Socialist Countries*, Routledge, London.

Dixon, J. and Scheurell, R. P. (eds) (1989) *Social Welfare in Developed Market Countries*, Routledge, London and New York.

Donnison, D. (1962) The Development of Social Administration, Chap 2 of W. D. Birrell, P. A. R. Hillyard, A. S. Murie and D. J. D. Roche (eds), *Social Administration*, Penguin, Harmondsworth.

Downs, A. (1957) *An Economic Theory of Democracy*, Harper and Brothers, New York.

Doyal, L. (1979) *The Political Economy of Health*, Pluto Press, London.

Doyal, L. and Gough, I. (1984) A theory of human needs, *Critical Social Policy*, Issue 10 (Summer), pp 6–33.

—— (1991) *A Theory of Human Need*, Macmillan, London.

Drucker, H., Dunleavy, P., Gamble, A. and Peele, G. (eds) (1986) *Developments in British Politics*, vol. 2, Macmillan, London.

Dunleavy, P. and O'Leary, B. (1987) *Theories of the State*, Macmillan, London.

Easton, B. (1980) *Social Policy and the Welfare State in New Zealand*, Allen & Unwin, Auckland.

Edwards, J. (1987) *Positive Discrimination, Social Justice and Social Policy*, Tavistock, London.

Elson, D. (1982) The Brandt Report: a programme for survival, *Capital and Class*, 16, pp 110–26.

Engels, F. (1962) *The Origins of the Family, Private Property and the State*, pp 185–327 of K. Marx and F. Engels, *Selected Works*, Vol. 2, Laurence & Wishart, London.

Eriksen, T. H. (1993) *Ethnicity and Nationalism*, Pluto Press, London.

Esping-Andersen, G. (1990) *The Three Worlds of Welfare Capitalism*, Polity Press, Cambridge.

Etzioni, A. (1969) *The Semi-Professions*, Free Press, New York.

—— (1993) *The Spirit of Community: Rights, Responsibilities, and the Communitarian Agenda*, Fontana, London.

—— (1995) Common values, *New Statesman and Society*, 12 May, pp 24–5.

Eysenck, H. (1973) *The Inequality of Man*, Temple Smith, London.

—— (1977) *Crime and Personality*, 3rd edn, Routledge & Kegan Paul.

Fagan, T. and Lee, P. (1997) New social movements and social policy, Chap 8 of M. Lavalette and A. Pratt, *Social Policy*, Sage, London.

Field, F. (1981) *Inequality In Britain*, Fontana, Glasgow.

Field, F., Meacher, M. and Pond, C. (1977) *To Him Who Hath*, Penguin, Harmondsworth.

Finch, J. (1984) *Education as Social Policy*, Longman, London.

Fitzgerald, T. (1983) The New Right and the family, pp 46–57 of M. Loney, D. Boswell and J. Clarke (eds), *Social Policy and Social Welfare*, Open University Press, Milton Keynes.

Fletcher, R. (1967) *Family and Marriage in Britain*, Penguin, Harmondsworth.

Forbes, I. and Smith, S. (eds) (1983) *Politics and Human Nature*, Frances Pinter, London.

Forder, A. (1974) *Concepts in Social Administration*, Routledge & Kegan Paul, London.

Fraser, D. (1973) *The Evolution of the British Welfare State*, Macmillan, London.

Frazer, E. and Lacey, N. (1993) *The Politics of Community: A Feminist Critique of the Liberal–Communitarian Debate*, Harvester Wheatsheaf, Hemel Hempstead.

Freeden, M. (1978) *The New Liberalism*, Clarendon, Oxford.

Friedlander, W. A. (1975) *International Social Welfare*, Prentice-Hall, Englewood Cliffs, NJ.

Friedman, M. (1962) *Capitalism and Freedom*, University of Chicago Press, Chicago.

Friedman, M. and Friedman, R. (1980) *Free to Choose*, Penguin, Harmondsworth.

Friedman, R. R., Gilbert, N. and Sherer, M. (eds) (1987) *Modern Welfare States*, Wheatsheaf, Brighton.

Friedson, E. (1970) *Professional Dominance*, Atherton, New York.

Galbraith, J. K. (1980) *The Nature of Mass Poverty*, Penguin, Harmondsworth.

Galston, W. A. (1991) *Liberal Purposes: Goods, Virtues, and Diversity in the Liberal State*, Cambridge University Press, Cambridge.

Gamble, A. (1981) *Britain in Decline*, Macmillan, London.

—— (1988) *The Free Economy and the Strong State*, Macmillan, London.

George, S. (1986) *How the Other Half Dies*, Penguin, Harmondsworth.

—— (1992) *The Debt Boomerang*, Pluto Press, London.

George, V. (1973) *Social Security and Society*, Routledge & Kegan Paul, London.

George, V. and Wilding, P. (1976) *Ideology and Social Welfare*, Routledge & Kegan Paul, London.

—— (1994) *Welfare and Ideology*, Harvester Wheatsheaf, Hemel Hempstead.

Geras, N. (1983) *Marx and Human Nature*, Verso, London.

Gerth, H. H. and Mills, C. W. (eds) (1970) *From Max Weber*, Routledge & Kegan Paul, London.

Gilbert, B. B. (1966) *The Evolution of National Insurance in Great Britain*, Michael Joseph, London.

Ginsburg, N. (1979) *Class, Capital and Social Policy*, Macmillan, London.

—— (1992) *Divisions of Welfare*, Sage, London.

—— (1993) Sweden: the social democratic case, Chap 7 of A. Cochrane and J. Clarke, *Comparing Welfare States*, Sage, London.

Glass, R. (1989) *Cliches of Urban Doom*, Blackwell, Oxford.

Glazer, N. (1986) Welfare and 'Welfare' in America, Chap 5 of R. Rose and R. Shiratori (eds), *The Welfare State: East and West*, Oxford University Press, Oxford.

Glennerster, H. (ed.) (1983) *The Future of the Welfare State*, Gower, Aldershot.

Goffman, I. (1961) *Asylums*, Penguin, Harmondsworth.

Goldberg, S. (1994) *Why Men Rule: A Theory of Male Dominance*, 2nd ed., Open Court, Chicago.

Gough, I. (1979) *The Political Economy of the Welfare State*, Macmillan, London.

Gould, A. (1988) *Conflict and Control in Welfare Policy: The Swedish Experience*, Longman, London.

—— (1993) *Capitalist Welfare States*, Longman, London.

Graham-Brown, S. (1991) *Education in the Developing World*, Longman, London.

Green, G. (1987) The new municipal socialism, in Chap 14 of M. Loney (ed.), *The State or the Market*, Sage, London.

Grunberger, R. (1974) *A Social History of the Third Reich*, Penguin, Harmondsworth.

Habermas, J. (1976) *Legitimation Crisis*, Heinemann, London.

Hadley, R. and Hatch, S. (1981) *Social Welfare and the Failure of the State*, George, Allen & Unwin, London.

Hall, P., Land, H., Parker, R. and Webb, A. (1975) *Change, Choice and Conflict in Social Policy*, Heinemann, London.

Hall, S. and Held, D. (1989) Left and Rights, *Marxism Today*, June.

Halsey, A. H. (1979) Social mobility and education, in D. Rubinstein (ed.) (1979), *Education and Equality*, Penguin, Harmondsworth.

Ham, C. and Hill, M. (1984) *The Policy Process in the Modern Capitalist State*, Harvester, Brighton.

Hambleton, R. (1979) Towards Theories of Public Learning, in C. Pollitt, L. Lewis, J. Negro and J. Patten, *Public Policy in Theory and Practice*, Hodder & Stoughton, Sevenoaks.

Hammoud (1987) Kuwait, in J. Dixon (ed.), *Social Welfare in the Middle East*, Croom Helm, London.

Hantrais, L. (1995) *Social Policy in the European Union*, Macmillan, London.

Hardiman, M. and Midgley, J. (1982) *The Social Dimensions of Development*, John Wiley, New York.

Harrison, P. (1983) *Inside the Inner City*, Penguin, Harmondsworth.

Harvey, D. (1973) *Social Justice and the City*, Edward Arnold, London.

Hatch, S. and Mocroft, I. (1983) *Components of Welfare*, Bedford Square Press, London.

Hay, J. R. (1975) *The Origins of the Liberal Welfare Reforms 1906–14*, Macmillan, London.

—— (1978) *The Development of the British Welfare State 1880–1975*, Edward Arnold, London.

Hayek, F. (1980) The principles of a liberal social order, in A. de Crespigny and J. Cronin (eds), *Ideologies of Politics*, Oxford University Press, Cape Town.

Hayter, T. (1976) *Aid as Imperialism*, Penguin, Harmondsworth.

—— (1983) *The Creation of World Poverty*, Pluto Press, London.

—— (1985) *Aid: Rhetoric and Reality*, Pluto Press, London.

Hearn, J. (1985) Patriarchy, professionalisation and the semi-professions, pp 190–206 of C. Ungerson (ed.), *Women and Social Policy*, Macmillan, London.

Heidensohn, F. (1987) Women and Crime: Questions for Criminology, in P. Carlen and A. Worrall, *Gender, Crime and Justice*, Open University Press, Milton Keynes.

Hendricks, J. and Calasanti, T. (1986) Social policy on ageing in the United States, Chap 12 of C. Phillipson and A. Walker (eds), *Ageing and Social Policy*, Gower, Aldershot.

Hennock, P. (1981) The origins of British national insurance and the German precedent 1880–1914, Chap 5 of W. J. Mommsen (ed.), *The

Emergence of the Welfare State in Britain and Germany, Croom Helm, London.

Hepburn, A. C. (ed.) (1980) *The Conflict of Nationality in Modern Ireland*, Edward Arnold, London.

Herrnstein, R. J. and Murray, C. P. (1994) *The Bell Curve: Intelligence and Class Structure in American Life*, Free Press, London.

Higgins, J. (1978) *The Poverty Business*, Robertson, London.

Higgins, J. (1981) *States of Welfare*, Blackwell, Oxford.

Hill, D. (1992) Rights and their realisation, Chap 1 of R. Beddard and D. Hill (eds), *Economic, Social and Cultural Rights*, Macmillan, London.

Hill, M. and Bramley, G. (1986) *Analysing Social Policy*, Basil Blackwell, Oxford.

Hobson, J. A. (1909) *The Crisis of Liberalism*, P. S. King and Son, London.

Hofsten, E. (1982) Population growth: a menace to what?, Chap 8 of V. Navarro (ed.), *Imperialism and Medicine*, Pluto Press, London.

Hogwood, B. W. and Gunn, L. A. (1984) *Policy Analysis in the Real World*, Oxford University Press, Oxford.

Holman, R. (1973) Poverty: consensus and alternatives, *British Journal of Social Work*, 3, 4, 431–46.

—— (1978) *Poverty*, Martin Robertson, London.

Humm, M (1995) *The Dictionary of Feminist Theory*, 2nd edn, Harvester Wheatsheaf, Hemel Hempstead.

Ignatieff, M. (1978) *A Just Measure of Pain*, Macmillan, London.

Illich, I. (1973) *Deschooling Society*, Penguin, Harmondsworth.

—— (1977a) *Tools for Conviviality*, Marion Boyars, London.

—— (1977b) *Limits to Medicine*, Penguin, Harmondsworth.

Illich, I., Zola, I. K., McKnight, J., Caplan, J. and Shaiken, H. (1977) *Disabling Professions*, Marion Boyars, London.

Ismael, J.S. (ed.) (1987) *The Canadian Welfare State*, University of Alberta Press, Alberta.

Jack, A. (1986) The future of the New Zealand welfare state, Chap 11 of E. Oyen (ed.), *Comparing Welfare States and their Futures*, Gower, Aldershot.

Jack, G. and Stepney, P. (1995) The Children Act 1989 — protection or persecution? Family support and child protection in the 1990s, *Critical Social Policy*, Issue 43, Vol 15, No 1, pp 26–39.

Jacobs, B. D. (1988) *Racism in Britain*, Croom Helm, London.

—— (1992) *Fractured Cities. Capitalism, Community and Empowerment in Britain and America*, Routledge & Kegan Paul, London.

Jencks, C., Smith, M., Acland, H., Bane, M. J., Cohen, D., Gintis, H., Heyns, B. and Michelson, S. (1973) *Inequality*, Allen Lane, London.

Jenkins, R. and Solomos, J. (eds) (1987) *Racism and Equal Opportunities in the 1980s*, Cambridge University Press, Cambridge.

Joe, T. and Rogers, C. (1985) *By the Few for the Few*, Lexington Books, Lexington.

Johnson, N. (1987) *The Welfare State in Transition*, Wheatsheaf, Hemel Hempstead.

—— (1990) *Reconstructing the Welfare State*, Wheatsheaf, Hemel Hempstead.

Jones, C. (1979) Social work education 1900–1977, in N. Parry, M. Rustin and C. Satyamuti, *Social Work, Welfare and the State*, Edward Arnold, London.

—— (1983) *State Social Work and the Working Class*, Macmillan, London.

Jones, G. (1980) *Social Darwinism and English Thought*, Harvester, Sussex.

Jones, H. (1990) *Social Welfare in Third World Development*, Macmillan, London.

Jones, M. A. (1992) *The Australian Welfare State*, Allen & Unwin, Sydney.

Jordan, B. (1974) *Poor Parents*, Routledge & Kegan Paul, London.

—— (1976) *Freedom and the Welfare State*, Routledge & Kegan Paul, London.

—— (1977) *Rethinking Welfare*, Blackwell, Oxford.

Jordan, B. and Parton, N. (eds) (1983) *The Political Dimensions of Social Work*, Blackwell, Oxford.

Joseph, K. (1974) Speech, 19 October, Press Release 509/74, Conservative Central Office.

Joyce, L. and McCashin, A. (1982) *Poverty and Social Policy: The Irish National Report*, Institute of Public Administration, Dublin.

Keane, J. (1988) *Democracy and Civil Society*, Verso, London.

Kerr, C., Dunlop, J. T., Hall, F. H. and Myas, C. A. (1973) *Industrialism and Industrial Man*, 2nd edn, Penguin, Harmondsworth.

Kincaid, J. (1973) *Poverty and Equality in Britain*, Penguin, Harmondsworth.

—— (1983) Titmuss, the committed analyst, *New Society*, 24 February.

King, A. (1975) Overload: problems of governing in the 1970s, *Political Studies*, 23 (2 and 3), pp 284–96.

—— (1976) *Why is Britain Becoming Harder to Govern?*, BBC, London.

Kinnear, D. and Graycar, A. (1983) Non institutional care of elderly people, Chap 5 of A. Graycar (ed.), *Retreat from the Welfare State*, George, Allen & Unwin, Sydney.

Kinnersley, P. (1973) *The Hazards of Work*, Pluto Press, London.

Krieger, J. (1986) *Reagan, Thatcher and the Politics of Decline*, Polity, Cambridge.

Lal, S. (1996) *Learning from the Asian Tigers*, Macmillan, London.

Langan, M. and Lee, P. (eds) (1989) *Radical Social Work Today*, Unwin Hyman, London.

Le Grand, J. and Robinson, R. (1984) *Privatisation and the Welfare State*, George Allen & Unwin, London.

Lea, J. and Young, J. (1982) The riots in Britain 1981, in D. Cowell, T. Jones and J. Young (eds), *Policing the Riots*, Junction Books, London.

—— (1984) *What is to be Done about Law and Order?*, Penguin, Harmondsworth.

Leach, R. (1991) *British Political Ideologies*, Philip Allen, Hemel Hempstead.

Leman, C. (1980) *The Collapse of Welfare Reform*, MIT Press, Cambridge, MA.

Lindblom, C. E. (1968) *The Policy-Making Process*, Prentice-Hall, Englewood Cliffs, N.J.

Lipsky, M. (1980) *Street Level Bureaucracy*, Russell Sage, New York.

Loney, M. (ed.) (1987) *The State or the Market*, Sage, London.

Lukes, S. (1973) *Individualism*, Blackwell, Oxford.

—— (1974) Socialism and equality, in L. Kolakowski and S. Hampshire (eds), *The Socialist Idea*, Weidenfeld & Nicolson, London.

Lusha, P. (1972) On theories of urban violence, in M. Stewart (ed.) (1972), *The City*, Penguin, Harmondsworth.

Macey, M. (1995) Towards racial justice? A re-evaluation of anti-racism, *Critical Social Policy*, Issue 44/45, Vol 15, No. 2/3, pp 126–46.

MacGregor, S. (1981) *The Politics of Poverty*, Longman, London.

Malik, K. (1996) The Beagle Sails Back Into Fashion, *New Statesman*, 6 December.

—— (1992) *The Making of an English Underclass*, Open University Press, Milton Keynes.

Mann, M. (1983) *The Macmillan Student Encyclopedia of Sociology*, Macmillan, London.

Manning, N. (1984) Social policy in the USSR and the nature of Soviet society, *Critical Social Policy*, Issue 11, Vol 4, No. 2, pp 74–88.

—— (1992) Social policy in the Soviet Union and its succesors, Chap 2 of B. Deacon (ed.), *The New Eastern Europe*, Sage, London.

Marcuse, H. (1972) *Eros and Civilisation*, new edn, Abacus, London.

Marshall, T. H. (1963) *Sociology at the Crossroads*, Heinemann, London.

—— (1975) *Social Policy*, 4th edn, Hutchinson, London.

Maruo, N. (1986) The development of the welfare mix in Japan, Chap 3 of R. Rose and R. Shiratori (eds), *The Welfare State: East and West*, Oxford University Press, Oxford.

Marwick, A. (1968) *Britain in the Century of Total War*, Penguin, Harmondsworth.

Marx, K. (1965) *The German Ideology*, Laurence & Wishart, London.

Marx, K. and Engels, F. (1962) *Selected Works Vol 1*, Foreign Languages Publishing House, Moscow.

Mazumdar, P. (1991) *Eugenics, Human Genetics and Human Failings: The Eugenics Society, its Sources and its Critics in Britain*, Routledge, London.

McCallum, J. (1989) Australia, pp 1–46 of J. Dixon and R. P. Scheurell (eds), *Social Welfare in Developed Market Countries*, Routledge, London and New York.

McIntosh, M. (1978) The State and the Oppression of Women, pp 255–89 of A. Kuhn and A. M. Wolpe (eds), *Feminism and Materialism*, Routledge & Kegan Paul, London.

McLaughlin, E. (1993a) Hong Kong: a residual welfare regime, Chap 5 of A. Cochrane and J. Clarke, *Comparing Welfare States*, Sage, London.

—— (1993b) Ireland: Catholic corporatism, Chap 8 of A. Cochrane and J. Clarke, *Comparing Welfare States*, Sage, London.

Mesa-Largo, C. and Roca, S. G. (1992) Cuba, in J. Dixon and D. Macarov (eds), *Social Welfare in Socialist Countries*, Routledge, London.

Miles, R. and Phizacklea, A. (1984) *White Man's Country*, Pluto Press, London.

Miliband, R. (1973) *The State in Capitalist Society*, Quartet Books, London.

Miller, D., Coleman, J., Connolly, W. and Ryan, A. (eds) (1987) *The Blackwell Encyclopedia of Political Thought*, Blackwell, Oxford.

Minford, P. (1987) The Role of the Social Services: A View from the New Right, in Chap 5 of M. Loney (ed.), *The State or the Market*, Sage, London.

Mishra, R. (1977) *Society and Social Policy*, Macmillan, London.
—— (1990) *The Welfare State in Capitalist Society*, Harvester Wheatsheaf, Hemel Hempstead.
Moore, S. (1993) *Social Policy Alive*, Stanley Thornes, Cheltenham.
Morgan, D. (1975) *Social Theory and the Family*, Routledge & Kegan Paul, London.
Morris, D. (1969) *The Naked Ape*, Corgi, London.
Morris, R. (ed.) (1988) *Testing the Limits of Social Welfare*, University Press of New England, London.
Mosse, J. C. (1993) *Half the World, Half a Chance: An Introduction to Gender and Development*, Oxfam, Oxford.
Mullen (1991) Which Internal Market?, Chap 7 of G. Thompson, J. Frances, R. Levacic and J. Mitchell, *Markets, Hierarchies and Networks*, Sage, London.
Murray, C. (1994) The New Victorians and the New Rabble, *Sunday Times*, 29 May.
Navarro, V. (1976) *Medicine Under Capitalism*, Prodist, New York.
Navarro, V. (ed.) (1982a) *Imperialism and Medicine*, Pluto Press, London.
—— (1982b) The international capitalist order and its implications for the welfare state, *Critical Social Policy*, Vol 2, No. 1, pp 3–62.
Nisbet, R. A. (1973) *The Sociological Tradition*, Heinemann, London.
Niskanen, W. A. (1971) *Bureaucracy and Representative Government*, Aldine-Atherton, New York.
Novak, M. (1982) *The Spirit of Democratic Capitalism*, Madison Books, Lanham.
Novak, T. (1984) *Poverty and Social Security*, Pluto Press, London.
O'Connor, J. (1973) *The Fiscal Crisis of the State*, St Martin's Press, New York.
Oakley, A. (1972) *Sex, Gender and Society*, Temple Smith, London.
—— (1982) *Subject Women*, Fontana, London.
Offe, C. (1984) *Contradictions of the Welfare State*, Hutchinson, London.
Oliver, M. (1990) *The Politics of Disablement*, Macmillan, London.
Olsson, S.E. (1990) *Social Policy and Welfare State in Sweden*, Arkiv, Lund.
Pahl, R. (1970) *Patterns of Urban Life*, Longman, London.
—— (1975) *Whose City?*, Penguin, London.
Papadakis, E. and Taylor-Gooby, P. (1987) *The Privatisation of Public Welfare*, Wheatsheaf, Brighton.
Parker, J. (1975) *Social Policy and Citizenship*, Macmillan, London.
Parsons, T. (1964) The professions and social structure, in T. Parsons, *Essays in Sociological Theory*, Collier Macmillan, Toronto.
Parsons, T. and Bales, R. F. (1956) *Family, Socialisation and Interaction Process*, Routledge & Kegan Paul, London.
Pascall, G. (1986) *Social Policy: A Feminist Analysis*, Tavistock, London.
Patterson, E. P. (1978) Native peoples and social policy, Chap 9 of S. A. Yelaja (ed.), *Canadian Social Policy*, Wilfred Laurier, Ontario.
Pearson, G. (1975) *The Deviant Imagination*, Macmillan, London.
Pearson, R. and Williams, G. (1984) *Political Thought and Public Policy in the Nineteenth Century*, Longman, London.
Peillon, M. (1982) *Contemporary Irish Society*, Gill and MacMillan, Dublin.

Phillipson, C. (1982) *Capitalism and the Construction of Old Age*, Macmillan, London.

Phillipson, C. and Walker, A. (eds) (1986) *Ageing and Social Policy*, Gower, Aldershot.

Phizacklea, A. and Miles, R. (1980) *Labour and Racism*, Routledge & Kegan Paul, London.

Pierson, C. (1991) *Beyond the Welfare State*, Polity, Cambridge.

Pinker, R. (1971) *Social Theory and Social Policy*, Heinemann, London.

—— (1990) *Social Work in an Enterprise Society*, Routledge, London.

Piven, F. F. and Cloward, R. (1972) *Regulating the Poor*, London, Tavistock.

—— (1982) *The New Class War*, Pantheon, New York.

Plant, R. and Barre, T. N. (1990) *Thatcher's Britain: Two Views*, Part 2 of Citizenship and Rights, Institute of Economic Affairs, Health and Welfare Unit, Choice in Welfare Series No. 3, London.

Powell, F. W. (1992) *The Politics of Irish Social Policy 1600–1990*, Edwin Mellen Press, Lewiston.

Pratt, A. (1997) Universalism or selectivism?, Chap 11 of M. Lavalette and A. Pratt, *Social Policy*, Sage, London.

Richards, J. R. (1980) *The Sceptical Feminist*, Routledge & Kegan Paul, London.

Rodgers, B. (1979) *The Study of Social Policy: A Comparative Approach*, George, Allen & Unwin, Sydney.

Rodmell, S. and Watt, A. (eds) (1986) *The Politics of Health Education*, Routledge & Kegan Paul, London.

Roebroek, J. M. (1989) Netherlands, pp 147–89 of J. Dixon and R. P. Scheurell (eds), *Social Welfare in Developed Market Countries*, Routledge, London and New York.

Room, G. (1979) *The Sociology of Welfare*, Basil Blackwell and Martin Robertson, Oxford.

Rose, M. E. (1972) *The Relief of Poverty 1834–1914*, Macmillan, London.

Roshier, B. (1989) *Controlling Crime*, Open University Press, Milton Keynes.

Rowbotham, S. (1973a) *Hidden from History*, Pluto Press, London.

—— (1973b) *Women, Resistance and Revolution*, Penguin, Harmondsworth.

—— (1975) *Woman's Consciousness, Man's World*, Penguin, Harmondsworth.

Rowntree, B. S. (1901) *Poverty: A Study of Town Life*, Macmillan, London.

Rudd, C. (1993) The welfare state: origins, development and crisis, Chap 12 of B. Roper and C. Rudd (eds), *State and Economy in New Zealand*, Oxford University Press, Oxford.

Ruxton, S. (1996) *Children in Europe*, NCH Action For Children, London.

Ryan, J. and Thomas, F. (1980) *The Politics of Mental Handicap*, Penguin, Harmondsworth.

Saggar, S. (1991) *Race and Public Policy*, Harvester Wheatsheaf, Hemel Hempstead.

Salter, B. and Tapper, T. (1981) *Education, Politics and the State*, Grant McIntyre, London.

Sarup, M. (1978) *Marxism and Education*, Routledge & Kegan Paul, London.

Saunders, P. (1981) *Social Theory and the Urban Question*, Hutchinson, London.

—— (1990) *Social Class and Stratification*, Routledge, London.

Saville, J. (1983) The origins of the welfare state, in M. Loney, D. Boswell and J. Clarke (eds), *Social Policy and Social Welfare*, Open University Press, Milton Keynes.

Schumacher, E. (1993) *Small is Beautiful*, Vintage Books, London.

Schumpeter, J. A. (1965) *Capitalism, Socialism and Democracy*, Unwin University Books, London.

Scott, A. (1990) *Ideology and the New Social Movements*, Unwin Hyman, London.

Scull, A. (1984) *Decarceration*, 2nd edn, Polity Press, Cambridge.

Searle, G. R. (1971) *The Quest for National Efficiency*, University of California Press, Berkeley.

—— (1976) *Eugenics and Politics in Britain 1900–1914*, Noordhoff, Leyden.

Seebohm, F. (1968) *Report of the Committee on Local Authority and Allied Personal Services*, Cmnd. 3703, HMSO, London.

Seidel, G. (1986) Culture, nation and race, in R. Levitas (ed.), *The Ideology of the New Right*, Polity, Cambridge.

Self, P. (1975) *Econocrats and the Policy Process*, Macmillan, London.

Semmel, B. (1960) *Imperialism and Social Reform*, Allen & Unwin, London.

Sen, K. (1994) *Ageing – Debates on Demographic Transition and Social Policy*, Zed Press, London.

Shakespeare, T. (1995) Back to the future? New genetics and disabled people, *Critical Social Policy*, Issue 44/45, Vol 15, No 2/3, pp 22–35.

Shaw, B. (1949) *Essays in Fabian Socialism*, Constable, London.

Shaw, J. W., Nordlie, P. G. and Shapiro, R. M. (1987) *Strategies for Improving Race Relations*, Manchester University Press, Manchester.

Sinfield, A. (1969) *Which Way for Social Work?*, Fabian Society, London.

Solomos, J. (1989) *Race and Racism in Contemporary Britain*, Macmillan, London.

Soper, K. (1981) *On Human Need*, Harvester Wheatsheaf, Brighton.

Sparr, P. (1994) *Mortgaging Women's Lives*, Zed Books, London.

Statham, D. (1978) *Radicals in Social Work*, Routledge & Kegan Paul, London.

Stedman Jones, G. (1971) *Outcast London*, Penguin, Harmondsworth.

Stern, V. (1987) *Bricks of Shame*, London, Penguin.

Stone, J. (1985) *Racial Conflict in Contemporary Society*, Fontana, Glasgow.

Sullivan, M. (1987) *Sociology and Social Welfare*, Allen & Unwin, London.

Takahashi, T. and Someya, Y. (1985) Japan, pp 133–75 of J. Dixon and H.S. Kim, *Social Welfare in Asia*, Croom Helm, London.

Taylor, S. (1984) The Scarman Report and the Explanation of the Riots, in J. Benyon (ed.), *Scarman and After*, Pergamon, Oxford.

Taylor-Gooby, P. (1985) *Public Opinion, Ideology and State Welfare*, Routledge & Kegan Paul, London.

Thompson, G., Frances, J., Levacic, R. and Mitchell, J. (eds) (1991), *Markets, Hierarchies and Networks*, Sage, London.

Thunhurst, C. (1982) *It Makes You Sick*, Pluto Press, London.

Timms, N. and Timms, R. (1982) *Dictionary of Social Welfare*, Routledge & Kegan Paul, London.

Tinker, A. (1984) *The Elderly in Modern Society*, 2nd edn, Longman, London.

Titmuss, R. (1968) *Commitment to Welfare*, Allen & Unwin, London.

—— (1970) *The Gift Relationship*, Penguin, Harmondsworth.

—— (1974) *Social Policy*, George, Allen & Unwin, London.

—— (1964) *Essays on the Welfare State*, 2nd edn, Allen & Unwin, London.

Touraine, A. (1971) *The Post Industrial Society*, Random House, New York.

Tout, K. (1989) *Ageing in Developing Countries*, Oxford University Press, Oxford.

Townsend, P. (1970) Introduction: does selectivity mean a nation divided?, Chap 1 of Fabian Society — *Social Services for All*, Fabian Society, London.

Townsend, P. (1975) The scope and limitations of means-tested social services in Britain, in P. Townsend, *Sociology and Social Policy*, Allen Lane, London.

—— (1979) *Poverty*, Penguin, Harmondsworth.

—— (1986) Ageism and social policy, Chap 2 of C. Phillipson and A. Walker (eds), *Ageing and Social Policy*, Gower, Aldershot.

—— (1993) *The International Analysis of Poverty*, Wheatsheaf, Hemel Hempstead.

—— (1995) *The Rise of International Social Policy*, Policy Press, Bristol.

Townsend, P. and Davidson, M. (1980) *Inequalities in Health*, Penguin, London.

United Nations (1994) *World Social Situation in the 1990s*, United Nations, New York.

United Nations Economic and Social Council (1991) *Final Report on Human Rights and Disability*, United Nations, New York.

Uttley, S. (1989) New Zealand, pp 190–227 of J. Dixon and R. P. Scheurell (eds), *Social Welfare in Developed Market Countries*, Routledge, London and New York.

Venable, V. (1966) *Human Nature: The Marxian View*, Meridian Books, Cleveland.

Vold, G. B. and Bernard, T. J. (1986) *Theoretical Criminology*, 3rd edn, Oxford University Press, New York.

Walker, A. (1987) The social construction of dependency in old age, Chap 3 of M. Loney (ed.), *The State or the Market*, Sage, London.

Walker, A. (1984) The political economy of privatisation, in J. Le Grand and R. Robinson (eds), *Privatisation and the Welfare State*, George Allen & Unwin, London.

Watkins, K. (1995) *The Oxfam Poverty Report*, Oxfam, Oxford.

Weale, A. (1978) Paternalism and social policy, *Journal of Social Policy*, No. 7, Part 2, pp 157–72.

Weeks, J. (1984) The fabians and utopia, Chap 6 of B. Pimlott (ed.), *Fabian Essays in Socialist Thought*, Heinemann, London.

Weiler, P. (1982) *The New Liberalism*, Garland, New York.

Westergaard, J. and Resler, H. (1975) *Class in a Capitalist Society*, Heinemann, London.

Wetherly, P. (1996) Basic needs and social policies, *Critical Social Policy*, Issue 46, Vol 16, No. 1, pp 45–65.

Wicks, M. (1987) *A Future For All*, Penguin, Harmondsworth.

Wiktorow, A. (1992) Soviet Union, Chap 8 of J. Dixon and D. Macarov (eds), *Social Welfare in Socialist Countries*, Routledge, London.

Wilding, P. (1982) *Professional Power and Social Welfare*, Routledge & Kegan Paul, London.

Wilensky, H. (1976) *The New Corporatism, Centralisation and the Welfare State*, Sage, London.

Wilensky, H. L. and Lebeaux, C. N. (1964) *Industrial Society and Social Welfare*, Free Press, New York.

Williams, F. (1987) Racism and the discipline of social policy, *Critical Social Policy*, Issue 20, Vol 7, No 2, pp 4–29.

—— (1989) *Social Policy: A. Critical Introduction*, Polity and Basil Blackwell, Cambridge and London.

Williams, R. (1976) *Key Words*, Fontana, Croom Helm, Glasgow.

Williams, S. (1981) *Politics is for People*, Allen Lane, London.

Wilson, E. (1977) *Women and the Welfare State*, Tavistock, London.

—— (1980) *Only Halfway to Paradise*, Tavistock, London.

—— (1983) Feminism and social policy, pp 33–45 of M. Loney, D. Boswell and J. Clarke (eds), *Social Policy and Social Welfare*, Open University Press, Milton Keynes.

Wilson, E. O. (1975) *Sociobiology: The New Synthesis*, Harvard University Press, Harvard, MA.

Wilson, J. Q. (1975) *Thinking About Crime*, Basic Books, New York.

Wilson, M. (1993) The German welfare state: a conservative regime in crisis, Chap 6 of A. Cochrane and J. Clarke, *Comparing Welfare States*, Sage, London.

Woodfield, A. (1989) Private versus public provision of social welfare services in New Zealand, pp 115–54 of M. James (ed.), *The Welfare State*, Centre for Independent Studies, New Zealand.

World Bank (1993) *The East Asian Economic Miracle*, Oxford University Press, Oxford.

Yelaja, S.A. (ed.) (1978a) *Canadian Social Policy*, Wilfred Laurier, Ontario.

—— (1978b) The elderly and social policy, Chap 8 of S. A. Yelaja (ed.), *Canadian Social Policy*, Wilfred Laurier, Ontario.

Young, J. (1981) Thinking seriously about crime, Chap 14 of M. Fitzgerald, G. McKennan and J. Pawson, *Crime and Society*, Routledge & Kegan Paul, London.

Younghusband, E. (ed.) (1964) *Social Work and Social Values*, Allen & Unwin, London.

Zapf, W. (1986) Development, structure, and prospects of the German social state, Chap 6 of R. Rose and R. Shiratori (eds), *The Welfare State: East and West*, Oxford University Press, Oxford.

Index